I0792795

PRAISE FOR INDEGENEITY AND DECOLONIAL RESISTANCE

"Challenging the tropes of dominant sociopolitical theory, *Indigeneity and Decolonial Resistance* is a bold, brazen and uncompromising collection of essays that stands at the cutting edge of decolonial studies."

—Peter McLaren, Distinguished Professor in Critical Studies, Attallah College of Educational Studies, Chapman University

"Boldly unmasking and challenging the colonial logic that underpins homogenizing classroom instruction across the disciplines and affirming the anti-colonial theoretical foundations of epistemic resistance rooted in indigenous spirituality, ways of knowing and being, this visionary collection offers vital conceptual tools and pedagogical possibilities that are bound to advance the global struggle for humanizing knowledge production and anti-racist education practice."

— Joyce E. King, PhD, Benjamin E. Mays Endowed Chair for Urban Teaching, Learning & Leadership, Georgia State University, USA

INDIGENEITY AND DECOLONIAL RESISTANCE

Indigeneity and Decolonial Resistance

Alternatives to Colonial Thinking and Practice

EDITED BY

George J. Sefa Dei

AND

Cristina Sherry Jaimungal

Myers Education Press

GORHAM, MAINE

Published by Myers Education Press, LLC
P.O. Box 424
Gorham, ME 04038

Myers Education Press is an academic publisher specializing in books, e-books and digital content in the field of education. All of our books are subjected to a rigorous peer review process and produced in compliance with the standards of the Council on Library and Information Resources.

LIBRARY OF CONGRESS CATALOGING-IN-PUBLICATION DATA AVAILABLE FROM LIBRARY OF CONGRESS.

13-digit ISBN 978-1-9755-0005-4 (paperback)
13-digit ISBN 978-1-9755-0004-7 (hardcover)
13-digit ISBN 978-1-9755-0006-1 (library networkable e-edition)
13-digit ISBN 978-1-9755-0007-8 (consumer e-edition)

Printed in the United States of America.

All first editions printed on acid-free paper that meets the American National Standards Institute Z39-48 standard.

Books published by Myers Education Press may be purchased at special quantity discount rates for groups, workshops, training organizations and classroom usage. Please call our customer service department at 1-800-232-0223 for details.

Cover design by Sophie Appel
Interior design and composition by Rachel Reiss

Visit us on the web at **www.myersedpress.com** to browse our complete list of titles.

Contents

Dedication

For our Elders, Ancestors, educators, professors, graduate students, undergrads, activists, and communities who shatter the boundaries of education and reimagine new possibilities.

Acknowledgments

We owe immense gratitude to our Ancestors, Elders, family, loved ones, colleagues, and peers who have consistently demonstrated their unwavering support, patience, and encouragement to do this work. Thank you for the countless ways you have challenged us to do better, shown us compassion and patience in times of need, and motivated us to keep on pushing for change. The support you show us in small and big ways makes a world of difference. Without you, this would not be possible.

With Humility, Gratitude, and Respect,
George J S Dei & Cristina Sherry Jaimungal

Back in the Day

Phyllis McKenna

Indigenous elders often say that memory is in the blood and bone, that our stories are passed not just verbally but through a kind of genetic memory

—BOMBAY & DEERCHILD, 2015

Teachings of years past
Generation to generation
Childhood memories tucked away
Deep within consciousness

Knowledge not found in books
Tokenized, appropriated, erasures
Living off the land
Possessing community values

Colonized, devalued, assimilated
Thoughts of inferiority
Broken people, families, communities
Infestation of trauma

Small acts of resistance
Skills of survival

Ensuring children possess
Identity, love, compassion, strength

Times of difficulty
Residential schools, illness, death
Having babies at 14
Caring for the sick and elderly

Back in the day
Elders talk simplicity
Complexity of separation
Land, language, culture

Ancestors' generations before
Knowledge racing through blood
1000 years past
Memories coded in veins

Healing within
Creation has meaning
Challenges turn to lessons
Lead only far as one journeyed

Reference

Bombay, A., & Deerchild, R. (2015, September 27). *Lasting effects of trauma reaches across generations through DNA*. CBC Radio Podcast. Retrieved from http://www.cbc.ca/radio/unreserved/buffy-sainte-marie-wab-kinew-and-how-dna-remembers-trauma-1.3242375/lasting-effects-of-trauma-reaches-across-generations-through-dna-1.3243897

CHAPTER 1

Indigeneity and Decolonial Resistance: An Introduction

George J. Sefa Dei and Cristina Sherry Jaimungal

We begin with some basic questions. How do we pursue alternatives to colonial thinking? What theoretical tools can be deployed? Where do we lodge the foundational basis for counter (and oppositional) knowledges? And, most importantly, how can it be ensured that our theoretical understandings translate to meaningful, practical decolonial practice in the educational system? These are not easy questions, but this book aims to offers some important lessons for decolonization. In writing on decolonization, we follow in the intellectual footsteps of many scholars whose works have informed our thinking over the years (see Asante, 1991, 2003; Escobar, 2004; Giroux & McLaren, 1989, 2014; Grande, 2015; Loomba & Orkin, 1998; Maldonado-Torres, 2004; Mignolo, 2007, 2009, 2012; Mignolo & Tlostanova, 2006; Pennycook, 2017; Quijano, 2000; Santos, 2007; Tuck & Yang, 2012, among many other prolific academic-activists who straddle the borders between the academy and action).

We see the important challenge of decolonization as subverting the taken-for-granted, everyday assumptions deeply held by society that work to routinely reinforce White power and privilege. Decolonization is about body, mind, soul, and spirit, and the transformation both within and outside. Decolonization is about developing and sharpening our thinking process and pursuing politics for transformative change. Decolonization is also about breaking with dominant practices and resisting subordination in all its forms. Decolonization is about the ability to define one's own agenda for a new future, and to relate our endeavors to a collective future. We link this understanding of decolonization with an anti-colonial lens (see Dei, 2000; Dei & Kempf, 2006; Dei & Lordan, 2016; among many others). While decolonization is about the power of nonhegemonic thinking and the transformative ideas we seek to engage with, an anti-colonial prism helps connect our thinking processes and thoughts with concrete political practice. The anti-colonial lens declares an open and unapologetic stance toward colonialism in its varied and complicated forms and calls for everyday resistance at and within all spaces. The anti-colonial is about open defiance, an outright opposition, and a clear declaration of an "against" stance toward colonization. Anti-colonialism is about an action-oriented engagement with knowledge and resistance to colonial and imperial forces and investments.

Following Dei (2016), this book is engaged from three stances: "(1) that our epistemological frameworks must consider the body of the knowledge producer, place, history, politics, and contexts within which knowledge is produced; (2) that the anti-colonial project is intimately connected to decolonization, and, by extension, decolonization cannot happen solely through western science scholarship; and (3) that the complex problems and challenges facing the world today defy universalist solutions" (p. 191). With these stances in mind, we must, therefore, work toward theoretical and pedagogical alternatives to colonial thinking and practice in ways that expand the search for a broader, more radical decolonial thinking and practice in education. A key principle of any decolonial practice is that in order to promote effective anti-colonial and decolonial education, we as scholars, educators, and community activists must begin to employ Indigenous epistemologies that seek to reimagine alternatives to colonial thinking and practice. Put simply, this book seeks to contribute to the search for a more radical decolonial educational practice, one that allows for the coexistence of—and conversation between—multiple epistemologies ("multiple-epistemes") (see also Cajete, 1994, 2000). We cannot decolonize our hegemonic ways of thinking and practice simply through dominant knowledge systems. We should look to counter (and offer oppositional) knowledges that offer different, contradictory, and frequently connected interpretations of our world and social realities. Western knowledge systems have often masqueraded as universal knowledges, shunning other ways of knowing, or appropriating such knowledges without due credit. Indigenous epistemes offer a different way of reading our worlds and the constitutive social, cultural, political, and spiritual relations. Indigenous knowledge systems stress relationality, connections, reciprocity, community building, appreciation, sharing, humility, social responsibility, and generosity as key or essential components facilitating the "coming to know" (see also Battiste & Henderson, 2009; Cajete, 1994, 2000; Chilisa, 2011; Gumbo, 2016, 2017; Mpofu, Otulaja, & Mushayikwa, 2014; Odora Hoppers, 2001, 2002; Smith, 1999; Wilson, 2001, 2008).

In this work, the assertion of Indigeneity is a politicized form of intellectual resistance. The push for politicizing (and radicalizing) Indigeneity is an affirmation of the power (as well as the relevance and utility) of Indigenous intellectual traditions in offering counter readings of schooling and education. Such readings help shape society in ways that subvert and resist the falsely constructed supremacy of western science knowledge.

To be clear, we do not refute claims that western intellectual traditions are relevant or useful to understanding our world today. No knowledge system offers a complete understanding of our world. In fact, we acknowledge that the western intellectual heritage and rich traditions, including philosophical ideas, have historically borrowed from and been influenced by other intellectual traditions, and vice versa. We recognize that western intellectual traditions illuminate a particular way of knowing and understanding our world. We also recognize that western science intellectual traditions are not homogenous bodies of knowledge and that they illuminate a very particular way (and interesting way) of understanding, examining, and knowing our world. The problem, as we see it, is the assumed dominance, supremacy, and legitimacy of western knowledge that works to oppress, suppress—and delegitimize—other ways of knowing, thinking, being, living, and imagining. We cannot underestimate the hegemonic power of western science and how a particular hegemony of knowing has been sustained and enforced in ways that have disproportionately discounted, devalued, and discredited other bodies of knowledge as well as damaged and denied our sense of collective humanity. By discounting, delegitimizing, and discrediting other bodies of knowledge, we have all been limited in understanding the complete history of ideas, events, practices, and occurrences that have shaped and continue to shape human collective growth and development. The hegemony of western science knowledge is revealed when we see Indigenous and colonized bodies dismissing (or outright refusing) knowledges and theorizations that are grounded in their local cultural contexts, histories, and identities.

In mounting resistance to our own cultural knowledge systems, Indigenous scholars are responding with critical intellectual rigor and mindful passion. Dei (2017) has argued that when racialized, Indigenous, and colonized scholars see a need to "write back," we are confronted with the hegemonic power of dominant knowledges to define what we see and how we choose to contest and resist, and what stories we tell about these experiences. For instance, we struggle with the question of what it means to "write back" when the very process of writing back to contest hegemony necessarily entails using eurocentric knowledge to situate analyses that critique, contest, and resist eurocentricity. The conundrum is that often this approach is inaccurately viewed as simply a reaction or resistance to Europe instead of being viewed as an academic contestation to white supremacist colonial logics that underpin and exert hegemonic power over knowledge production in imperialistic ways. We see this much of the time when confronted with the challenge to prove the "theory" behind our assertions. We must resist this intellectual posture and posturing. Aligned with scholars such as Mignolo (2012; 2007) who sharply examines and reveals the ways in which "[t]he modern foundation of knowledge is territorial and imperial" (p. 205) and Escobar (2004) who astutely analyzes subaltern intellectual communities and their "potential to foster alternatives to Western modernity" (p. 210), we agree with the assertion that we must delink colonial modes of knowledge production in order to decolonize knowledge, and, we further add, to decolonize education practices. In the present volume, therefore, we encourage readers who are new to anti-colonial, Indigenous, and decolonial scholarship not only to view our discussion as a way to challenge and resist such hegemony, but also—and just as important—to begin to reimagine and create new futurities. By interrogating and challenging the conventional privileging and legitimacy of western knowledge production, we assert that "something different, something else is possible" when it comes to reading and making sense of human experiences. This assertion drives us to not only examine but also to challenge oppressive structures in the academy, in our schools, and in community, and even within activist spaces. We recognize that some readers may find this approach and assertion too bold or "radical"; however, we respond by emphasizing that our intention is to contribute to and expand scholarship, theory, and pedagogical thought that go beyond the limits of western knowledge production, a conversation that illuminates a way forward, a politics of futurity that engages multiple-epistemes of "Indigeneity." For this work to be meaningful and achievable, it is necessary for readers to not only understand but also to employ multiple forms of knowledge, knowledge that aims to delink, or what Mignolo (2007, 2012) and Mignolo & Tlostanova (2006) refer to as "border thinking": that is, thinking beyond the limited, imperialistic western modes of knowledge production.

For example, we want readers to think about scholarship such as critical pedagogy (Giroux & McLaren, 1989, 2014), and most importantly, its connection to real, on the ground struggles (Grande, 2015) as well as classroom spaces (King, 1991, 2006). It is through scholarship and its connection to the lived social realities and institutions that we can reveal the ways systems of privilege are upheld in order to make them visible so that we can resist and redefine them. We, therefore, strive to demonstrate that more comprehensive and complex engagement with multiple epistemologies (not just the ones mentioned in this text) can illuminate and stimulate new pedagogical and theoretical directions that meaningfully resist and reimagine the possibilities of going beyond purely western knowledge production and education practices. Part of this push forward involves rethinking and centering "resistance" as it relates to conceptions of Indigeneity, the Land, and decolonial thought.

To understand Indigeneity as a political form of intellectual resistance, we must first broach what it means to insist on one's Indigenousness and Indigeneity as a source of knowing and knowledge politics. As suggested already, we must be critical of the frames of reference we use to interrogate our Indigenous realities. As Battiste and Youngblood Henderson (2000) explain, "Eurocentric thought demands universal definitions of Indigenous knowledge, even though Indigenous scholars have established no common usage of the term" (p. 36). Therefore, we cannot demand fixed definitions of *Indigeneity* nor can we interrogate Indigenous realities using a eurocentric lens. In fact, we must be extremely critical of the frames of reference we use to interrogate our Indigenous knowledges and must continuously be mindful that "[s]urvival for Indigenous peoples is more than a question of physical existence; it is an issue of preserving Indigenous knowledge systems in the face of cognitive imperialism. It is a global issue of maintaining

Indigenous worldviews, languages, and environments" (Battiste and Youngblood Henderson, 2000, p. 12). In this light, asserting Indigeneity and engaging in Indigeneity as a political form of resistance to cognitive imperialism inherent in eurocentric ways of knowing must be recognized. Indigeneity is about history, culture, identity, politics, and resistance. Furthermore, Indigeneity is a recourse to ancient and historical landscape and the lessons of the Land and place as knowledges that are not fossilized or essentialized in time and space. The Land is also intricately tied to Indigeneity, and the saliency of Indigeneity and its connection to the Land is crucial to highlight. Land is taken both concretely and metaphorically, allowing bodies to implicate space and learning. Land evokes more than a physical presence. It is a spiritual place and a spiritually centered understanding of social space. Land is social, physical, and cultural, as well as spiritual and metaphorical, constructions. It is about place, environments, water, sky, and soils. Land is about physical and emotional attachment. It is a place where we define a sense of belonging and identity, a place that bestows on us culture, histories, and memories. We understand the Land as an embodiment of Earth teachings, a necessary and relevant aspect that will aid in transforming and situating what education ought to be. The role of Land ownership and Land dispossession as the central issue within Indigenous knowledge production bring to the fore why education should engage the social and physical context of the learners.

The question of Land and pedagogy has been addressed very comprehensively by many Indigenous scholars. Examples are the works by Simpson (2014), Deloria (2011), Coulthard (2014), among others who speak in direct reference to the Turtle Island context. For any education to be deemed "Indigenous" it must be rooted in the Land, specifically, the workings of the Land and Earthly teachings (see also Deloria, 2001). It is enthused that Land offers spiritual, emotional, cultural and political connections between peoples, Nature, their cosmological beliefs and practices. As well, for Indigenous peoples, being cognizant of these connections points to how we must act responsibly within our communities. Through the engagement with the Land, learning becomes a lifelong sacred activity helping to educate about and convey Indigenous peoples' thought processes and the philosophical systems, which, although distinct, are connected with other ways of knowing (see also Alfred, 1999, 2005). As Simpson (2014) writes, "we cannot carry out the kind of decolonization our ancestors set in motion if we don't create a generation of land-based, community-based intellectuals and cultural producers who are accountable to our Nations and whose life work is concerned with the regeneration of these systems, rather than meeting the overwhelming needs of the Western academic industrial complex or attempting to 'Indigenize the academy' by bringing Indigenous Knowledges into the academy on the terms of the academy itself" (p. 13). We cannot decolonize without a rootedness on the Land. The Land is the anchor for our decolonization practice. We need to reclaim stolen and dispossessed Lands as a starting point of any decolonization politics. As has also been opined to acknowledge "[L]and as pedagogy, as a life practice inevitably means coming face-to-face with settler colonial authority, surveillance and violence because, in practice, it places Indigenous bodies between settlers and their money (see Coulthard, 2014, p. 36, quoted in Simpson, 2014, p. 19). Developing a critical understanding of Land ownership and Land dispossession as central issues within Indigenous knowledge production highlights the significance of why education must engage the social and physical milieu of learners. Furthermore, by politicizing Indigeneity—across Lands—we create meaningful opportunities to problematize and resist education practices and discourse that rely heavily on limited (and damaging) conceptions of "development," narratives of "social mobility," and teleological notions of "progress" that prevent us from reimagining alternatives to knowledge production and education in ways that push this work forward.

Our choice, then, to consistently focus on resistance is a strategic and necessary part of the work and discussion being put forth here. We cannot ignore the fact that the western canon—and, by extension, western forms of knowledge—continues to be the most powerful, insidious tool of colonization. Under the guise of "education," schools have historically been (and still are) sites of assimilation, domination, and inculcation of values, beliefs, and practices. There is nothing neutral about the project of education. It is in school where we first begin to see how certain bodies are deemed violent, disruptive, exemplary, or deficient. Schools actively cultivate, maintain, and exacerbate social hierarchies and inequity. Notions of citizenship, belonging, and place are produced by the state and amplified by schools. Therefore, in this collection, the reader will find that we bring to the fore what it means to claim Indigeneity, recognizing that current education trends aimed at creating "inclusiveness" and "diversity" are bound to fail without addressing the power relations at play in the ways that Black, Indigenous, and racialized students experience and understand schooling philosophies, attitudes, and culture. Higher suspension and push-out rates, low teacher expectations, and inadequate and underresourced curricular sophistication are all well-documented symptoms of systemic issues in education that are a direct result of schools not being responsive to the social identities of the learners (Dei, 2008; Dei, Holmes, Mazzuca, McIsaac, & Campbell, 1995; Dei, 2008). These notions are particularly detrimental to racialized students. Though such observations are not new to scholars who work to advance anti-racism, anti-colonialism, and decolonial projects, we must continue to build awareness and share knowledges about the ways in which our colonial legacies have drastically shaped our views of the world—from the way we organize schooling and normalize notions of borders and mobility, to the way we structure our sense of place, belonging, and time, as well as understand conceptions of ownership, progress, and healing. In doing so, it is imperative that anti-colonial and decolonial projects challenge our views and beliefs about what it means to learn, how learning can take place, and what we can do to reimagine alternatives to colonial thinking and practice in ways that recenter the learner, take stock of the political context of the learner and the Land, and focus on the saliency of resisting and delinking knowledge production and practices.

In taking a critical decolonial approach to knowledge production and educational practice, we focus on those subordinated bodies and regimes of knowledge that are usually consigned to the margins of academic discussions and so-called "deeply intellectual" conversations in the elite halls of the western academy. Our goal is to help resurrect these "Otherized knowledges" by pointing to how they can be deployed to offer counter visions of schooling and education. The complex "geopolitics of knowledge" (Mignolo, 2012) supports the contention that all knowledges are not neutral but rather sociopolitical and cultural constructions of knowing. By bringing a decolonial lens to knowledge and educational resistance, we are also questioning what is often presented as "valid" and "legitimate" knowledge and the ways such knowledges ought to be produced, interrogated, and disseminated both internally and externally. The questions of who and what are left out—and how, why, and when—are huge questions for investigation. These questions make us all complicit in the marginalization of certain voices, experiences, and knowledges in academia. We must uphold the idea of multiple knowledge constructions to ensure that we bring a deeper understanding of both the differences and similarities among knowledge systems. The epistemic frameworks we deploy to understand schooling and education also reveal a constant struggle for the learner to navigate, engage, and appreciate the plurality of knowledge traditions in the academy and to challenge how these knowledges are differentially valued in the educational system.

Within every learning space there is always the colonial presence and the possibility of anti-colonial resistance. This colonial presence is marked by power and privilege as accorded on particular bodies and experiences. The anti-colonial presence is marked by the resisting voice, insisting on being heard and challenging the meta and master narrative. This voice of resistance is demanding to be heard on its own terms, even as colonial and colonizing relations continually rear their heads. The politics of decoloniality requires an understanding that colonialism did not end with the formal departure of the colonizer from the Lands of the colonized (Quijano, 2000; Santos, 2007; see also Phillipson, 1992). Anything to the contrary is intellectual and political dishonesty on the part of a learner. Colonialism still manifests itself both by the presence and absence of the colonized. There is the colonizer within who continually works with the tropes and ideas of Western modernity, liberalism, and human material progress. There is a coloniality of power that simultaneously operates while masking itself in the ongoing search for "excellence," "merit," "standards, "and "scholarly knowledge" as something that can be marked on specific bodies and particular geographies. These specificities of knowledge underpin the bodies and geographies that pinpoint to a very curious dynamic of the intersections of power and knowledge along the lines of race, gender, class, sexuality, and disability.

With such issues and contestations in mind, this book stems from intensive discussion (over the course of a year) with graduate students, community activists, and education scholars who recognize the urgent need to decolonize knowledge production and schooling on some key questions about knowledge, resistance, and decolonization. We utilize an anti-colonial framework to challenge normative practices within current school policies and education practices. The book examines a broad range of issues in education, particularly the neocolonial practices that inhibit true learning. The need to decolonize knowledge, school classrooms, and educational curricula cannot be overlooked, especially in light of the educational disengagement of Indigenous, Black, and racialized youth. Despite the existence of research that advocates for educational transformation and change, schools still remain oppressive spaces. It is within the classrooms and the epistemologies that underpin the curricula that particular kinds of learners are marginalized and oppressed. It is important that there be an intellectual shift away from culturally deficient and paternalistic ideas that inhibit the learner from exercising openness and creativity in thought that challenges the colonial production of knowledge. By expanding and reimagining the possibilities inherent in the field of education, each of the papers in the collection probe how we, as scholars, educators, and community activists, can challenge and subvert processes of colonization across a range of geopolitical spaces. Each author utilizes anti-colonial thought to challenge normative practices within current school policies and education practices, offering insightful nuances that ask readers to take stock of current education landscapes and reimagine the potentialities of what true learning could be. By expanding and reimagining the possibilities inherent in the field of education, this collection probes how we, as scholars, educators, and community activists, can challenge and subvert processes of colonization across a range of geopolitical spaces.

To open the discussion, Phyllis McKenna's poetic essay "Back in the Day" challenges readers to reflect on memory, colonialism, trauma, and healing. McKenna's poem is an apt starting point, as it politicizes identity—the body and the Land—and creates a path forward that focuses on healing, growth, and transformation. She compels us to think about blood memory, what she describes as "memories coded in veins." Her captivating words echo the importance of the Land, identity, and healing, emphasizing the importance of being open to new challenges, new journeys, and new ways of knowing and learning—themes that run deep through each of the chapters.

In "Decolonial Latinx Feminist Spiritual Practices in Processes of Decolonization" Carolina Rios Lezama contributes to the discussion with a theoretical groundedness, specifically espousing the power of decolonial Latinx feminist epistemologies. The author discusses how Latinx women negotiate identity, remember, and reclaim Indigenous knowledge. She challenges the damaging dichotomy of the western body and spirit that leads to the fragmentation of Latinx women's subjectivities. Rios Lezama carefully demonstrates how subjugated knowledges that center spirituality can engage in processes of decolonization by reconfiguring cultural and knowledge production. Rios Lezama ends her chapter by outlining precisely how decolonial Latinx feminist epistemology can not only enhance understandings of the learner but also inform broad issues of schooling and education to create transformative change.

A cornerstone of decolonial feminist theorizing that engages Indigenous knowledges is the anchor in spiritual ontologies and epistemologies. Janelle Brady's essay,

"(Re)Claiming Spirituality as Anti-Colonial Resistance and Decolonial Praxis," expands discussions on spirituality and decolonial knowledge, arguing that spirituality grounded in Afrocentric epistemologies is an intentional and political project that can help transform and recreate educational spaces and relationships. Brady's essay is important in that it explores the pedagogical implications of spirituality, offering new insights into reclaiming and understanding spirituality from a place of relationality. She asserts that it is critical to reclaim spirituality in ways that allow for holistic and multicentric ways of knowing. Her questions and analysis bring to light the importance of creating culturally relevant pedagogy in ways that holistically connect learners and educators to education and the larger political world. Afrocentric epistemologies constitute one of the counter discourses intended to subvert the dominance of eurocentric knowledge.

In her essay "Reflections on the Implications of Western Theories on Indigenous Populations: Decolonizing and Indigenizing the Classroom," Cristina Bianchi looks at a western-dominant knowledge system as expressed in mental health. The author examines western theories of mental health, mental wellness, and human development in order to challenge readers to address the limitations of eurocentric healing philosophies and methods. Bianchi articulates the importance of using multiple teaching strategies, self-reflecting methods, and identity-building strategies that center Indigenous knowledges, decolonization, and multiple worldviews. She draws on her experience in childhood studies and interprets different ways of decolonizing and Indigenizing the classroom through early childhood development practices.

The spatial geography classroom is an important learning space. Jessica Peden, in her study "Decolonizing the Geography Classroom: A Call to Action for Educators to Reimagine Pedagogy of Place," critically examines the colonial logic that underpins the discipline of geography. It is argued that geography is more than space with a given physicality—that geography itself is a socially and politically constructed understanding. Peden's astute analysis sheds light on the capitalist lens used to determine and teach conceptions of the environment and place, articulating how the curriculum itself embeds, maintains, and reproduces notions of capitalism. The author's emphasis on decolonizing the classroom is a direct call to action to create anti-colonial spaces for students to explore connectivity, reciprocity, and community. Land, place, and environment always enter into the discussion of different geographies.

Indigenous knowledges often face the problem of not just being heard and respected, but also of being misappropriated and misconstrued. Such knowledge can be co-opted to serve narrow and parochial interests other than what was originally intended. Mandeep Jajj's article, "'Indigenous Knowledges': Issues of Commodification, Privatization, and Intellectual Property Rights," reveals and problematizes the privatization of Indigenous knowledges in India, exposing the colonial operation of appropriation, privatization, commodification, commercialization, and monopolization of the Land and its renewable resources. Jajj demonstrates how Indigenous knowledges are turned into "economic necessities" in order to control, subjugate, and further oppress marginalized bodies. Her work interrogates the way in which neocolonial agendas seek to normalize the manipulation, misuse, and extraction of Indigeneity as a source of capital and points to the importance of reclaiming knowledges of the Land in order to fight against such hegemony.

But there are also hopeful signs in the engagement of such knowledges. Rachel Buchanan's study, "Decolonization Through Decentralization," draws attention to the structures that maintain oppression and divisiveness under the guise of unity in the context of Africa. Arguing for decolonization through decentralization in education, she critiques euro-western knowledges' inability to coexist. By critiquing the approach of western "development experts" to education in Africa through science, research, and education policies that rely on western imperialism frameworks of knowledge production, Buchanan calls for an end to the standardized and homogenized curricula that maintain the supremacy of the elite and naturalize oppression using discourses of development and unity. Her analysis is duly informed by an Indigenous epistemological framework.

Moving toward a particular facet of education, Hagger Said's "The Role of English Education in Post-Colonial Egypt: Criticisms and Solutions for the Future" explores the role of English-language education in North Africa (Egypt). The author disrupts the neutrality of English-language education in Egypt and illuminates its colonial entanglements and legacies. In particular, Said's work challenges the dominance and pervasiveness of English education and usage, offering useful critiques and solutions that provide new pedagogical possibilities that resist linguistic hegemony and reaffirm Indigenous knowledges and languages.

Recognizing that education is closely wedded to western paradigms of development and notions of economic progress, Shukri Hilowle's "Education in Somalia: The Role of International Organizations in Formal Education" uses an anti-colonial framework to examine the role of international organizations (IOs) in Somalia. By uncovering historical colonial dimensions of state collapse, she demonstrates how education projects such as "Operation to Restore Hope" of 1993 reveal the dysfunctional nature of IOs, incisively pointing out the failure to achieve meaningful education and state stability. Hilowle ultimately calls on policymakers, educators, and IO stakeholders to re-examine the intended (and unintended) repercussions of a development-driven education agenda.

Expanding the dialogue and critique of development practices in education, Wambui Karanja's essay, "Development, Research, and the Commodification of Poverty in Africa," examines colonialist conceptualizations and constructs of Africa and Africans using anti-racist, decolonial, and Afrocentric frameworks (Asante, 1991, 2003). Karanja's apt analysis problematizes and exposes the way in which research and development projects commodify poverty in Africa. In the pursuit of western-based development and modernization goals, she argues that research about Africa perpetuates negative stereotyping of Africa and Africans, calling for action on alternatives to decolonizing research approaches to address issues of complicity and implication in perpetuating the colonial project.

The search for genuine development options for the Global South is a perennial issue. It can be argued that spirituality ought to remain as the axis for the implementation of genuine development agendas, particularly in the Global South. Spirituality allows us to dream about new futures, whether in education or development. Kimberly L. Todd's essay, "Dreaming Our Way to New Decolonial and Educational Futurities: Charting Pathways of Hope," uses dreaming as spiritual praxis to reframe the possibilities in educational futurities. Her work re-envisions an education system that places connection and spirituality at the heart of its pedagogy in order to lead to decolonial futurities. Steeped in decolonial frameworks, Indigenous epistemologies, and transformative education research, Todd focuses her discussion on the interconnection and interdependence of all life forms, pushing readers to think about schooling as transformative sites that hold potential to inspire decolonial futurities.

Phyllis McKenna's second poem centers Indigeneity through the assertion of identity, the triumph of resiliency, and strategies of resurgence. Powerful and moving, Mckenna's words nod to colonial histories and thoughtfully gesture toward new futurities: self-determination, collective identity, community resistance, and Indigenous resurgence. The use of poetry must be understood as a highly political and deeply theoretical process that actively employs a strategic form of resistance to colonial knowledge production in the academy. As a closing piece, it is helpful for us to reiterate how McKenna's words speak directly to educators, emphasizing how vital it is to engage decolonizing education in ways that do not tokenize Indigenous identities and experiences. While simultaneously challenging readers to ponder questions of Indigenous survival, resistance, resurgence, strength, and kindness in the face of colonialism, genocide, and Land dispossession, McKenna makes a bold call to action that demands the attention of educators. With generations of wisdom and knowledges embedded in her mind, body, and spirit, McKenna is cautious yet hopeful that decolonization—as a process, not an end goal—can happen through education and knowledge production.

In conclusion, this collection has succeeded in blending poetry, scholarly papers, and think-tank writing styles to engage scholars, educators, and community activists in critical ideas that intend to rethink and contribute new understandings of decolonizing education. Our learning objective has been to produce a book that helps us theorize and reframe Indigeneity and decolonial resistance projects in education using anti-colonial, anti-racist, and decolonial scholarship. We have utilized an anti-colonial framework to challenge normative practices within current school policies and education practices in a range of geopolitical spaces: Latin America, Africa, Somalia, Egypt, Hawaii, and Canada. We believe that this compilation encourages continuous spiritual and intellectual growth, offering thought-provoking insights that lead readers to challenge, question, and reimagine the possibilities for decolonial futurities through various sites of education—Latinx identity-making, a geography classroom in Canada, Afrocentricity, international organizations in Somalia, English schooling in Egypt, intellectual property in India, charter schools in Hawaii, and identity-making in Canada. While this collection encourages the reader to acknowledge and bear witness to the insidious nature of colonial education practices and philosophies, the ultimate goal is geared toward reinvigorating current topics in education in ways that bring about a renewed sense of energy, spirit, and intellectual rigor to those that continue to reveal colonialism, reimagine futurities, and work toward decolonizing the academy, education, community, and activist spaces.

References

Alfred, T. (1999). *Peace, power and righteousness: An Indigenous manifesto*. Toronto, ON: Oxford University Press.

Alfred, T. (2005). *Wasáse: Indigenous pathways of action and freedom*. Toronto, ON: University of Toronto Press.

Asante, M. (1991). The Afrocentric idea in education. *Journal of Negro Education, 60*(2), 170–180.

Asante. M. (2003). *Afrocentricity: The theory of social change*. Chicago, IL: African American Images.

Battiste, M., & Henderson, J. (2009). Naturalizing Indigenous knowledge in eurocentric education. *Canadian Journal of Native Education, 32*(1), 5–18.

Cajete, G. (1994). *Look to the mountain: An ecology of Indigenous education*. Skyland, NC: Kivaki Press.

Cajete, G. (2000). *Native science: Natural laws of interdependence*. San Diego, CA: Clear Light Publishers.

Chilisa, B. (2011). Resisting dominant discourses: Implications of Indigenous, African feminist theory and methods for gender and education research. *Gender and Education, 22*(6), 617–632.

Coulthard, G. (2014). *Red skin, white masks: Rejecting colonial politics of recognition*. Minneapolis, MN: University of Minnesota Press.

Dei, G.J.S. (2000). Rethinking the role of Indigenous knowledges in the academy. *International Journal of Inclusive Education*, 4(2), 111–132.

Dei, G. J. S. (2016). Indigenous philosophies, counter epistemologies and anti-colonial education. *Education and Society*, 190–206.

Dei, G.J.S. (2017). Black like me: Reframing Blackness and decolonial politics. R. Freeman Butts Distinguished Lecture, annual meeting of the American Educational Studies Association (AESA), Omni William Penn Hotel, Pittsburgh, PA, November 1–5.

Dei, G.J.S., & Kempf, A. (Eds.). (2006). *Anti-colonialism and education: The politics of resistance*. Rotterdam, Netherlands: Sense Publishers.

Dei, G.J.S., & Lordan, M. (2016). *Anti-colonial theory and decolonial praxis*. New York, NY: Peter Lang.

Dei, G. J. (2008). Schooling as community: Race, schooling, and the education of African youth. *Journal of Black studies, 38*(3), 346–366.

Dei, G. J., Holmes, L., Mazzuca, J., McIsaac, E., & Campbell, R. (1995). Drop out or push out? The dynamics of Black students' disengagement from school. In annual meeting of the American Educational Research Association.

Deloria, V., Jr. (2001). Traditional technology. In V. Deloria, Jr. & D. Wildcat (Eds.), *Power & place: Indian education in America*. Golden, CO: Fulcrum Resources.

Escobar, A. (2004). Beyond the Third World: Imperial globality, global coloniality and anti-globalisation social movements. *Third World Quarterly, 25*(1), 207–230.

Giroux, H. A., & McLaren, P. (Eds.). (1989). *Critical pedagogy, the state, and cultural struggle.* Albany, NY: State University of New York Press.

Giroux, H. A., & McLaren, P. (Eds.). (2014). *Between borders: Pedagogy and the politics of cultural studies.* Routledge.

Grande, S. (2015). *Red pedagogy: Native American social and political thought.* Lanham, MD: Rowman & Littlefield.

Gumbo, M.T. (2016). A model for Indigenising the university curriculum: A quest for educational relevance. In V. Msila & M. Gumbo (Eds.), *Africanising the curriculum: Indigenous perspectives and theories* (pp. 33–56). Stellenbosch, South Africa: Sun Media.

Gumbo, M.T. (2017). Alternative knowledge systems. In J. Williams & K. Stables (Eds.), *Contemporary issues in technology education: Critique in design and technology education* (pp. 87–105). Singapore: Springer.

King, J. E. (1991). Dysconscious racism: Ideology, identity, and the miseducation of teachers. *The Journal of Negro Education, 60*(2), 133–146.

King, J. E. (Ed.). (2006). *Black education: A transformative research and action agenda for the new century.* New York, NY: Routledge.

Loomba, A., & Orkin, M. (Eds.). (1998). *Post-colonial Shakespeares.* New York, NY: Routledge.

Maldonado-Torres, N. (2004). The topology of being and the geopolitics of knowledge: Modernity, empire, coloniality. *City, 8*(1), 29–56.

Mignolo, W.D. (2007). Delinking: The rhetoric of modernity, the logic of coloniality and the grammar of de-coloniality. *Cultural Studies,* 21(2–3), 449–514.

Mignolo, W.D. (2009). Epistemic disobedience, independent thought and decolonial freedom. *Theory, Culture & Society, 26*(7–8), 159–181.

Mignolo, W.D. (2012). *Local histories/global designs: Coloniality, subaltern knowledges, and border thinking.* Princeton, NJ: Princeton University Press.

Mignolo, W.D., & Tlostanova, M.V. (2006). Theorizing from the borders: Shifting to geo- and body-politics of knowledge. *European Journal of Social Theory, 9*(2), 205–221.

Mpofu, V., Otulaja, F.S., & Mushayikwa, E. (2014). Towards culturally relevant classroom science: A theoretical framework focusing on traditional plant healing. *Cultural Studies of Science Education, 9*(1), 221–242.

Odora Hoppers, C.A. (2001). Indigenous knowledge systems and academic institutions in South Africa. *Perspectives in Education, 19*(1), 73–86.

Odora Hoppers, C.A. (2002). Top of form Indigenous knowledge and the integration of knowledge systems: Towards a conceptual and methodological framework. In C.A. Odora Hoppers (Ed.), *Indigenous knowledge and integration of knowledge systems towards philosophy of articulation.* Claremont, South Africa: New Africa Books.

Pennycook, A. (2017). *The cultural politics of English as an international language.* New York, NY: Taylor & Francis.

Phillipson, R. (1992). *Linguistic imperialism.* Oxford, UK: Oxford University Press.

Quijano, A. (2000). Coloniality of power and Eurocentrism in Latin America. *International Sociology, 15*(2), 215–232.

Santos, B.D.S. (2007). Beyond abyssal thinking: From global lines to ecologies of knowledges. *Review* (Fernand Braudel Center), 31, 45–89.

Simpson, L.B. (2014). Land as pedagogy: Nishnaabeg intelligence and rebellious transformation. *Decolonization: Indigeneity, Education & Society, 3*(3), pp. 1–25.

Smith, L. (1999). *Decolonizing methodologies.* London, UK: Zed Books.

Tlostanova, M., & Mignolo, W.D. (2007). The logic of coloniality and the limits of postcoloniality. In R. Krishnaswamy & J.C. Hawley (Eds.), *Post colonial and the global* (pp. 109–123). Minneapolis, MN: University of Minnesota Press.

Tuck, E., & Yang, K.W. (2012). Decolonization is not a metaphor. *Decolonization, Indigeneity, Education and Society, 1*(1) [online journal].

Wilson, S. (2001). What is Indigenous research methodology? *Canadian Journal of Native Education, 25*(2), 175–179.

Wilson, S. (2008). *Research is ceremony: Indigenous research methods.* Halifax, NS: Fernwood Publishing.

CHAPTER 2

Decolonial Latinx Feminist Spiritual Practices in Processes of Decolonization

Carolina Rios Lezama

Colonialism involved the dispossession of Indigenous peoples from their Land and the imposition of western authority over already-existing systems of government. The colonial project was and continues to be the institutional violence of armies, law courts, and the prison-industrial complex that deprives Indigenous and racialized people of their Land and contributes to their disenfranchisement. Moreover, colonialism involves the imposition of western knowledges over Indigenous cultures, history, language, and their systems of government, and has sought to eradicate non-western knowledges. The impact of colonialism on the subjectivities of colonized peoples has been devastating. Wa Thiong'o (1986) explains that colonialism "makes [the colonized] see their past as one wasteland of non-achievement and it makes them want to distance themselves from that wasteland" (p. 3). In order to challenge the negative impacts colonialism had on the colonized and their subjectivities, decolonization of the mind, body, and soul is necessary (Dei, 2012). In what follows, I will argue that through the reclaiming of Indigenous knowledges and engaging in Indigenous spiritual practices, Latinx[1] and Chicana women are participating in processes of decolonization that are reconfiguring cultural and knowledge production. I will begin by locating myself within this chapter to help the reader understand how I became involved in this topic. I will then explain why I chose a decolonial feminist epistemology and will define the terms *Indigenous* and *decolonization* as used throughout the chapter. Then I will demonstrate how Chicana and Latinx women are engaging in processes of decolonization through the reclaiming of

Indigenous knowledges and spiritual practices. Further, I will argue that by centering spirituality and the spirit, Latinx women are challenging the western body/spirit dichotomy and the split of the sex and spirit that has contributed to the fragmentation of Latinx women's subjectivities. I will conclude with a discussion of how this decolonial Latinx feminist epistemology can inform broad issues of schooling and education to create transformative change.

Locating Myself

I will begin by locating myself within the chapter. I am a cysgender[2] Latina with Indigenous Quechua[3] roots. I was born in Peru and moved to Turtle Island when I was 13 years old. My research interests, which stem from my experiences living in Toronto and Peru, are Latinx women/women-identified organizing, anti-racism, and Indigenous knowledges. My experiences living in Toronto as a Latinx-identified woman have strongly shaped my consciousness of the socioeconomic barriers that racialized women face. My family's historical struggle against anti-Indigenous racism in Peru and experiences of discrimination, racism, and socioeconomic barriers faced in Peru and on Turtle Island have also influenced my research interests.

After completing my undergraduate training, I became involved in community activism in the Latin American community through MUJER, a Latin American women's organization. Much of my work centered on violence prevention, leadership training, and Latinx feminist pedagogy. After engaging in community activism for over five years, I decided to pursue academic activism because I realized the community activism being led by Latin American women/women-identified in Toronto was not being shared and passed on to future generations. I remember meeting university-educated Latin American women who would express how disappointed they were that Latinx voices were not included in the gender studies curriculum. Those who were enrolled in graduate school would share how much they struggled to find literature on Latin American women's activism in Toronto. All of this served as motivation to organize a course available to the Latin American community that would introduce Latin American women to feminist traditions in Latin America, the United States, and Canada. Together with some powerful and inspiring participants in the course, we read intellectual feminist writers such as Gloria Anzaldúa, Cheri Moraga, Chela Sandoval, Magaly San Martín, and many more. Through the work of these Latinx women intellectuals, we see our experiences represented and reflected. This serves as further inspiration to pursue academic work inclusive of Latinx experiences and to contribute to documenting Latinx feminist traditions in Toronto. Yet despite the incredible intellectual and emotional work I have witnessed, I felt there was something missing—something deep within myself that needed nurturing and nourishing that I later came to understand as a spiritual connection. But I was not sure where or how to begin my journey.

I recall visiting a couple of Spanish-speaking Catholic churches where I might be able to find a way to nurture my spirit. At the first church I visited, the priest began his sermon with his thoughts on Cuba. He called Cuba "hell in this world." I was highly disappointed with his comments, not because I think Cuba is a perfect place, but because he was speaking about Cuba uncritically. He was not considering the challenges Cuba has faced as a result of the embargo placed on it by the United States, or the fact that despite this embargo Cuba has been able to provide free education and healthcare to its population. Moreover, I was very uncomfortable with the whiteness of the church, with its white angels and white Virgin Mary statue, something that did not reflect the ethnically and racially diverse Latinx community. I was also left very uncomfortable by the overall structure and institution, which reinforced patriarchal values by not allowing women to hold leadership positions.

However, I did not give up on the Catholic Church after this one visit, as I wanted to remain open to the idea that it was possible to undermine the patriarchal, predominantly white views within the church. I reminded myself that Indigenous people in Latin America have undermined the church by inserting their own religious practices. This strong belief in people's agency led me to visit a second church that preached liberation theology. Unfortunately, I was again disappointed, this time because the church was engaged in censoring conversations about abortion at a local radio station that was using church space. This, in turn, pushed me out of the church, and I continued my search for spiritual connectivity.

I began to read books by bell hooks on self-care and self-love. In these books, hooks claims that one cannot be a liberated feminist until one develops, or at least consciously works toward cultivating, a healthy self-esteem and self-love. For example, in *All About Love*, hooks (2001), using Erich Fromm's definition of *love*, defines it as "the will to extend one's self for the purpose of nurturing one's own or another's spiritual growth" (p. 4). I found this definition to be immensely powerful, because I had always understood love to be an emotion rather than an act and a choice. I had never connected love to spiritual growth. According to hooks, spiritual awakening is an awakening to love. An awakening to love and spirituality involves nurturing our spirits and challenging social injustices. In the pages of *All About Love* I found what I needed, what my spirit needed. I was so glad to have found this type of work and wanted to share it with other women. However, I remember discussing this experience with a community organizer and being shocked at her response. According to this organizer, bell hooks had become less radical and less political for writing about self-care—that is, her writing about love and spirituality had made her less political and "soft." I later came to realize that this is a belief that many community organizers shared. However, for me, spirituality and the spirit became important, indeed fundamental, to community organizing and to helping me navigate academia. My spiritual practices and the nurturing of my spirit serve as a source of strength to help me maintain hope that social transformation is possible and that we must continue to fight injustice. Thus, for me to be able to engage in processes of transformation at an individual and social level requires that my spirit be nurtured and centered.

Other authors who have helped me understand the importance of the spirit and spirituality are Shahjahan (2005), Cynthia B. Dillard (2008), Njoki Wane (2006), and George J. Sefa Dei (2002, 2012), who explore spirituality as a valid source of knowledge in academia. Engaging the spirit can help us transform and create social change. If, as these authors argue, the spirit can never be conquered, then we can be certain that we can access our true selves and begin to heal from the wounds of colonialism and neocolonialism. This healing will be difficult, considering that colonialism keeps changing and transforming itself. But if we center the spirit and tap into our own Indigenous practices, traditions, and beliefs, we may be able to create transformative changes within ourselves and our communities.

Decolonial and Anti-Racist Feminist Framework

This chapter is informed by a decolonial perspective of anti-racist feminism that will utilize Indigenous knowledges, experiences, and traditions of Latinx and Chicana women to counter dominant eurocentric views. This approach counters the dominant eurocentric views that negate, seek to erase, and subjugate Indigenous knowledges. Dominant eurocentric views strip Indigenous peoples of their agency and resiliency in order to ensure that the current system of domination is sustained. Thus, decolonization is imperative.

> Decolonization, which sets out to change the order of the world, is, obviously, a program of complete disorder. But it cannot come as a result of magical practices, nor of a natural shock, or of a friendly understanding. Decolonization, as we know, is a historical process: that is to say it cannot be understood, it cannot become intelligible nor clear to itself except in the exact measure that we can discern the movements which give it historical form and content. (Fanon, 1963, p. 36)

In the quotation, Frantz Fanon describes the process of decolonization as an attempt to fundamentally restructure the world. It involves undoing the systems of violence perpetuated by colonialism that have dispossessed Indigenous peoples from their Land and the epistemological violence Indigenous people have experienced. Indigenous presence and experiences must be foundational in this decolonial approach and analysis. Failure to make Indigenous experiences foundational to an anti-racist feminist framework results in placing colonialism in the past, while failing to address the multiple projects of continuing colonialism (Dhamoon, 2015, p. 21). Consequently, to decolonize we must examine the trajectory that led to the struggles of people fighting to challenge the systems of violence and how these systems are interconnected and constantly changing.

An anti-racist feminist framework allows me to place Latinx and Chicana women at the center of my inquiry. By focusing on their perspectives and experiences, I seek to acknowledge their agency and ground their identities within their social realities. Understanding their social realities allows me to explore the multiplicity of ways and factors that shape their experiences. For Latinx and Chicana women, experiences are not only shaped by their gendered experiences but also by social categories such as class, race, ethnicity, and even religion. These social categories intersect in their individual experience to reflect multiple "interlocking systems of privilege and oppression" at the social level (Collins, 2000, p. 277). These systems of oppression, including racism, sexism, heterosexism, and misogyny, work together and support each other in order to maintain the systems of violence that attempt to control Latinx and Chicana women's bodies and identities. Consequently, an intersectional approach would "disrupt the interacting multiplicities of gendered racisms and colonialism that aggregately consolidate white supremacy, colonialism, racism, hetero-patriarchy, and capitalism" (Dhamoon, 2015, p. 34). Moreover, the "matrix of domination is constantly shifting, appropriated, and being re-made in response to various centers of power and... resistances" (Dhamoon, 2015, p. 34). This constant shifting and being remade requires that our feminist practice undertake different political projects.

A decolonial, anti-racist feminist framework would allow me to examine how multiple forms of colonialism have affected Latinx and Chicana women. It would allow me to deconstruct the epistemological violence forced on Latinx and Chicana women by centering their experiences and grounding their identities on their social realities to counter this violence. This framework also acknowledges their agency, which they exert through the re-membering and reappropriating of their Indigenous knowledges and spiritual practices. It is through the reappropriation of Indigenous goddesses that Latinx and Chicana women construct new identities that challenge dominant discourses that have claimed superiority and universality.

The Colonial Project

The colonial project deployed various tools to control and subdue Indigenous peoples and dispossess them of their lands. Andrea Smith (2005) argues that sexual violence against Indigenous and racialized women extended to their lands and territories, which became violable (p. 55). According to Smith, "the project of colonial sexual violence established the ideology that Native bodies are inherently violable—and, by extension, that Native lands are also inherently violable" (p. 12). The colonialists claimed possession of the Land under the doctrine of *terra nullius*, or "Land belonging to nobody." By asserting that the Land did not belong to anyone, they were able to claim and confiscate shared

Indigenous Lands. The colonizers used military force to remove Indigenous peoples from their Land and physical violence to subdue Indigenous bodies. Indigenous women in particular were the targets of sexual violence. Smith states that "the colonial/patriarchal mind that seeks to control the sexuality of women and Indigenous peoples... also seeks to control nature" (p. 55). Anne McClintock (1995) also explains that Indigenous women were seen as "the earth that is discovered, entered, named, inseminated and, above all, owned. Symbolically reduced, in [European] male eyes, to the space on which male contests are waged" (p. 31). These racist ideologies, as presented by McClintock and Smith, intersect with sexist ideologies of control over women's bodies and their Land.

McClintock argues that the colonial encounter was not only gendered and racialized; it also melded all histories into a linear, universal, and single understanding that privileged the colonizer's culture and story. In this linear understanding of history, non-European cultures were constructed as backward, ahistorical, fixed, and static, while European cultures were constructed as modern, rational, and having achieved progress. However, the existence of Black, Indigenous, and other non-Europeans who were supposed to occupy a place somewhere in the past created contradictions. According to McClintock, "colonized peoples... do not inhabit history proper but exist in a permanently anterior time within the geographic space of the modern empire as anachronistic humans, atavistic, irrational, [and] bereft of human agency..." (p. 30). McClintock argues that the West constructed the idea of a linear social evolution wherein societies have to move up and follow certain stages from "savagery" to "civilization." Since western civilizations had already passed through these stages, their colonial subjects were not just less developed; they were also windows into the past. This idea of the colonial subjects being at an earlier stage of progress served to justify European intervention as part of a civilizing project to "help" non-European people achieve progress from their place of "inferiority."

In Canada, these same racist ideologies were used to justify state intervention in the lives of Indigenous communities. Indigenous children were taken away from their homes, families, and communities and forced to assimilate into the dominant culture through residential schools. Residential schools were part of the state's civilizing project, which sought to isolate Indigenous children from their communities because their communities' culture and traditions were considered inferior. In 2008, the Indian Residential Schools Truth and Reconciliation Commission (TRC) was formed with a mandate to create a public record of the policies, operations, and legacy of residential schools. The TRC carried out an investigation into the residential schools and interviewed over 6,000 witnesses, most of whom were survivors. In its final report, the commission drafted "Calls for Action," among them that Indigenous people's history be included within the school curriculum. Of course, the exclusion and erasure of Indigenous histories within educational institutions is not limited to Indigenous peoples. Education has also erased the experiences and contributions of African, Japanese, Chinese, Latin American, and other racialized communities.

The racist and sexist ideologies constructed during colonialism to subdue Indigenous peoples have become deeply embedded within our education system, media, and society. For example, fields of knowledge such as literature and art are considered objective knowledge without any political ideology or agenda. However, Edward Said (1979) argues that, in fact, knowledge produced by western scholars in literature and the arts in fact reinforces colonial power relations. According to Said, the Arab world (or Orient) was constructed as inferior and backward through the work of western scholars of literature and art, who portrayed the Arab world as inferior. As a result, he argues that western scholars cannot be read without considering the configurations of power that shape the relationship between the West and the Other (p. 5). One of the devastating effects of constantly being bombarded by eurocentric messages of superiority is that it "annihilates [non-European] people's belief in their names, in their languages, and in their environment, in their heritage of struggle, in their unity, in their capacities and ultimately in themselves" (wa Thiong'o, 1986, p. 3). This epistemic violence is part of a concerted attempt to colonize the minds and souls of non-European peoples. Given this bombardment of eurocentric messages and the devaluing and erasure of non-European traditions, beliefs, and stories, how do we begin to negate all that colonialism has done to our bodies and minds? How do we decolonize from the negative impacts of cultural imperialism and colonial knowledge production?

Defining Decolonization and Indigenous Knowledges

Linda Tuhiwasi Smith (1999) argues that decolonization cannot be limited to the deconstruction of the dominant story; rather, it must also involve the indigenizing of research and research methodologies. Thus, in order to construct knowledge, we have to engage with our Indigenous knowledges, our elders, and our traditions. But what is meant by Indigenous knowledges? Indigenous knowledges are about a worldview that is cognizant of a deep spiritual connection to animals, plants, water, and other living things, making Indigenous knowledges inherently tied to the Land. The Indigenous worldview understands Land in a context of culture and self-determination that is based on reciprocity, which contradicts the eurocentric worldview that emphasizes Land as property (Sunseri, 2000, p. 145). In the Indigenous worldview, Land is a source of knowledge; it is collectively shared, and everyone has a responsibility to care for and protect the Land. However, this characteristic of Indigenous identity, which connects it to Land, becomes problematic when it excludes Indigenous people that have been completely removed from their Land, as is the case with African and other communities (Adefarakan, 2011, p. 37). Indigenous identity is sometimes restricted to those who, although forcibly removed from their Land, remain residents of that geographical space—for example, the Mohawk and various other Indigenous groups in Canada who are Indigenous to the land. However, Adefarakan (2011) argues that while the relationship to the Land is critical to

Indigenous identity, it does not have to manifest as a physical marker (p. 37). She proposes that a rearticulation of Indigeneity that moves away from essentialist notions of "Indigenous peoples" is necessary. This rearticulation allows space for the inclusion of multiple histories and realities of different Indigenous people, including those groups that are part of the diaspora (p. 38). This characterization of Indigenous identity and Indigenous knowledges as not being confined to a geographic space is important for the experiences of Latin American people who have also been forcibly removed from their Land, but engage in processes of reclaiming and relearning of their Indigenous languages, food, soul, and spirituality. In this chapter, therefore, Indigenous knowledges

> represent essentially a "speaking back" to the production, categorisation and positions of cultures, identities, and histories. These knowledges challenge the conventional discursive frameworks and practices that seemingly present unquestionable "truths" about social existence. (Dei, 2008, p. 6)

Reclaiming Indigenous knowledges is thus essential to the decolonizing process of African, Latinx, and other communities, as it helps to challenge dominant discourses that attempt to invisibilize white privilege. Njoki Wane (2006) states that in order to uproot herself from colonial ideology, she had to relearn and reclaim her history, culture, and spiritual practices by listening to the elders of her community (p. 101). Engaging in the reclaiming of our own stories, we can begin to see the value of our own traditions in helping us to rebuild, heal, and recover from colonialism (Battiste, 1998, p. 24). Alfred and Corntassel (2005) argue for a self-conscious and individual kind of traditionalism that reconstructs traditional communities based on original teachings. The recommitment and reorientation of the self to original teachings will manifest over time in broad social and political movements (Alfred & Corntassel, 2005, p. 611). Individual work designed to reconnect and reclaim Indigenous roots will manifest outward into family, community, and society. Since individuals are part of a whole, affirming Indigenous knowledges will, in turn, affect the whole. By affirming and reconstructing Indigenous knowledges, Indigenousness becomes an actively lived resurgence (Alfred & Corntassel, 2005, p. 612). It is also important to note that Indigenous knowledges are not fixed. On the contrary, Indigenous knowledges are dynamic and undergo constant change as people negotiate their relations to Land, culture, and society (Dei, 2008, p. 7).

Defining Spirituality

Castellano (2000) explains that one of the sources of Indigenous knowledges is spiritual in origin. This spiritual knowledge is learned through the connection to Land, nature, and all living things. Such interconnectedness to everything in the environment allows for an appreciation and sense of purpose and responsibility to maintain harmony.

As George Sefa Dei (2000) explains: "Indigenous epistemologies are grounded in an awareness and deep appreciation of the cosmos and how the self/selves, spiritual, known and unknown worlds are interconnected" (p. 115). The sense of interconnectedness is born out of a deep appreciation for the cosmos and everything around us, including that which is known and unknown. This informs Indigenous knowledges and epistemologies.

According to Parker Palmer, spirituality is "the ancient and abiding human quest for connectedness with something larger and more trustworthy than our egos" (cited in Dei, Karumanchery, James-Wilson, & Zine, 2000, p. 93). According to Palmer's perspective, spirituality is not solely about the individual and internal. It is also not completely external. For example, for Native Americans, spirituality "evolves from exploring and coming to know and experience the nature of living energy moving in each of us, through us, and around us" (Cajete, 1994, p. 42). Spirituality, then, is experienced internally, but it also extends outward to everything around us, resulting in a more holistic view of spirituality. Rahnema summarizes this skillfully in her definition of *spirituality*:

> the art of listening to the world at large and within one, from the hegemony of a conditioned "me" constantly interfering in the process; the ability to relate to others and to act, without any pre-defined plan or ulterior motives; and the perennial qualities of love, compassion and goodness which are under constant assault in economized societies. (Rahnema, cited in Dei, 2002, p. 6)

Based on Rahnema's definition, spirituality is experienced internally and externally. It is about experiencing the energy of the world at large within us, which requires that we listen deeply to the world around us. This deep listening allows the individual to develop a deep connection to all living energy in the world. An important aspect of experiencing spirituality in this manner is that by understanding the individual as part of a whole, we take responsibility for our environment. Moreover, if we have the ability to relate to others and to act, we will also stand up for those who may not have the resources to do so on their own. This relatedness to others while cultivating qualities of love, compassion, and goodness also reinforces humility and a commitment to challenging a capitalist system that creates impoverishment and destroys the environment.

Using an African-centered lens, spirituality is defined as the essence of people regardless of where they are in the world (Dillard, 2008, p. 278). Vanzant defines *spirituality* as "the truth of who we are at the core of our being [...] the consciously active means by which we can recognize, activate, and live the impartial, non-judgmental, consistent truth of who we are" (Vanzant, cited in Dillard, 2008, p. 278). If spirituality were at the core of our being and the truth of who we are, then this would mean that the mind could not be separated from the spirit or the body from the spirit. Consequently, engaging the spirit is crucial for Indigenous people to be able to connect with their true selves and be their authentic selves. The authentic self means understanding who we are and where we come from, and operating from a sense of self that is defined by one's own self instead of being defined by others (Salter, 2011, p. 160). When the spiritual connection is broken, or weakens, one becomes susceptible to internalizing negative views about Indigenous cultures, histories, and languages. This makes it extremely important for colonized individuals to remember, share, and participate in their traditional spiritual practices. Western epistemologies tend to separate the body, mind, and spirit and privilege the intellect over the body and spirit, which is not only incongruous with Indigenous views of spirituality but allows continued colonialism of the minds of the colonized.

George J.S. Dei (2012) further argues that centering the spirit creates powerful possibilities for the oppressed to reclaim their spirituality and souls and to resist colonial domination. Centering the spirit serves as a form of resistance that challenges colonial domination by reinforcing interconnectedness to everything around us, including people. For example, when Catherine Dillard (2008) centers the spirit in her researcher, she provides a counter-practice that breaks away from research as solely academic practice; research thus becomes a practice that serves humanity (p. 278). Centering the spirit allows the researcher to develop a sense of purpose of giving back to her/his/their community, a strategy that challenges dominant research practices in which the researcher is the only one who benefits from the research. By centering the spirit, the research project becomes a tool for serving humanity and one's community and not something that serves oneself at the expense of others. Individualistic views, which are so prevalent within academia, reinforce individual success at the expense of others and place an emphasis on material success. This creates a race-to-the-top environment in which researchers are concerned about their number of publications and less concerned about giving back to their communities. But when the spirit is centered in research or community activism, one cannot do this work for the sake of personal self-growth; instead, it must be done with the purpose of serving the needs of the community.

Consequently, using Indigenous epistemologies and centering the spirit requires that we understand ourselves as part of a whole. We need to "surrender our sense of separateness, to see ourselves in the lives of another" (Dillard, 2008, p. 288) and to develop compassion, love, humility, goodness, and a responsibility to making the world a better place for others and us. In addition, we must also understand this spiritual practice as a connection to Land, nature, and all other living things. As has been stated earlier, we do not exist in a vacuum, and life is not present only in the people around us. Life is present in plants, Land, animals, and all that makes up nature and our environment. Holistic Indigenous knowledges seek to create balance in individual lives and society by uniting people (Castellano, 2000, p. 30). As Paulo Freire and Antonio Faundez (1989) argue: "Indigenous knowledges is a rich social resource for any justice-related attempt to bring about social change" (cited in Kincheloe & Steinberg, 2008, p. 3). Thus, the possibilities for social transformation through Indigenous knowledges and the spiritual practices that are so deeply embedded in Indigenous epistemologies and ontologies can lead to radical social transformation.

Latinx and Chicana Spirituality and Decolonization and Social Justice

For Latinx and Chicana women, spirituality is deeply connected to social justice and both a commitment to and responsibility for supporting their communities. According to C. Alejandra Elenes (2014), spirituality is more than a connection to the Creator; it is tied to struggles for gender equality and social justice (p. 44). She explains that it is her life journey and experiences of sexist and patriarchal rules that have shaped her outlook on spirituality and the reason behind her choice to engage with Chicana feminist epistemologies and pedagogies. Elenes (2014) adds that "spirituality is a way of understanding someone's (or a community's) position in the world by trying to make sense of unfair economic conditions and gender inequality, and to do something about it" (p. 44). For Latinx and Chicana women, then, spirituality is also a critical lens that helps them understand their position in the world and that of their community. Latinx and Chicana women use a decolonizing feminist perspective on spirituality. Irene Lara (2008b) explains that a decolonizing feminist perspective to spiritual work of Chicana and Latinx women means "that their work is grounded in a critical historical consciousness that aims to resist and transform the negative impact of racist and sexist ideologies on the lives of women of color" (p. 22). Thus, this decolonial understanding of spirituality grounded in the lived experiences of Latinx and Chicana women allows them to develop a commitment and responsibility to challenge the oppressive conditions they observe and experience.

The decolonial spiritual practices of Latinx and Chicana women are grounded in their lived experiences because, as Anzaldúa explains, "the spirit evolves out of the experiences of the body" (as cited in Keating, 2000, p. 8). For Latinx and Chicana women, the spiritual is rooted in the body, which allows them to recognize that the body is therefore divine. Understanding the body as divine serves as a source of strength and empowerment to counter the sexist, patriarchal, and racist views that are constantly placed on Latinx and Chicana women's bodies. For example, Anzaldúa, by recognizing the body as divine, was able to counter the conventional religion's rejection of the female body (p. 9). Moreover, for Anzaldúa, "spirituality and being spiritual means being aware of the interconnectedness between things" (p. 9). This interconnectedness serves to create reciprocity and compassion with all those who are oppressed. We become what Anzaldúa calls "kindred spirits," or citizens of the universe who can see beyond borders and differences that separate us. Instead of reinforcing the differences, Anzaldúa calls for compassion and reciprocity. She states that "if something happens to the people in India or Africa—and they're starving to death and dying—then that's happening to us, too" (p. 10). Anzaldúa wants us to focus on the cosmic energy that unites us in order to develop a sense of responsibility to help all those who are marginalized and oppressed, as well as to maintain a sense of interconnectedness. Further, she adds:

> I didn't have the money, privilege, body, or knowledge to fight oppression, but I had this presence. Spirituality—through ritual, meditation, affirmation, and strengthening myself—was the only way I could fight the oppression. Spirituality is oppressed people's only weapon and means of protection. Changes in society only come after the spiritual. (as cited in Keating, 2000, p. 11)

For Anzaldúa, spirituality is a weapon of protection for Latinx and Chicana women. It is a form of resistance. To her, spirituality is about activism, resistance, and countering dominant practices that have led to the separation of the body, mind, and spirit. It is the holistic and decolonial understanding of spirituality grounded in Latinx and Chicana women's lived experiences and the interconnectedness with everything around them that serves to counter the fragmentation of body, mind, and spirit. For Anzaldúa, her "whole struggle in writing, in this anticolonial struggle, has been to [...] put us back together again [...] to connect up the body with the soul and the mind with the spirit" (as cited in Keating, 2000, p. 11). Thus, she uses her writing to rewrite stories that have disempowered Chicana and Latinx women. By rewriting these stories, she is embodying her spiritual vision and activism. She is drawing from her spiritual weapon to counter hegemonic practices.

Dolores Delgado Bernal (2001) argues that Chicana college students develop spiritual practices as self-care defenses against oppression and as tools for daily survival on college campuses (p. 635). She explains that Chicana college students experience several barriers in college, including silencing, being viewed as a liability because additional English-language programs have to be developed for them, and socioeconomic barriers at home. These barriers make it challenging for Chicanas to succeed in college. However, Chicana college students draw on their community's spiritual practices to help them overcome these barriers. These spiritual practices and traditions become woven into their identities and worldviews (p. 634). According to Gonzalez, these spiritual practices and traditions become tools for negotiating and navigating the day-to-day college experience (as cited in Bernal, 2001, p. 634). It helps them to challenge norms of dominant culture and to resist the various forms of oppression within and outside their communities. Moreover, for these college students their spirituality is connected to their commitment to the betterment of their communities. Spirituality is a tool for resistance that supports the healing process at the personal and communal levels.

Spirituality for Latinx and Chicana women is about protection, self-care, resistance, and survival. It is not apolitical or a form of escapism. On the contrary, it is very much political. Their "holistic" view of spirituality connects the body, mind, and spirit and understands that individuals must experience themselves in a connected way, which allows Latinx and Chicana women to act in socially just ways (Lara, 2008b, p. 23). Moreover, because their spirituality is rooted in their lived experiences, it includes the experiences of racism, classism, sexism, and homophobia. Thus, this spirituality is rooted in a critical consciousness of the devastating effects of colonialism and imperialism on the bodies, minds, and spirits of colonized peoples (p. 23). "For these women of color colonialism is not abstract or long-ago history. Its legacy is alive, intersecting with sexism, classism, homophobia and other oppressions. It manifests in daily lives through institutional and internalized oppression and domination" (p. 23). Thus, decolonization is an ongoing process, and the spirit can play a key role in protecting and countering these "interlocking systems of oppression."

According to Sendejo (2014), Chicana spiritual practices seek out a holistic and decolonial way of living and understanding the world by looking to the past and ancient practices to make sense of the present. In her poem "A Mindful Invitation," the Latinx feminist writer Inez Talamantez (2014) invites us to root ourselves in our culture, Land, language, spiritual practices, and her-stories.

> The ancestors knew we were coming
> They left work for us
> Now we carry their wisdom forward
> Know who you are, sabe quien eres
> Know your Land, conoce tu tierra
> Learn your language, aprende tu idioma
> Follow the beliefs of your people, your spiritual culture
> Do not let spells affect you. (p. xi)

According to Gloria Anzaldúa (2002), the path to *conocimiento* (deep consciousness) involves *desconocer* (unlearning) what we have been programmed to believe and the opening of our senses to everything around us by connecting with our ancient practices (p. 543). Relearning ancestors' knowledges and unlearning colonial education and ideologies is part of how Chicanas and Latinx women counter "spells," or the colonizing of the mind. Lara Medina (1998) explains:

> The spiritual practices of many Chicanas emerge from a purposeful integration of their creative inner resources and the diverse cultural influences that feed their souls and their psyches..... Chicanas define and decide for themselves what images, rituals, myths, and deities nourish and give expression to their deepest values. (p. 189)

Reclaiming Indigenous Chicana Goddesses

For many Chicanas, reclaiming their Indigenous roots and spirituality has entailed the appropriation of La Virgen de Guadalupe and challenging the patriarchal Christian images of the Virgin Mary (the *marianismo ideal*). In the Catholic Church, La Virgin de

Guadalupe (or Virgin Mary—known as La Virgen de Guadalupe in Mexico and among Chicanos) is venerated as a divine being, free of "original sin," who is nurturing, pure, subservient, and self-sacrificing for herself, for her family, and for others. Chicanas have reappropriated Guadalupe and reconceptualized the ideal of Chicana womanhood as more reflective of the actual role that many Latinas play in their families and communities—that is, as symbols of strength, autonomy, and dignity (Campesino & Schwartz, 2006, p. 73).

Chicanas associate three Aztec goddesses with La Virgen de Guadalupe: Tonantzin, Tlazolteotl, and Coatlicue. Tonantzin, which means "Our Sacred" in the Nahuatl language, symbolizes fertility and the Earth. Tlazolteotl is linked to the cycle of life, birth, growth, undoing, and renewal. She is the guardian of midwives, pregnant women, and infants. Coatlicue is known as La Hija Rebelde (the rebel daughter) (Elenes, 2014, p. 45). Coatlicue is represented wearing a skirt of writhing snakes and a necklace of hands, hearts, and skulls. She has a deadly side that is capable of destruction. Elenes (2014) argues that the interrelationship of these three goddesses helps construct a multifaceted identity for Guadalupe. It allows Chicana and Latinx women to engage in processes of decolonization that challenge the unattainable marianismo ideal. In rediscovering these Indigenous goddesses, Chicanas can associate strength and women's freedom with Guadalupe. For example, Sandra Cisneros (1996) writes that "maybe it's my Coatlicue-Lupe attitude that makes it possible for my mother to tell me, 'No wonder men can't stand you.' Who knows? What I do know is this: I am obsessed with becoming a woman comfortable in my skin" (p. 50)

The Catholic Church's representation of La Virgen de Guadalupe as pure, virgin, and completely devoid of sexuality created an unrealistic and unattainable ideal of womanhood. While the pure and virgin qualities were venerated, anything related to sexuality was considered evil, with the result of denying Chicana and Latinx women their sexuality. The Catholic Church's patriarchal ideology that configures the virtuous virgin as one to be venerated, unlike the pagan *puta* (whore), is used to control Chicana women's bodies, identities, and sexuality (Lara, 2008a, p. 99). However, Chicana feminists have challenged the dichotomy of the virgin versus *la puta* by reinforcing the connection beween spirituality and sexuality. For example, Lara (2014) embraces the "serpentine conocimiento," a concept inspired by Anzaldúa, engaging with the power of the serpent when reclaiming Indigenous goddesses (p. 115). The serpent is associated with the three Indigenous goddesses, each representing creation, destruction, sexuality, and motherhood (p. 116). Furthermore, "serpentine conocimiento" includes "conocimientos (knowledge) related to sex, sexuality, and the erotic" (p. 116). Sandra Cisneros (1996) describes Guadalupe as "the sex goddess, a goddess who makes me feel good about my sexual power, my sexual energy, who reminds me that I must... [speak] from the vulva... speak the most basic, honest truth" (p. 50). In recreating a multifaceted Guadalupe and connecting spirituality with sexuality, Chicanas are countering monolithic ways of representing Chicana womanhood.

Reconfiguring Cultural and Knowledge Production

In reclaiming Indigenous goddesses, Chicana and Latinx women are helping to heal themselves from fragmentation of their identities and oversimplified identities that the Catholic Church and the mainstream media impose on them. Molina Guzman and Valdivia (2004) explain that, in the mainstream media, a Latina woman's body is framed as animalistic, primitive, and irresistibly dangerous to the Anglo-American male characters (p. 213). This representation of Latinx women reinforces colonial racist ideologies imposed on Black and Indigenous women, and reclaiming Indigenous goddesses allows Chicana women to reconceptualize their identity and counter these popular images promulgated in the media and by the Catholic Church. Through the Indigenous goddesses, Chicanas construct complex and multifaceted identities on their own terms. They challenge sexist and racist ideologies by constructing identities grounded on Indigenous and spiritual knowledge that reflects their social reality, her-stories, and experiences.

Further, by using subjugated knowledge, Chicanas are challenging the knowledge-production process. This challenge calls into question what is considered valid knowledge and who is a legitimate producer of knowledge. By drawing on their Indigenous knowledges and spiritual practices to construct complex identities, Chicanas and Latinx women become knowledge producers. Sendejo (2014) explains that writing about Chicana goddesses and spirituality within academia challenges the academic space that has traditionally excluded them and the importance of spiritual practices and knowledge (p. 90). Moreover, their theorizing comes from the everyday lives and bodies of Chicanas and not from abstract perspectives that are detached from the realities (Saavedra & Nymark, 2014, p. 257). According to C. Alejandra Elenes (2014), "recognizing that spirituality has a central place in the way people construct their subjectivity is a necessary step in the formation of Chicana feminist pedagogies" (p. 54).

Our education system, television shows, and even museums play a major role in constructing representations of non-Europeans that distort and mask the oppression of those they supposedly represent, which serves to mask ideological messages as "truths" (Durrans, 2005, p. 11). When ideological messages are presented as "truths," white privilege is invisibilized and normalized. For example, research demonstrates that stereotypes prevalent in the media about Latinx people being prone to violence, theft, and laziness are taken as "truth" by educators and impact how Latinx youth are treated in the classroom (Gaztambide-Fernandez, 2011, p. 68). According to the Proyeto Latino Report (2011), educators express to their Latinx students stereotypes prevalent within the media. This, in turn, impacts Latinx youths' relationships with their teachers, leads to Latinx youth disengagement, and contributes to the high "push out" rate among Latinx youth.

A Latinx/Chicana decolonial feminist epistemology allows students and teachers to undo dualist, essentialist, and oversimplified thinking because it involves the formulation of knowledge capable of deconstructing and decentralizing hegemonic practices (Elenes, 2001, p. 691). Moreover, centering Indigenous and spiritual knowledge allows learners to resist oppression by strengthening their individual selves. For many racialized students across Canada, the United States, and Europe who struggle with lack of representation in the classroom and in the curriculum, finding ways to strengthen their individual selves can prove to be an excellent way of overcoming feelings of inferiority and a sense of feeling lost that colonialism creates. However, engaging the spirit involves more than resistance because "to resist is to remain in a male-energy mode; to heal is to transform, and transformation involves the feminine principle. The decolonization of our bodies and the reclaiming of our spirits is a struggle for our human rights as women" (Facio, 2014, p. 70).

To engage in Latinx/Chicana decolonial feminist pedagogy is to engage in the processes of healing and transformation. It requires the construction of a theoretical and political movement based on a multiplicity of identities, resistances, and ambiguities (Elenes, 2001). This is where a sense of purpose and meaning for education becomes crucial. Education becomes a means to give back to family and community by creating political movements that seek to better the community and thereby transform it. This political movement has to be accepting of the multiplicity of identities and ambiguities that are open to the diversity that exists within the classroom and within each individual. It also reconceptualizes traditional notions of education by recognizing that knowledge production is not limited to the classroom and the teacher. Rather, it takes place in different spaces: at home, at a *maquiladora* factory, on the streets, and in everyday life (Elenes, Gonzalez, Bernal, & Villenas, 2001). Consequently, Latinx/Chicana decolonial feminist epistemology seeks to empower and transform learners, particularly those that are excluded and marginalized in the classroom.

To conclude, Chicana and Latinx women use feminist decolonial spiritual practices to engage in a process of decolonization. These feminist, decolonial spiritual practices begin with Chicana and Latinx women as the knowledge producers of their own complex and multifaceted identities. They ground their knowledges on their lived experiences, their Indigenous knowledges, and their spiritual practices. Because their decolonial practices are grounded on their lived experiences and within their bodies, Chicana and Latinx women develop a critical lens or political consciousness that is tied to their experiences of gender oppression within their communities and the social injustice experienced by their communities. The recognition and realization of the social injustice may begin at a personal level, but it then extends outward to their communities and beyond. These decolonial practices challenge western, patriarchal, and racist projects designed to maintain the status quo. Through these decolonial practices, knowledge production is challenged, and new identities are constructed that are grounded in the remembering of Indigenous goddesses and the validation of Indigenous and feminine knowledge that is often subjugated by western views. Finally, their holistic understanding of spirituality also challenges the binaries that act to place the body and mind in opposition to each other, which only results in fragmentation. However, by connecting sexuality, spirituality, body, and mind through feminist decolonial practices, Chicana and Latinx women are engaging in a process of transformative decolonization.

Notes

1. *Latinx* is a gender-neutral pronoun that allows us to move beyond gender binaries such as "femininity" and "masculinity" found in the Spanish language. The word is inclusive of trans people.
2. *Cysgender*: denoting or relating to persons whose self-identity conforms with the gender that corresponds to their biological sex; not transgender.
3. *Quechua*: one of the largest Indigenous groups in the central Andes of South America. I am Quechua on my father's side.

References

Adefarakan, T. (2011). (Re)Conceptualizing "Indigenous" from anti-colonial and Black feminist theoretical perspectives: Living and imagining Indigeneity differently. In G.J.S. Dei (Ed.), *Indigenous philosophies and critical education: A reader* (pp. 34–52). New York, NY: Peter Lang.

Alfred, T., & Corntassel, J. (2005). Being Indigenous: Resurgences against contemporary colonialism. *Government and Opposition*, 40(4), 597–614.

Anzaldúa, G.E. (2002). "Now let us shift…the path of conocimiento…inner work, public acts." In G. Anzaldúa & A. Keating (Eds.), *This bridge we call home: Radical visions for transformation* (pp. 540–778). New York, NY: Routledge.

Battiste, M. (1998). Enabling the autumn seed: Framing a decolonized currricular approach toward aboriginal knowledge, language and education. *Journal of Native Education*, 22(1), 16–27.

Bernal, D.D. (2001). Learning and living pedagogies of home: The mestiza consciousness of Chicana students. *Qualitative Studies in Education*, 14(5), 623–639.

Cajete, G. (1994). *Look at the mountain: An ecology of indigenous education*. Skyland, NC: Kivaki Press.

Campesino, M., & Schwartz, G. (2006). Spirituality among Latinas/os: Implications of culture in conceptualization and measurement. *ANS: Advances in Nursing Science*, 29(1), 69–81.

Castellano, M.B. (2000). Updating aboriginal traditions of knowledge. In G.J.S. Dei et al. (Eds.), *Indigenous knowledges in global contexts* (pp. 21–36). Toronto, ON: University of Toronto Press.

Cisneros, S. (1996). Guadalupe the sex goddess. In A. Castillo (Ed.), *Goddess of the Americas: Writings on the Virgin of Guadalupe* (pp. 48–51). New York, NY: Riverhead Books.

Collins, P.H. (2000). *Black feminist thought: Knowledge, consciousness, and the politics of empowerment*. New York, NY: Routledge.

Dei, G.J.S. (2000). Rethinking the role of Indigenous knowledges in the academy. *International Journal of Inclusive Education*, 4(2), 111–132.

Dei, G.J.S. (2002). Spiritual knowing and transformative learning. New approaches to lifelong learning. NALL Working Paper #59. Retrieved from https://files.eric.ed.gov/fulltext/ED478139.pdf

Dei, G.J.S. (2008). Indigenous knowledges studies and the next generation: Pedagogical possibilities for anti-colonial education. *Australian Journal of Indigenous Education*, 37, Supp. 5–13.

Dei, G.J.S. (2012). "Suahunu": The trialectic space. *Journal of Black Studies*, 43(8), 823–846.

Dei, G.J.S., Karumanchery, L. L., James-Wilson, S., & Zine, J. (2000). *Removing the margins: The challenges and possibilities of inclusive schooling*. Toronto, ON: Canadian Scholars' Press.

Dhamoon, R. (2015). A feminist approach to decolonizing anti-racism: Rethinking transnationalism, intersectionality, and settler colonialism. *Fera Feminism Journal* (4), 20–37.

Dilliard, C. (2008). When the ground is black, the ground is fertile: Exploring endarkened feminist epistemology and healing methodologies of the spirit. In N. Denzin, Y. Lincoln, & L.T. Smith (Eds.), *Handbook of critical and Indigenous methodologies* (pp. 277–292). Los Angeles, CA: Sage Publications.

Durrans, B. (2005). Behind the scenes: Museums and selective criticism. *Anthropology Today, 8*(4), 11–15.

Elenes, C.A. (2001). Transformando fronteras: Chicana feminist transformative pedagogies. *Qualitative Studies in Education, 14*(5), 689–702.

Elenes, C.A. (2014). Spiritual roots of Chicana feminist borderland pedagogies: A spiritual journey with Tonantzin/Guadalupe. In E. Facio & I. Lara (Eds.), *Fleshing the spirit: Spirituality and activism in Chicana, Latina, and Indigenous women's lives* (pp. 43–58). Tucson, AZ: University of Arizona Press.

Elenes, C.A., Gonzalez, F.E., Bernal, D.D., & Villenas, S. (2001). Introduction: Chicana/ Mexicana feminist pedagogies: Consejos, respeto, educacion in everyday life. *Qualitative Studies in Education, 14*(5), 595–602.

Facio, E. (2014). Spirit journey: "Home" as a site for healing and transformation. In E. Facio & I. Lara (Eds.), *Fleshing the spirit: Spirituality and activism in Chicana, Latina, and Indigenous women's lives* (pp. 59–72). Tucson, AZ: University of Arizona Press.

Fanon, F. (1963). *The wretched of the earth*. New York, NY: Grove Press.

Gaztambide-Fernandez, R. (2011). *Proyecto Latino. Year 1: Exploratory research*. Report to the Toronto District School Board.

hooks, b. (2001). *All about love: New visions*. New York, NY: HarperCollins.

Keating, A. (2000). Risking the personal. In G.E. Anzaldúa (Ed.), *Interviews/entrevistas* (pp. 1–15). New York, NY: Routledge.

Kincheloe, J., & Steinberg, S. (2008). Indigenous knowledges in education: Complexities, dangers and profound benefits. In N. Denzin, Y. Lincoln, & L.T. Smith (Eds.), *Handbook of critical and Indigenous methodologies* (pp. 135–156). Los Angeles, CA: Sage Publications.

Lara, I. (2008a). Goddess of the Americas in the decolonial imaginary, beyond the virtuous virgin/pagan puta dichotomy. *Feminist Studies, 34* (Spring–Summer), 99–128.

Lara, I. (2008b). Latina health activist-healers bridging body and spirit. *Women and Therapy, 31*(1), 21–40.

Lara, I. (2014). Sensing the serpent in the mother, dando a luz la madre serpiente: Chicana spirituality, sexuality, and mamihood. In E. Facio & I. Lara (Eds.), *Fleshing the spirit: Spirituality and activism in Chicana, Latina, and Indigenous women's lives* (pp. 113–134). Tucson, AZ: University of Arizona Press.

McClintock, A. (1995). *Imperial leather, race, gender, and sexuality in the colonial contest*. New York, NY: Routledge.

Medina, L. (1998). Los espiritus siguen hablando: Chicana spiritualities. In C. Trujillo (Ed.), *Living Chicana theory* (pp. 189–213). Berkeley, CA: Third Woman Press.

Molina Guzman, I., & Valdivia, A.N. (2004). Brain, brow, and booty: Latina iconicity in U.S. popular culture. *Commission Review, 7*, 205–221.

Saavedra, C., & Nymar, E.D. (2014). Borderland-Mestizaje feminism: The new tribalism. In N.K. Denzin, Y.S. Lincoln, & L.T. Smith (Eds.), *Handbook of critical and Indigenous methodologies* (pp. 225–276). Thousand Oaks, CA: Sage Publications.

Said, E. (1979). *Orientalism*. New York, NY: Random House.

Salter, N. (2011). Holding relationships as sacred responsibilities: A journey of spiritual growth and being. In N.N. Wane, E.L. Manyimo, & E.J. Ritskes (Eds.), *Spirituality, education and society: An integrated approach* (pp. 157–168). Rotterdam, Netherlands: Sense Publishers.

Sendejo, B. (2014). Methodologies of the spirit: Reclaiming Our Lady of Guadalupe and discovering Tonantzin within and beyond the *Neplanta* of academia. In E. Facio & I. Lara (Eds.), *Fleshing the Spirit: Spirituality and activism in Chicana, Latina, and Indigenous women's lives* (pp. 81–101). Tucson, AZ: University of Arizona Press.

Shahjahan, R.A. (2005). Spirituality in the academy: Reclaiming from the margins and evoking a transformative way of knowing the world. *International Journal of Qualitative Studies in Education, 18*(6), 685–711.

Smith, A. (2005). *Conquest: Sexual violence and American Indian genocide.* Cambridge, MA: South End Press.

Smith, L. (1999). Colonizing knowledges. In *Decolonizing methodologies: Research and Indigenous peoples* (pp. 58–78). New York, NY: Zen Books.

Sunseri, L. (2000). Moving beyond the feminism versus nationalism dichotomy: An anti-colonial feminist perspective on aboriginal liberation struggles. *Canadian Woman Studies, 20*(2), 143–148.

Talamantez, I. (2014). A mindful invitation/Una invitación consiente. In E. Facio & I. Lara (Eds.), *Fleshing the Spirit: Spirituality and activism in Chicana, Latina, and Indigenous women's lives* (p. xi). Tucson, AZ: University of Arizona Press.

Wane, N. (2006). Is decolonization possible? In J.S. Dei & A. Kempf (Eds.), *Anti-colonialism and education: The politics of resistance* (pp. 87–105). Toronto, ON: Sense Publishers.

wa Thiong'o, N. (1986). *Decolonising the mind: The politics of language in African literature.* Portsmouth, NH: Heinemann Educational Books.

CHAPTER 3

(Re)Claiming Spirituality as Anti-Colonial Resistance and Decolonial Praxis: An Africana-Feminist Discussion on Spirituality and Indigenous Knowledges in Education

Janelle Brady

Introduction

Reflecting on my time spent in the kitchen with my grandmothers and mother from an early age while they cooked, and I washed, passed, and cleaned, I have come to realize that those years of experience with women in my family have shaped the person I am today. As a child, I did not participate in countless after-school and costly weekend activities; rather, I spent hours with my cousins and with my aunties, who would braid our hair lovingly, test us on mathematics, and give us all a sense of self, history, identity, and purpose. Having lost parts of my history since my ancestors were stolen from Africa and brought to the Caribbean, I was still grounded in my Afrocentricity through the passing down of stories. Having grown up as a young, Black person with limited education about Indigenous people in Turtle Island, I feel as though that history, like my own, has also been robbed from people like me and packaged in a grand narrative of erasure through the eurocentric project. My knowledges, my ancestors' knowledges, and my community's Indigenous knowledges have been and continue to be delegitimized by colonial and neocolonial forms of domination, a point that will be further examined in the following pages. This chapter views spirituality as a decolonial tool of resistance, reclaiming, and embeddedness of a collective that is larger than myself and is grounded in my community and my history. Often eurocentric knowledge has dislocated and dismembered our histories and stories. However, I seek out interconnectedness in all things as a way of reclaiming my history and identity. I will not be dismembered, disjointed, and fragmented through the celebration of hybridity and my own self-indulgent subjectivities that risk losing sight of larger collectivities and community.

Spirituality, as will be discussed in detail in the following pages, is about relationality, interconnectedness, and community, so to disengage myself from a larger political project against anti-Blackness would be hollow and de-spiriting (Dillard, 2006; Mazama, 2002). Often, in very individualistic projects, people indulge in the self and looking at difference. Difference is very important in challenging projects of racism, sameness, and colorblindness. However, while drawing upon difference, it is important to find fluidity, spirituality, and connectivity between and among communities so as to build solidarity. Sometimes people cite difference as a way of preventing the Black community from having a larger conversation about anti-Black racism, because they state that race is a social construct. It definitely is, but it is also important to draw on a spiritual epistemological and ontological pursuit of interconnectedness within and across communities. My own history of coloniality is not a single story, but is instead connected to a larger network of world Indigenous peoples (Alfred & Corntassel, 2005) fighting and resisting Euro-colonialism and "contemporary colonialism." As of late I have experienced an urgency to theorize through a spiritual lens. I must not deny it, as to do so would lead to a fragmentation of my soul.

In this chapter I will explore the idea of spirituality by beginning with a review of the literature, highlighting the similarities and differences among various thinkers (Abdi, 2011; Dei, 2012; Dillard, 2014; Este & Bernard, 2006; Mazama, 2002; Miller, 1994; Palmer, 2003; Schneiders, 2003; Shahjahan, 2009; Ver Beek, 2001). In the following section I will discuss some of the historical junctures in the de-spiriting of Indigenous peoples. I will follow that with some thoughts on my own subject-location as it relates to spirituality in Indigenous knowledges. After the discussion on historical junctures of de-spiriting, I will present the concept of *suahunu* (Dei, 2012) as a possibility for new imaginaries and engage with the pedagogical implications for education. In the course of my discussion I will pose these questions: What does it mean to be spiritually engaged in reclaiming Indigenous knowledges as anti-colonial resistance to dominant knowledge? How can educators move away from reproducing the dominant forms of knowledge? In decolonial educational pursuits, how can educators spiritually engage both epistemologically and ontologically?

Visiting the Literature: Understanding the Convergences and Divergences for Spirituality in Indigenous Knowledges

Here I offer a conversation on the convergences and divergences for spirituality in the broader discussion of Indigenous knowledges.

Depending on the subject-positions and localities, spirituality can be approached differently. In the following paragraphs I engage with Ver Beek (2000) and Schneiders (2003) on spirituality because it provides a good starting point for an examination of the literature. Following that, I include the voice of Mazama (2002), who takes an Afrocentric approach to spirituality.

First, Ver Beek (2001) defines *spirituality* (for most people in the South) as "integral to their understanding of the world and their place in it, and so central to the decisions they make about their own and their communities' development" (p. 31). His definition demonstrates that spirituality is not merely compartmentalized. For him, spirituality is constant and relevant to a way of being, knowing, and doing. Ver Beek reminds us that spirituality is important to the ontological and epistemological realization and reclaiming of Indigenous knowledges.

Unlike Ver Beek, who focuses on the ways of knowing and being in spirituality, Sandra Schneiders calls for an infusion of religion and spirituality while debunking the idea that the two must be mutually exclusive. She critiques the role of corruption of religious institutions and works toward a scenario in which religion and spirituality can go hand in hand in bridging the role of community and the individual. Schneiders (2003) defines spirituality as "the experience of conscious involvement in the project of life-integration through self-transcendence toward the ultimate value one perceives" (p. 166), thus describing the very personal development that people live and experience. In this definition, she attributes spirituality to "religious or non-religious or secular spiritualities" (p. 166), thereby highlighting that spirituality and religion are not always synonymous. Mazama's work further reifies this idea in the context of Afrocentricity.

One of the major tenets of Afrocentricity vis-à-vis African freedom and creativity is African resistance, which relies heavily on African spirituality (Mazama, 2002). This is particularly important because African spirituality concerns the ways in which African people—both those living on the continent and those that are part of the diaspora—are connected. Thus, African spirituality is a tool of resistance that has been and continues to be key to the global survival of Africans (Este & Bernard, 2006). Such unity and interconnectedness is about spirituality. However, unlike Schneiders, who finds hope in the fact that religion and spirituality are compatible, Mazama (2002) highlights that Christianity is incompatible with Afrocentricity because, as a worldview, it seeks universalism and is part and parcel of white supremacy. Mazama's articulation disrupts western eurocentricity and white supremacy; further, however, it examines the role that Christianity has played in ongoing forms of colonialism, white supremacy, brutality, and slavery. Mazama is more upfront than many scholars in her approach to an African spirituality that questions and disrupts the role of Christianity. Though I will revisit Mazama's work in a later section on an Africana-Black feminist perspective, it is important to note here the divergences between thinkers whose work looks at spirituality.

Parker Palmer (2003) defines *spirituality* as "the eternal human yearning to be connected with something larger than our own egos" (p. 377). He looks at ways of teaching and learning from our hearts and souls and highlights the significance of interconnectedness in spirituality beyond pursuits of the individual. Importantly, Palmer reminds us to always be aware of community, action, and interconnectedness. In this vein, J.P. Miller (1994) calls for contemplation that goes beyond the self and the ego, and describes contemplation "as a non-dualistic form of experience where we experience a deep connection to the ground of being" (Miller also cites Merton's 1972 definition; p. 56). Miller seeks out contemplation as an ontological way of being, and when using the term *contemplation*, his work engages ideas of spirituality, particularly when it comes to higher education. Rather than contemplation, I would simply call it spirituality. However, the rationale for coming to a contemplative place in higher education is important and adds to the larger conversation about spirituality and the pedagogical implications for education.

Shahjahan (2009) defines *spirituality* in terms of its ability to bring people to a critical awakening and action. Many use the word *woke* for such a critical awakening and movement to action. Dei (2009) states that there must not be a divide between teaching and activism in the pursuit of "professionalism and objectivity" (cited in Rostan, forthcoming). Spirituality is a way of being and a connection to one's knowledge and to other beings—both within the community as living or transcended—allowing for movement from "inward to outward action" (Shahjahan, 2009, p. 122). Shahjahan also looks at spirituality within the educational context as movement to action, and in his 2009 essay he describes it in the context of the anti-oppressive higher education. Often equity, social justice, and anti-oppressive discourses forget the importance of naming and working with and through spirituality. Thus, Shahjahan's work reminds us of the connectedness to spirituality in anti-oppressive and educational contexts. Abdi (2011) provides a similar definition of *spirituality* that goes beyond general domains of religion and compartmentalized aspects of one's life, but is constitutive of all aspects of being (p. xi). Though many of the scholars discussed here have differences of opinion, a major area of agreement is the interconnectedness of spirituality, spirituality as epistemology and ontology, and its overall implications for education.

The De-Spiriting of Indigenous Peoples and Knowledges in the Making of the Euro-Colonial-Modern Dominant Knowledge

The Euro-colonial expansion project is the antithesis of Indigenous knowledges and the realm of spirituality. Eurocentrism and contemporary white supremacy are about the fragmentation of people from one another, from their Land, from their ancestors, and from their history. The fragmentation of Indigenous peoples is not only de-spiriting; it also works to break down the mind-body-soul connection that individuals gain by igniting their own spirituality. In the context of science, universality, modernity, and the seeking of a truth—or even postmodernity on the quest of seeking multiple truths—the spirit is often left unawakened in the current schooling project. Indigenous knowledges are pushed to the margins and are taught in a compartmentalized way that centers western-colonial scientific knowledge as universal. Abdi (2011) states:

> Whose rationalizing, de-spiritualizing life systems are being advanced in current relations of the schooling project? If these enlightenment and[,] by extension, modernist-driven ways of learning and teaching are representative of seeing the world, then the epistemic enfranchisement of spirituality in educational research and schooling platforms should and will delightfully disturb such hegemonic edifice of monocultural scientism which has dominated the learning landscape for too long. (p. xii)

Abdi calls into question who benefits from a Euro-colonial project that centers universality under the guise of objectivity. He highlights the notion that the epistemological project of spirituality in educational realms will disrupt hegemonic, dominant ways of knowing and universality. Spirituality, then, is not just an individual pursuit, but instead a decolonial praxis. Dei (2012) posits that "we cannot downplay spiritual identities in education" and that "we must reclaim our spirituality to help resist colonial and intellectual domination" (p. 9). Spirituality as a tool of resistance and for reclaiming histories for ancestors, Land, and community through the awakening of spiritual identities is important in anti-colonial and decolonial pursuits that disrupt dominance and universalism in education. Since spirituality is associated with tradition, rationalist-enlightenment thinkers would purport that such ideas are "backward" or "bizarre." As such, modern colonial thinkers have negated the significance of oral histories and tradition in educational practices (Wane, 2000). The very underpinnings of spirituality, especially in the context of African spirituality, assume community. Dillard (2014) states:

> Spirituality, in African-centered thought is the very essence of African people, regardless of where we are in the world. It is a kind of cosmological spirituality that holds central the notion that all life is sacred and moral virtue of individuals and that of the community is the same. (p. 228)

Contemporarily those who follow the tenets of Indigenous knowledges, such as folks who ground their work in community-centered organizing and principles often come under attack by post-colonialists who insist that we are in an era of "post-" rather than collectively organizing an "anti-" colonial theoretical and praxis pursuit. Ideas of community are critiqued by postmodernists, who insist on ongoing, multiple truth-seeking pursuits while claiming that community collectivity and consolidated responses ought to be tied to essentialism, as it does not take into account the myriad subjectivities. In this mess of trying to constantly claim messiness, spirituality often gets pushed aside when its underpinnings come up against divide-and-conquer politics that keep Indigenous bodies separate and apart.

Spirituality cannot be a political tool of decolonial resistance if it is fragmented among many disjointed and disconnected communities. In African-centered or Afrocentric thought, spirituality is foundational for African people regardless of location. This is important to thinking about Land. The connecting and unifying force in bringing together African people beyond time and space is spirituality. This reminds people of their Indigeneity and localized knowledge passed down through ancestral history and helps us think through Indigeneity as an international category (Dei, 2017). The cosmological spirituality that holds African people together goes beyond the imposition of colonial borders.

An Africana-Black Feminist Conversation About Spirituality

In interrogating my own subject-position, it is important to discuss the fragmentation of people like me who came from the Caribbean to Turtle Island. As someone who was stolen from the continent, questions of Indigeneity as international category (Dei, 2017) are crucial to me. I articulate my experiences through an Africana-Black feminist perspective. By drawing on the work of many scholars, I use Africana and Black feminism to demonstrate the fluidity of Blackness across contexts. Borrowing from the work of Collins (2000), for example, I believe that self-definition of Black women's experiences is important to understanding and interrogating our lived experiences. Crenshaw (1991) uses the term *intersectionality* to demonstrate the double form of oppression based on the racial and gendered experience of Black women. Megwe (2007) uses African feminism to go beyond a U.S.-based articulation of the African woman experience. Norwood (2013) uses the term *Africana* to encapsulate the experiences of African women across diasporic contexts, going beyond a U.S.-based articulation of lived experiences as developed in Black feminist thought. The fluidity of conversation in Africana-Black feminism demonstrates the rejection of a dominant, single-story "intervention" of white feminism, which masquerades as universal (Collins, 2000; hooks, 1991; Megwe, 2007; Oyewumi, 2003). This type of decolonial approach to theorizing from subject-locations other than the dominant is important in that it demonstrates the multiple ways of knowing entrenched in Indigenous knowledge forms which is an active critique to "universal" dominant ways of knowing and theorizing. As such, this explains why, for my own situated knowledge (Collins, 1990; Dei & Kempf, 2006; hooks, 1991) and perspective, it is important that I enter the conversation from a Caribbean feminist perspective grounded in Afrocentricity, placing Blackness at the forefront when articulating and reclaiming spirituality.

The articulation of an Africana-Black feminism must be undertaken in relation to—and in connection with—Land. As a diasporic African woman, it is important for me to re-examine and highlight that we must think about Africa beyond the continent (Dei, 2004). It is important to look at the ways in which African people are connected. Mazama (2002) would remind us that African people are united through our spirituality and that Afrocentricity and spirituality go hand in hand. Also, Afrocentricity provides a connectedness, a consciousness, and a sense of being and is a cosmological and metaphysical element that unites African people. This is key in bringing forth important questions when it comes to Afrocentricity as yielding a connection and sense of being for African people globally, uniting a community beyond the Land.

In articulating an Africana-Black feminist perspective within a discussion of spirituality, it is important to look at the experiences of Black women in relation to research, teaching, and community. King (2015) discusses Black women's perspective and responsibility to bring forth our situated knowledge rather than purporting to be "objective" and "neutral," since that sense of neutrality is very disconnected and fragmented from Indigenous ways of knowing. Instead, having a locally contextual knowledge base and historical cultural memory is essential to articulating multiple ways of knowing. King (2015) talks about her experiences and the cultural memory that was passed down from her grandmother. As an Africana-Black feminist, I draw on the experiences and teaching of my mother, grandmother, and aunts. Such a knowledge base provides me with a sense of being and a spiritual connection to my past and to my ancestors.

Dillard (2006) writes about the stress that African women feel in relation to their research methodology. She discusses the tensions and issues around traditional research methodology and how they can create a dialectic for Black women scholars. Similar to the work of King, Dillard's writing critiques the removed position that researchers must have from their "research subjects" and methodological process, something that demonstrates the extension of Euro-colonialism in research. Dillard instead calls for an "Endarkened feminist epistemology" rooted in an African-based cosmology that includes spirituality, community, and praxis (p. 278). An endarkened feminist epistemology draws on the long-standing history of Black feminist thought—specifically Collins—but also works to explain Black women's knowing and the "patterns of epistemology that undergird it" (Dillard, 2006). Dillard's work is similar to that of Mazama in her articulation of an African/Afrocentric connection of being that must include spirituality.

Articulating a Black feminist/Africana perspective is an important step in moving away from white feminism, which has historically excluded the rights of Black women from the movement. Thus, white feminism shows how the ongoing forms of neocolonialism morph into everyday conversations and organizing. Marbley (2005) demonstrates the ways in which first-, second-, and third-wave feminism have often omitted the saliency of race from the conversation. White feminism has neglected the experiences of Black women and experiences of "intersectionality" to examine how racism and sexism are linked. Further, from an African diasporic perspective, white feminism is presented in the guise of being universal and is seen and described as the saving grace of African women and Third World countries (Megwe, 2007; Nilliasca, 2011; Norwood, 2013). However, African women have embodied forms of feminism and womanism for centuries and continue to articulate such local knowledges for those who care to listen. It is important to question ideologies and epistemologies that pose as dominant and all-knowing. Such an articulation has led to a moving away from white mainstream forms of feminism, which can be de-spiriting.

It is important to extend conversations of spirituality to the Land in order to examine the ways in which spirituality has been articulated through forms of self-definition, as practiced by Africana-Black feminists and womanists. I return to questions of the Land based on my own subject-position. Aidoo (1992) states:

> Given . . . a heroic tradition, it is no wonder that some of us regard the docile mendicant African woman of today as a media creation. But if she does exist, she is the result of the traumas of the last five hundred years' encounter with the West, the last one hundred years of colonial repression, the current neo-colonial disillusionment, and of a natural environment that is now behaving like an implacable enemy. (p. 320)

Coming from a history that was ruptured by colonialism, it is important that I always return to questions about the Land. How can we extend conversations about spirituality to questions about Land from Afrocentric and Indigenous ways of knowing? It is important to think as well about how colonial ruptures and 500 years of repression, as Aidoo (1992) highlights, have an effect on the lived realities of Black women. It is important to look at the impact colonialism has had on spirituality. For those on the continent, the Land currently is described as being disastrous, malnourished, and disorganized. For those in the diaspora, the Land comes with a sense of loss and disconnect from histories that were stolen. However, a reclaiming of the Land through spirituality, the connection of African communities both in the continent and in the diaspora, is a way of building solidarity and community, and of fighting eurocentric divide-and-conquer tactics.

With the loss of the physicality of the Land, it is important to see how there is knowledge residing in the body of an African woman and to understand how Black women are the foremothers and knowledge producers in the women's liberation movement (Rodgers, 2017). What are the implications for African diasporic women who experience loss? How can we initiate a conversation between African diasporic experiences and African continental feminist experiences? How can storytelling as knowledge production, transformation, and healing be a means for reclaiming spirituality? How can our own subjectivities as researchers (Dillard, 2006; King, 2015), as educators (Ladson-Billings, 1996) help move us toward a reclaiming of spirituality in Euro-colonial contexts?

A Discursive Framework for Spirituality Grounded in Indigenous Knowledges and a Trialectic Space

To provide a discursive framework for spirituality grounded in and guided by Indigenous knowledges, the guiding principles of *suahunu,* or a "trialectic space" (Dei, 2012), will be highlighted in this section.

Dei (2012) uses the "trialectic space" (*suahunu*) concept to reframe an approach to decolonizing education for contemporary young learners. Trialectic space is not solely temporal—a feature of modern-colonial logic and postmodern logic—but works with embedded and interconnected histories and is not made up of partitioned bodies of knowledge (p. 2). This space calls upon the interconnectedness of histories and moves away from a linear production of knowledge toward a circular and holistic embrace of knowledges. In relation to spirituality,

> trialectic space provides a spiritually grounded, anticolonial approach to education that can dialogue with how African and Indigenous learners become alienated from their local surroundings and social environments and, conversely, also to counter Eurocentric cycles of knowledge production. (p. 4)

Thus, trialectic space carves out a place for African and Indigenous learners to reclaim an anti-colonial education that, unlike our current Euro-colonial schooling system centers their knowledges. Euro-colonial schooling poses as universal and liberal, a system in which all students can thrive within the benchmarks of equality and merit. However, educational institutions are fraught with an anti-Blackness that is designed to "push out" Black, Native, and Brown bodies (Dei, Mazzuca, McIsaac, & Zine, 1997). A trialectic space provides African and Indigenous learners with a holistic view of education grounded in myriad principles that center the intellectual, emotional, and spiritual growth and awareness of the learner. For example, trialectic space in education focuses on a body-mind-soul connection, a society-nature-culture interface, the sacredness of intellectual activity, the importance of spirit-centered space, the power and efficacy of ancestralism, bringing an "embodied connection" to knowledge production, the self and collective implication in creating decolonizing spaces, and sharing Indigeneity and multicentric knowledges (Dei, 2012). Entering the trialectic space allows for the mind-body-soul connection in ways that can attempt to mend the fragmentation of community and the self by colonialism. The rational-modern project of colonialism advocates for mastery of emotions and aspects of the spirit, leading to fragmentation. Dei (2012) highlights that we ought to move away from Cartesian mastery and intellectual reasoning of one's body. Wane speaks about our fragmented souls (Wane, personal communication, May 2016). This fragmentation leaves our own spirits unawakened and lends assistance to the justifications of colonialism.

In contemplating justifications, it is important to think about society-nature-culture. Mazama (2002) states that the fundamental philosophical principle is the principle of unity of being, which means that our connectedness to humans, other beings, plants, and minerals transcends ourselves. This is not unique to African Indigenous knowledge. It is, in fact, similar across many Indigenous knowledges—thus the sacredness of Land, Sky, and Water. We are all connected and interconnected. Returning to the idea of colonial justification and advocacy of mastery of knowledge, as opposed to sharing of knowledges, the Euro-colonial expansion was void of the society-nature-culture principle—and thus lacked spirituality—in the ongoing pursuit and dismemberment of Land, people, nature, and things. Similar to the colonial usurpation of Land, the Euro-colonial projects are also about ways of knowing vis-à-vis appropriation. This leads me to the next section, which considers the sacredness of intellectual activity.

Dei (2012) highlights the sacredness of intellectual activity as part of the trialectic space. This touches upon one of the major principles of Indigenous knowledges—that is, humility of knowing. Knowledge is not about pursuit of self-interest or for consumption. Knowledge is to be shared. In spirituality, though personal, it is not solely about the individual, but about the interconnectedness of community, Ancestors, and all beings, including inanimate objects. However, these characteristics, such as the sharing of knowledge and the interconnectedness of community, were not tenets of the modern-colonial project as its emphasis was on the pursuit of knowledge and the ongoing consumption of knowledge for individual benefit. Instead of sharing knowledge, colonial relations and new forms of colonialism abet the consumption of the Global South by the Global North. Spirituality is also compartmentalized and consumed by the North. York (2001) highlights the commodification of spirituality, which can be bought and sold in accordance with "free"-market principles and thence appropriated (p. 361). Again, this demonstrates the ways in which spirituality can become compartmentalized for utilitarian purposes. York does not describe whiteness in his analysis of free-market appropriation, but it is essential to thinking about the "use" of spirituality through the means of appropriation. The exoticized "Other" gets tasted, tried, and mediated into nonexistence, leading to the justification of ongoing forms of colonization. Moving away from mastery to humility is important for a spiritual space and for reclaiming spirituality. The spirit-centered space moves people away from simply serving the body and the mind and connects one's spirit to the humanity of others. Such a connectedness calls into account relationality and unity.

Moreover, such interconnectedness also speaks to the power and efficacy of ancestralism. Without a connection to Ancestors, we are fragmented parts. However, this connection reminds us that we must be humble and learn from and show gratitude to our Ancestors. Spirituality is about connectedness not only to ourselves and to one another, but respect for and connectedness to our Ancestors. A tenet of Euro-colonial expansionism was the severing and disjointedness of African and Indigenous people's histories. I draw my strength from my aunts and grandmothers, the holders of my ancestral history.

In the area of knowledge production, I have an "embodied connection" (Dei, 2012). This means that scholarship for me is not just about scholarship, but about activism, and thus I owe my work to my community and the communities with which I "coproduce" knowledge. This creates a lot of responsibility for me as a researcher and activist. What does it mean to embody this connection? Academia can make us dismembered, fragmented parts, but in (re)claiming spirituality, we can have a holistic view of knowledge production and pay careful attention to our ethical responsibility to our community, which we learn from and work with. There is a self- and a collective implication in creating decolonial spaces, and this means that we also have a commitment and responsibility to the community with which we work. The community with which we work on decolonial projects must strive not to reproduce power and hierarchal relations of power and domination. Finally, sharing Indigeneity in multicentric[1] knowledges is part of a discursive framework of trialectic space (Dei, 2012), and also key to spirituality as anti-colonial. This is important in thinking about spirituality, which calls on articulation of the self through connection to elders, Sncestors, and community—and, importantly, by identifying multicentric ways of knowing so as to build a community grounded in anti-colonial resistance.

Thus, the foregrounding of a trialectic space provides a strong basis for understanding spirituality as a discursive framework in the epistemological and ontological tenets of Indigenous knowledges.

Pedagogical Implications for Education

Dillard (2006) discusses the implications of integrating spirituality into methodology, and they are very similar to spirituality's connection to education and the pedagogical implications of such. Ladson-Billings (1996) discusses her refusal to apologize for bringing her own subjectivities into her pedagogical practice. Dillard describes love, embracing compassion, seeking reciprocity, ritual as methodology, and gratitude as guiding principles for methodology from an endarkened feminist epistemological standpoint. I would say that these major principles are key to spirituality as well, and must be placed front and center for pedagogical practices.

Because Euro-colonial schooling and education have de-spirited Black children and led to fragmentation by silencing our identities, histories, and communities, it is important to bring in a spiritual pedagogy in order to allow students to have an awakened experience in the education system. The histories and stories of Black children are not told in the classroom, a situation that leads to a hollow educational system that focuses solely on a single and universal eurocentric narrative. Shahjahan (2005) reminds us of the importance of bringing spirituality into education, as do scholars such as Wane, Manyimo, and Ritskes (2011) and Shields (2005). Such a connecting way of education reminds students that we care. Further, it is important that we draw on our own lived experiences and realities as educators in order to nourish a sense of harmony with our students. As such, teaching as all-knowing "objective" Black women in educational contexts leads to fragmentation. Our students see themselves in us, so it is important to illuminate our own situated knowledge and subjectivity so that they, too, can be comfortable with their own. I ask: What are the new imaginaries/possibilities in education when we look at (re)claiming spirituality from an Africana-feminist perspective? How can we draw on a trialectic space in order to articulate Indigenous knowledges and ways of knowing? What are the possibilities for looking at Land and Indigeneity beyond Land through spiritual cosmologies and connectivity? How can we look at spirituality as decolonizing Euro-colonial schooling and education?

For example, as a college educator I have worked to deploy some very simple but important Africana-feminist strategies in the classroom that were grounded in spirituality and sharing. Having lost a student in our class to suicide, we collectively decided that things needed to change in our classroom. We needed to have a space where students could collectively learn and grow. So rather than sitting in rows, we sat in a circle, a practice that is grounded in African and Indigenous knowledge systems. Circles certainly deconstruct hierarchies and single, all-knowing dynamics wherein teachers hold knowledge that the students are devoid of. We found that sitting in a circle created space for having difficult conversations, sharing, laughing, and collectively passing on our various knowledges as a group. Students seemed to be much more at ease with this, and by the end of the course they were thankful for that small and simple change. As well, when people talk about equity and inclusion in the classroom, a common rebuttal questions the percentage of students from a diverse background that an educator needs in order to incorporate equitable class practices. I find this thought process very problematic in that it reinforces the idea that the histories and stories of people from racialized backgrounds are othered in and compartmentalized in a larger eurocentric narrative. Instead, as an educator, I did not need to quantify and justify the number of students from diverse—that is, nonwhite—backgrounds in the classroom in order to integrate Indigenous and Black history into my teaching. Also, I had only had one student who was Indigenous from Turtle Island, and I made it a point to do a Land-acknowledgment reading in each class, read by different students. That student appreciated this gesture, because it was the first time in her educational experience that her history and her lived reality were embedded in the curriculum. These are some of the ways that I incorporated Indigenous knowledges grounded in spirituality. The importance of such grounding was that, as an educator, I was able to use the experiences, questions, debates, and conversations of my students to grow, learn, and unlearn.

Concluding Thoughts

As an educator and a learner, reclaiming my spirituality as anti-colonial resistance and decolonial practice is important for me in the educational context. I ask what spirituality might look like in an educational context. Many scholars have looked at spirituality in education (Miller, 1994; Palmer, 2003; Shahjahan, 2004, 2005; Shields, 2005; Wane et al., 2011). I ask: How can we look at spirituality through the lens of a trialectic space in hope and new imaginaries? How can we reclaim our spirituality as a form of anti-colonial resistance? And what does it mean to spiritually engage with a community of knowledge coproducers grounded in the sharing and reciprocal principles of Indigenous knowledges? It is important for me to draw on my own subject-location as an Africana-Black feminist and to draw on thinkers who have experiences of similar pain and love, and who have asked related questions. As an educator, I will work continuously to critically re-think Euro-colonial schooling and education and to examine all challenges and tensions. The larger question presented here reminds us that Indigeneity is a decolonial tool and that in action and resistance to colonial-dominant knowledge, in reclaiming spirituality, in reclaiming Blackness, we are challenging 500 years of colonization and trauma. As an educator, I have learned that having such difficult conversations takes time. It engenders much emotion and pain, and it does not happen instantly. However, by engaging in conversations with mentors, friends, and family and by staying connected with others beyond myself, I have learned and unlearned.

Throughout this chapter I have engaged with various definitions of *spirituality* within the larger conversation of Indigenous knowledges while examining the convergences and divergences, explored the historical traumas and de-spiriting of colonization, presented my own subject-location, and looked toward new imaginaries for hope in *suahunu* and the pedagogical implications for education. In all, I am continuing to remember that decolonization is a process of learning and unlearning and am seeking new ways to reclaim spirituality as an educator and as a part of a larger web of community, Land, the sky, water, and all beings.

Note

1. Multicentric knowledge is not interested in the subsuming of one knowledge by another. Rather, it is about respecting multiple knowledges, from multiple entry points and localities. As such, multicentric knowledge is not about the mastery of knowledge, but about sharing and reciprocity.

References

Abdi, A.A. (2011). Foreword. In N.N. Wane, E.L. Manyimo, & E.J. Ritskes (Eds.), *Spirituality, education and society: An integrated approach* (pp. xi–xiii). Rotterdam, Netherlands: Sense Publishers.

Aidoo, A.A. (1992). The African woman today. *Dissent, 39*, 319–325.

Alfred, T., & Corntassel, J. (2005). Being Indigenous: Resurgences against contemporary colonialism. *Government and Opposition: An International Journal of Comparative Politics, 40*(4), 597–614.

Collins, P.H. (1990). *Black feminist thought: Knowledge consciousness and the politics of empowerment.* New York, NY: Routledge.

Collins, P.H. (2000). *Black feminist thought: Knowledge, consciousness, and the politics of empowerment* (2nd ed.). New York, NY: Routledge.

Crenshaw, K. (1991). Mapping the margins: Intersectionality, identity politics, and violence against women of colour. *Stanford Law Review, 43*, 1241–1299.

Dei, G.J.S. (2004). Theorizing Africa beyond its boundaries. In G.J.S. Dei (Ed.), *Teaching Africa: Towards a transgressive pedagogy* (pp. 47–60). London, UK: Springer.

Dei, G.J.S. (2009). The anticolonial theory and the question of survival and responsibility. In A. Kempf (Ed.), *Breaching the colonial contract* (pp. 251–257). Dordrecht, Netherlands: Springer Science & Business Media B.V.

Dei, G.J.S. (2012). "Suahunu," the trialectic space. *Journal of Black Studies, 20*(10), 1–24.

Dei, G.J.S. (2017). *Reframing blackness and black solidarities through anti-colonial and decolonial prisms*. Cham, Switzerland: Springer.

Dei, G.J.S., & Kempf, A. (2006). *Anti-colonialism and education: The politics of resistance*. Rotterdam, Netherlands: Sense Publishers.

Dei, G.J.S., Mazzuca, J., McIsaac, E., & Zine, J. (1997). *Reconstructing 'drop-out': A critical ethnography of the dynamics of Black students' disengagement from school*. Toronto, ON: University of Toronto Press.

Dillard, C.B. (2006). *On spiritual strivings: Transforming an African American woman's academic life*. Albany, NY: State University of New York Press.

Dillard, C.B. (2014). When the ground is black, the ground is fertile: Exploring endarkened feminist epistemology and healing methodologies in the spirit. In N.K. Denzin, Y.S. Lincoln, & L.T. Smith (Eds.), *Handbook of critical and Indigenous methodologies* (pp. 277–292). Thousand Oaks, CA: Sage Publications.

Este, D., & Bernard, W.T. (2006). Spirituality among African Nova Scotians: A key to survival in Canadian society. *Critical Social Work, 7*(1).

hooks, b. (1991). *Feminist theory: From margin to center*. Boston, MA: South End Press.

King, J.E. (2015). *Dysconscious racism, Afrocentric praxis, and education for human freedom: Through the years I keep tolling*. New York, NY: Routledge.

Ladson-Billings, G. (1996). Your blues ain't like mine: Keeping issues of race and racism on the multicultural agenda. *Theory Into Practice, 35*(4), 248–255.

Marbley, A.F. (2005). African-American women's feelings on alienation from Third-Wave feminism: A conversation with my sisters. *Western Journal of Black Studies, 29*(3), 605–614.

Mazama, M.A. (2002). Afrocentricity and African spirituality. *Journal of Black Studies, 33*(2), 218–234.

Megwe, P. (2007). Theorizing African feminism(s): The "colonial" question. *Matatu, 35*(1), 165–174.

Merton, T. (1972). *New seeds of contemplation*. New York, NY: New Directions.

Miller, J.P. (1994). Contemplative practice in higher education: An experiment in teacher education. *Journal of Humanistic Psychology, 34*(4), 53–69.

Nilliasca, T. (2011). Some women's work: Domestic work, class, race, heteropatriarchy, and the limits of legal reform. *Michigan Journal of Race and Law, 16*(2), 377–410.

Norwood, C. (2013). Perspectives in Africana feminism: Exploring expressions of Black feminism/womanism in the African diaspora. *Sociology Compass, 7*(3), 225–236.

Oyewumi, O. (2003). *African women and feminism: Reflecting on the politics of sisterhood*. Trenton, NJ: Africa World Press.

Palmer, P.J. (2003). Teaching with heart and soul: Reflections on spirituality in teacher education. *Journal of Teacher Education, 54*(5), 376–385.

Rodgers, S. (2017). Womanism and Afrocentricity: Understanding the intersection. *Journal of Behaviour in the Social Environment, 27*(1–2), 36–47.

Rostan, Y. (Forthcoming). Co-creating thriving biocultural communities: An anticolonial framework for community wellness, resilience and innovation. In F. Villegas, & J. Brady, (Eds.) (Forthcoming). *Critical schooling and education: Transformative theory and praxis*.

Schneiders, S.M. (2003). Religion vs. spirituality: A contemporary conundrum. *Spiritus: A Journal of Christian Spirituality, 3*(2), 163–185.

Shahjahan, R.A. (2004). Centering spirituality in the academy: Towards a transformative way of teaching and learning. *Journal of Transformative Education, 2*(4), 294–312.

Shahjahan, R.A. (2005). Spirituality in the academy: Reclaiming from the margins and evoking a transformative way of knowing the world. *International Journal of Qualitative Studies in Education, 18*(6), 685–711.

Shahjahan, R.A. (2009). The role of spirituality in the anti-oppressive higher education classroom. *Teaching in Higher Education, 14*(2), 121–131.

Shields, C.M. (2005). Liberating discourses: Spirituality and educational leadership. *Journal of School Leadership, 15*, 608–623.

Ver Beek, K.A. (2000). Spirituality: A development taboo. *Development in Practice, 10*(1), 31–43.

Wane, N.N. (2000). Indigenous knowledge: Lessons from the Elders—A Kenyan case study. In G.J.S. Dei, B.L. Hall, & D.G. Rosenberg (Eds.), *Indigenous knowledges in global contexts: Multiple readings of our world* (pp. 54–69). Toronto, ON: University of Toronto Press.

Wane, N.N., Manyimo, E.L., & Ritskes, E.J. (Eds.). (2011). *Spirituality, education and society: An integrated approach.* Rotterdam, Netherlands: Sense Publishers.

York, M. (2001). New age commodification and appropriation of spirituality. *Journal of Contemporary Religion, 16*(3), 361–372.

CHAPTER 4

Reflections on the Implications of Western Theories on Indigenous Populations: Decolonizing and Indigenizing the Classroom

Cristina Bianchi

I HAVE ALWAYS marveled at the difference between *having knowledge* and *being educated* and what these mean to different individuals. This can be based on how one defines "to be with knowledge" and "to be educated." An example of this relationship can be seen by observing the classroom environment. An educator is educated to teach students a predetermined school curriculum that is based on each school's philosophy and mandatory government standards. Yet educators become unique and influential only when they use their knowledge to teach important academic and social skills to help their students relate to the real world.

Brook (2013) considers education to be an overall intrinsic motivation, where lessons are learned and passed on to other individuals who form identities that further influence community understanding. This definition provides the learner with the power of intrinsic motivation to influence the environment with new knowledge that is learned through experience, cultural practice, and direct instruction. However, defining knowledge through a Euro-Canadian/American lens (which will be referred to as *western* throughout this chapter) creates challenges since, though *knowledge* is used in everyday language, there is no formal definition regarding its meaning. Furthermore, those in different professions—for example, philosophers, economists, and educators—all have different perspectives on knowledge as well, a factor that needs to be acknowledged as we seek to understand the term. For example, the *Stanford Encyclopedia of Philosophy* mentions that the notion of knowledge is a way of acknowledging and recognizing an idea, and gaining a path toward truth in a concept (Ichikawa & Steup, 2017). O'Grady (2012) defines knowledge and information as interchangeable, yet determines knowledge to be "created collaboratively by this process [information], context dependent and constructed by the users" (p. 951). As such, knowledge can be described as the facilitation and exploration of truth on the part of the individual by using information from external or internal influences. One component that is missing from this definition is the culture from which the truth is derived. Culture is considered a knowledge asset that is continuously developing a spatio-temporal set of practices and beliefs that is shared within a collective memory among a community (Boisot, 1998; George & Reid, 2005). The knowledge created through different culture-specific practices provides sustainability to communities and allows future generations to thrive (Throsby & Petetskaya, 2016). Hence, culture has great importance, influence, and implications for how individuals interact in assigning meaning to their world. In this chapter, I will draw on Boisot (1998), George & Reid (2005), and Throsby & Petetskaya's (2016) notion of culture in order to reflect on the ways in which culture is *made*.

Throughout this chapter I will first define the terms *Indigenous, western knowledge, Indigenous knowledges*, and *Indigeneity*. Next, I will explore different definitions of *human development* and *identity* from western and Indigenous perspectives. These will include definitions from academia as well as understandings that I have formulated on my own. Similarly, I will define *mental health* and *identity* within the human development context for individuals from different regions with different cultural identities. This will be done by using different texts from Indigenous scholars and western scholars and connecting the possible implications of using different knowledge on Indigenous populations. Finally, I will present some of the different ways of decolonizing and indigenizing classrooms through an elementary school philosophy.

At this point I would like to locate myself within this chapter. I am a white, female, second-generation Canadian, born and raised in Toronto (acknowledging that I was raised on traditional territory of the Haudenosaunee [Iroquois]), and recently graduated with a specialty in early childhood. I have always had an interest in environmental influences on child development. Working and volunteering with professionals in multiple child-based settings through my undergraduate and current studies has furthered my interest in how educators holistically influence their students within the elementary school setting. I developed an interest in Indigenous culture, knowledge, and history as I approached the end of my undergraduate studies. Combining my passion for the importance of holistic child development and Indigenous knowledges has allowed me to create a new knowledge space for educating others about different knowledges that lead to enhanced self-empowerment and identity. I will locate myself within the different sections of the chapter to point out where my knowledge of the topic was gained.

Defining Indigenous and Indigenous Knowledges

Indigenous

The original definition of the term *Indigenous* was constructed by two sets of researchers who set out to create a term for communities who engaged in distinct ways of problem-solving by using their own ideologies and knowledge about the environment around them (Warren et al., 1980, as cited in Agrawal, 1995). Since then, the term *Indigenous* has come into such wide international use that it has made a clear reference in western academia to individuals and communities that take part in common culture to identify themselves in terms of ancestral territory (Purcell, 1998). *Indigenous* has also been twisted into a political and economic context that has allowed western society to gain control over the term. The word as originally defined was powerful, but it has been manipulated in a multitude of ways to fit the need of academics to categorize people. An example of this is the term *aboriginal* (a colonial category), which blankets the population with a western definition of the term *Indigenous* with the objective being to continue taking away individuals' right to be Indigenous and to fully practice their cultures (Alfred & Corntassel, 2005). I will use the term *Indigenous* in its original meaning: representing empowering individuals and communities that use ways of knowing that are different and untouched by western culture.

Indigenous knowledges and western knowledge

Western knowledge (i.e., Euro-Canadian/American knowledge) reflects an understanding of the world through scientific knowledge and observation. Additionally, it is not seen as "culturally grounded," although western scientists explain that ethnoscience has been a way to claim Indigenous seeing (Kincheloe & Steinberg, 2014; Purcell, 1998). On the other hand, Indigenous knowledges are emic (Purcell, 1998) and emerge from collective experiences (Dei, 2008). Language carries extreme importance in Indigenous knowledges, as the "structure and composition is designed to articulate Indigenous worldviews, values, conceptualizations, and knowledge" (Simpson, 2004, p. 377). Many authors and researchers agree that Indigenous knowledges comprise the necessary attachment to a physical location, Land, or space that allows communities and individuals to develop a pure understanding of the relationships that surround them, including natural and social environments (Dei, 2008; Throsby & Petetskaya, 2016). Indigenous people's connection to the Land is extremely important, as "without intact ecosystems, [they] cannot nurture these relationships" (Simpson, 2004). Yet Indigenous knowledges can be described as the multicategorical body of understanding that involves relationships with the physical environment, history, culture, and all aspects of life to form ideologies, epistemologies, and ontologies that construct their distinct knowledge within them (Kincheloe & Steinberg, 2014).

Another aspect of Indigenous knowledges is the Fourth World, which can be defined as viable relationships with the spiritual and cultural heritage left by Ancestors that are planted in Indigenous behavior, thought, and knowledge (Manuel & Posluns, 1974a). The Fourth World is a unifying way to connect the Indigenous with prior and future generations and cannot be replaced by other ways of knowing. However, the Fourth World becomes present when:

> People develop customs and practices that link it to the Land as the forest is linked to the soil, and as people stop expecting that there is some unnamed thing that grows equally well from sea to sea. As each of our underdeveloped nations begin to mature, we may learn to share this common bed without persisting in a relationship of violence and abduction. Such mutuality can come only as each respects the wholeness of the other, and also acknowledges his own roots. (Manuel & Posluns, 1974b, p. 265)

Western knowledge relies heavily on science, deems to be organized and linear, and is in constant need of validation of the unknown. Indigenous knowledges, on the other hand, are fluid, constantly changing to fit the individual, and do not need scientific validation or reasoning to prove the unknown (Agrawal, 1995). Comparing knowledges are difficult as each knowledge has shared and separate historical struggles and cultural rite, since there has always been a domination of knowledge (western over Indigenous) throughout history. Purcell (1998) explains that "once these dimensions are made explicit, we can begin to bridge the gap between methodology and ideology by showing the hidden interdependence that has existed all along" (p. 268).

I was introduced to and educated about the term *Indigenous* when, in my third year of undergraduate studies, I took a field study course that examined mental health in northern Canadian communities. Two professors and ten students travelled to Moosonee and Moose Factory, Ontario. To summarize my experience in words is impossible; I saw a reality that is only briefly mentioned in textbooks. I heard stories from residential school survivors, elders, community members, and activists about how some were marginalized by the Northern Canadian community, and from children who believed they did not have the ability to pursue education beyond the elementary grades. One lesson I took back to Toronto was never to romanticize the experience I had. The trip was impactful and provided me with the foundation that sparked my interest in Indigenous communities, knowledge, and the different ways in which to decolonize. Having been introduced to different readings from different Indigenous and western scholars, I see the terms *Indigenous* and *Indigenous knowledges* as ones that are used to refer to people who are not part of western thinking and, as a result, are given a negative connotation in their own category.

Western and Indigenous Theories of Human and Identity Development

Western theory of human development and identity

Human and identity development are both chronologically based as a series of steps and stages that correlate to physical and mental growth and that are influenced by environmental factors (Erikson, 1968; McAdams, 2013; Mclean & Syed, 2015). Western theory of human development is recognizably linear, either showing an individual's progression or regression in his or her own development, or compared to standardized assessments of a group of individuals (Welzel, Inglehart, & Kligemann, 2003). Human development can be examined from any angle, but there is a focus on physical, biological, and social perspectives that, in turn, leads to identity building. Alfred and Corntassel (2005) define *identity* as the choices that individuals make in response to their environment, whether they be influenced by economic, political, or social reasoning. Hence, as external events influence the internal formation of identity, it ultimately affects multiple aspects of the individual's life.

One western human development theory was formulated by Urie Bronfenbrenner, who is well known for his bioecological *process-person-context-time* model. He was responsible for three major theory developments, all with a focus on ecology as the "adjustment between organism and environment" (Bronfenbrenner, 1975, p. 439). His main work included a focus on the interaction among different ecological levels that the individual experiences throughout human and identity development. These different levels include the *microsystem* (which directly influences the individual), the *mesosystem* (the interaction of the influences on the individual), the *exosystem* (which encompasses other social factors that influence intermediate contact), the *macrosystem* (which holds culture and ideologies that continuously evolve), and the *chronosystem* (a measure of time and historical event influence). Additions to Bronfenbrenner's ecology theory included the biological understanding of how individuals' genetics affect their environment, as well as the process of interaction that takes place (Bronfenbrenner & Ceci, 1994). The final development of the *process-person-context-time* model summarized the importance of all factors having a bidirectional role in human and identity development. *Process* describes the interactions occurring between individual objects and people. *Person* is the recognition that individuals bring their own personal characteristics into activities and interaction. *Context* is the environment in which the interaction is occurring. *Time* could be historical or confined to a specific occasion (Bronfenbrenner, 1995, 2005; Bronfenbrenner & Morris, 1998).

Although Bronfenbrenner's research model has been applied to the field for decades, the theory has always been in a continuous state of development (Tudge, Mokrova, Hatfield, & Karnik, 2009). One concern with this theory is its limitation as to where factors can be placed in the model (i.e., at which level). Another is how much a factor truly impacts an individual in the model. Investigating western theory of identity is closely linked to human development because of the physical and chronological time and "proposed characteristics" that are categorized to fit each age in the model. Though Bronfenbrenner did not think of his model in a linear fashion, the model of time is always moving forward, and thus the model "grows" with the individual.

Following Bronfenbrenner's ecological theory, Erik Erikson developed a new model that focused on identity. This focus on identity analyzed the psychosocial stages of the individual's orientation toward the self and others and included social and conflictual aspects in the interaction between individuals and their social environments (Gerrig, Zimbardo, Desmarais, & Ivanco, 2012). Erikson's (1965) main contribution was the psychosocial stages and formation of identity, as well as identity crisis. Identity was described as the balancing of the intrinsic wants and needs for social roles to find "the inner sameness and continuity of one's meaning for others" (p. 253). If an individual were unable to fully complete the set life-stage test for each age bracket, he or she would be psychologically underdeveloped, a condition that would lead to identity diffusion (Erikson, 1968). Identity diffusion occurs when an individual's identity is paused in development or when an individual has not succeeded in creating a definite identity. Erikson's identity theory has been extended into religious and spiritual categories that examine how psychology meets theology in identity development in adults (Hoare, 2009). Religion and spirituality play an important role in identity development as the moral code of what is right and wrong. Since religion and spiritual development are introduced from birth, the introduction of other belief systems can add to the life-stage test of identity and role confusion, which begins during adolescence and then extends into ethical adult identity (Hoare, 2009).

Both theories incorporate the use of social and environmental surroundings developing within an individual's context. These theories can be classified as either *individualistic* or *collectivist* cultures. Individuals in *individualistic* cultures strive for and prioritize their personal goals, making the culture more autonomous during their identity development (Triandis, Bontempo, Villareal, Asai, & Lucca, 1988; Watkins et al., 1998). *Collectivist* cultures include individuals whose emphasis is on achieving goals that would be most beneficial to the community as a defining factor in their identities (Triandis et al., 1988; Watkins et al., 1998). *Individualistic* and *collectivist* cultures relate to human and identity development, because both cultures place an emphasis on individuals influencing their environment for their personal development. It is how the individual is engaging in the experience, within the specific culture, that determines and defines the direction of his or her identity building. Overall, these theories merely scratch the surface of the human experience. Given the multitude of cultural and historical contexts, it is not possible for any one theory to summarize all aspects of human development (Forte, 2009).

Indigenous perspective of human development and identity

Locating myself within this knowledge, I was educated in the colonial western education system and thus have limited knowledge of Indigenous perspectives of human development. With that said, the only way I can explain some major concepts within Indigenous theories about human development and identity is by drawing on Indigenous literature. An article written by Cross (1991) examined the life stages of Black Indigenous populations, which Mihesuah (1998) later adapted to focus on development of Indigenous populations.

Both Life Stage models of identity development encompass four stages. However, Mihesuah (1998) itemizes different factors that must be considered before using Cross's (1991) model with Indigenous populations: different tribes have different methodologies, histories, languages, physical looks, and definition of *Indian*. Therefore, the overall environmental and personal needs for individuals will differ.

Stage one is considered the *Pre-encounter* to identity development. There is a heavy influence that is predominantly in the hands of western culture. In Cross's (1991) model, stage one is where an individual understands that he or she is Black but is exposed to a different portrayal of Blackness—often a negative one—and accepts a white worldview. First exposure to social norms and values is provided by the family. It is not until individuals are older that they discover other aspects of their identities from friends, communities, and media influences (Mihesuah, 1998). If the individual has family members who have fostered different aspects of their identity (such as tribal or cultural), the individual is more likely to adopt these same views of cultural identity. Within the Indigenous perspective, cultural identity refers to the cultural standards and expressions that one subscribes to (Mihesuah, 1998; Schouten, 1996) and which provide an individual with a collective identity, a past, and a shared destiny (Green, 1995). Thus, depending on the environment that individuals are raised in, as well as external colonial influences, they may compare themselves to the dominant culture because it is the "imposed norm."

Stage two is the *Encounter*. This takes place when an individual is inspired to explore his or her cultural history and identity. Cross (1991) held this stage to be "the switch" that individuals experience when their frame of reference for forming their identity becomes incomplete or weak. Mihesuah's (1998) model holds that individuals will eventually pursue three possible identities: *becoming Indian, becoming more Indian/rediscovering Indianness, or becoming less Indian.* This stage involves building their identity, depending not only on their mental and physical perceptions of what it means to be "Indian," but also the feedback they receive from their community and the world at large about what it means to be "Indian" (Mihesuah, 1998; Taylor, 1994). At this stage, individuals become conscious actors searching for Indigenous identity, developing their identity through discussion with others who either agree or are still struggling with their own recognition of their identity (Taylor, 1994). Root (1990) created a series of identity resolutions for individuals who are biracial, or for anyone considering this stage in identity development (Root, 1990). The various resolutions include accepting what society decides is the identity, multiple identification to different cultural groups, identification with a new cultural group, or identification with a single group. Each resolution has its attractions, but the effects of resolutions depend on what the individual feels he or she is in agreement with.

Stage three is the *Immersion-Emersion*. This is completed when individuals try to construct a new concept of themselves from a new reference point in their community or themselves. Cross (1991) explains that the individual becomes fully immersed in Black "everything" (styles, clothing, mannerisms, etc.) and addresses the fact that the individual may have insecurities as he or she "begins to demolish the old perspective and simultaneously tries to construct what will become his or her new frame of reference" (p. 202). Like Cross, Mihesuah (1998) focuses on the choice that is made by individuals to pursue their version of "Indian" by seeking others who may be from the same tribe or different cultures. Individuals will notice recognition or absence thereof from others, which can cause a negative or positive reaction on the individual's newly constructed identity (Mihesuah, 1998; Taylor, 1994). Reinforcing the notion that as identity formation is occurring, Hegel (1977) comments that only when the Indigenous identity is acknowledged in another being will it exist.

Because of historical considerations, oppression, and domination, Indigenous individuals may identify with the dominant political institution's definition of Indigenous identity (Alfred & Corntassel, 2005). As individuals build new identities, a focus on tradition will develop through identity exploration. Linnekin's (1985) framework of the interpretation of tradition explains that every new generation will not necessarily interpret traditions the same way that previous generations did, due to the differences in internal or external influences at any given time. Furthermore, traditions holding the same significance through generations will always be interpreted differently and provide new meaning to each individual. This allows culture and tradition to remain static while developing within each generation and to grow and express group and individual cultural identity in different ways.

The last stage is *Internalization*. For both Cross (1991) and Mihesuah (1998), the inner security of individuals' identity is seen in their location within the world and their own communities. This will ultimately allow them to be *comfortable* and *accepting* of their identity (Mihesuah, 1998). An observation made by Cross (1991) and Mihesuah (1998) showed that the stages presented are not always definitive in either population, as there is a chance that an individual may remain in one stage throughout his or her lifetime. It is important to note that some individuals never make it past the pre-encounter stage, as "identities are (re)constructed at multiple levels—global, state, community, individual—it is important to recognize these multiple sites of resistance to state encroachment" (Alfred & Corntassel, 2005, p. 600). The Life Stage model offers flexibility in terms of how long the identity process can take, but also carries with it the disadvantage of different colonial-imposed factors whose presence will require more time to get through each of the stages.

There are very few differences between the Life Stage models. One important difference between Cross (1991) and Mihesuah (1998) can be seen in stage two. In Cross's model, encounter is identified as the "jolt" that inspires the individual to make the change. Mihesuah creates stage two as the determinant of the path that an individual may choose to pursue in the immersion-emersion stage. Overall, both Life Stage models are important to individuals in developing their own culture identities. Culture is complex and multidimensional, as it influences the practices of individuals' actions and habits (Bader, 2001). Schouten (1996) describes cultural identity as a "living force" that "will eventually prove itself as a powerful counter-trend against the global cultural domination of the West and the cultural uniformity it brings with it" (p. 54).

Reflecting on the different versions of the Life Stage model, researchers are interpreting human development as identity development and the journey for clarity of their external world to reflect what they want from their internal world. The western perspective of identity development shows that individuals can have multiple determining factors, including the bidirectional influence of environment and genetics. However, Indigenous identity building has a certain type of strength that considers the historical/colonial dialogue on top of other factors (Dei, 2008; Kincheloe & Steinberg, 2014). Yet Indigenous individuals are able to find themselves by discovering their own identity without the overarching colonial influence.

The proper use of the term *Indigenous knowledges* within identity spaces can be defined as *Indigeneity*. To summarize, Indigenous knowledges refers to collaborating with the Land, different spaces, and different people for knowledge that is different from western knowledge. Indigeneity is the process of identifying within no category or binaries by using empowerment and resistance without influence from colonial powers (Dei & Asgharzadeh, 2001; Kincheloe & Steinberg, 2014). Indigenous knowledge and Indigeneity share a connection in their resistance to the continuous colonial influence and oppression on the Indigenous individual. This can be viewed as shared experience from the community to a global perspective. Indigeneity is holistic when referring to the "trialectic space" to decolonize education, with the main purpose of using the body-mind-soul connection to locate oneself in western academia (Dei, 2012).

Under the constant judgmental gaze of a western perspective, Indigenous people have additional influential factors that are present during identity development and empowerment, including their government, Land, and culture (Akena, 2012). As individuals understand the sacredness of ceremonies, spiritual power, and relationships with past and future generations, the connections become "crucial to living a meaningful life for any human being" (Alfred & Corntassel, 2005, p. 599). In order to hold on to the sacredness of healing and ceremonies, individuals must find support both within the community and themselves. Western knowledge must acknowledge their disruption of the development of Indigeneity, identity, ceremony, and knowledge.

Finally, Indigenous knowledge and Indigeneity use the power of spirituality. *Spirituality* cannot be defined in any one simple way; it can be a collection of understandings that create an individual's spirituality over time. It is personal and distinctive and can use connections within a religious figure(s) and Ancestors, as well as different physical elements of knowledge such as nature and the environment (Cajete, 1994; Dei, James, Karumanchery, James-Wilson, & Zine, 2000; Mazama, 2002; Shahjahan, 2004; Wane, 2002). Spirituality also addresses the myth of supernatural/natural dichotomy, created where the difference between "the spirits and the world of the living is essentially one of degree of visibility, the spiritual world being largely invisible but nonetheless quite real" (Mazama, 2002, p. 221). Overall, an important component of identity, Indigenous knowledges, and Indigeneity is the connection to the spiritual and cultural messages from the Ancestors and the Land (Alfred & Corntassel, 2005).

By observing both western and Indigenous ideologies, one can see the concerns in both aspects of development. Western society shows evidence of theories, and in exploring identity, western society has overlooked the vast amount of thought and knowledge to be found within actual identity development. Because they embody a variety of factors that have created an impediment to their development, Indigenous perspectives have been unable to flourish. This resistance was the result of a change in domination, as western knowledge viewed Indigenous knowledges as unfamiliar (Akena, 2012). Yet returning to my earlier definitions of *education* and *knowledge*, individuals should want to expand their knowledge to include the different ways in which people have been living and building collective knowledge for hundreds of years.

Mental Health

I was once told that if society were to view mental health as an entity that is as important as physical health, the world would work differently. That statement resonated with me as I completed my undergraduate degree, and I continue to believe that there is more knowledge to be acquired in the service of mental health when working with individuals across all cultural identities. To simply define *mental health* from one perspective would not encompass the wide influence and significance that the mind can offer. Mental health is a vast, complex topic that can range from day-to-day psychological and behavioral processes to severe mental illness, with a focus on well-being when handling stress, ultimately fostering the understanding of these processes within the promotion of well-being and resilience (Kirmayer & Valaskakis, 2009; Overton & Medina, 2008). However, mental illness can be classified as a pattern of symptoms that "can be measured and studied in a common language" (Glied & Frank, 2008, p. 114). Not only does mental illness affect the individual; it also affects the family and supporters, and can be socially alienating, dehumanizing, and culturally dispossessing (Glass, 1989; Johnstone, 2001). Mental illness was stigmatized and deemed unnatural until 1974, when Thomas Szasz found that mental illness caused physical symptoms in the body, and hence the classification of psychiatric illnesses began (Overton & Medina, 2008).

The age of technology has provided a new approach to reaching out to and educating audiences about mental health through TV, radio, the internet, and social media (McClellan, Ali, Mutter, Kroutil, & Landwehr, 2016; Peek et al., 2015). Social media have had both positive and negative effects on mental health intervention and mental health education, and were found to be a contributing factor in an individual's mental health (Gkotsis et al., 2017; Hanna, Langdon, & Vanclay, 2016; Lau et al., 2016). What will ultimately determine how the media will influence an individual is the use of social media, the information presented, and the state of mind that an individual possesses.

For the purposes of this chapter, mental health and mental illness will be combined under the umbrella term *mental health*, because both terms ultimately affect day-to-day interactions and behaviors. I do recognize the true severity of mental illness. A definition of *mental health* incorporating explanations from Johnstone (2001), Overton and Medina (2008), and Kirmayer and Valaskakis (2009) is the spectrum and continuum of emotions, resilience, behaviors, and cognitive functions that interfere with everyday tasks and regular routines.

In western ideologies of mental health there is a consensus that different factors within the individual's daily life will influence his or her mental health (Walsh, 2011). These factors include the influence of genetics and an individual's lifestyle choices, including exercise, diet, media, and religious or spiritual development. There is also a focus on the individual's influence on his or her own mental health (Kirmayer & Valaskakis, 2009), which places the responsibility for mental health on individuals, rather than looking to their environment as the ultimate determinant. Since *mental health* has a broad definition, Kirmayer and Valaskakis (2009) characterized the major difference in Indigenous mental health as "the shared history and social predicament that has made many communities vulnerable to a range of social problems that, in turn, increase the risk of emotional suffering" (p. xv). These circumstances can be individual ones, or an amalgam of (in)direct influences of colonial past and present oppression, ethnic and cultural identity development, historical/intergenerational trauma, and current political and economic contexts (Kirmayer & Valaskakis, 2009; Wesley-Esquimaux & Smolewski, 2004). The major differences between Indigenous and western mental health definitions are the factors that immediately influence the individual—proximally or distally—and the chronological order of influential events.

Because of one's exposure to different extreme and historic factors, mental health from an Indigenous perspective is viewed more in terms of individual empowerment and self-determination. Different methods of empowerment and self-determination can be identified by using collective healing methods from a lost culture and tradition, connection to family and culture, life experiences, and identity building using traditional ways of healing (Archibald, 2006; Kilcullen, Swinbourne, & Cadet-James, 2016; Kirmayer & Valaskakis, 2009; Nagel, Hinton, & Griffin, 2012). Two other aspects of mental health that can influence both western and Indigenous populations are resilience and learned helplessness. *Resilience* can easily be described by using the example of a raincoat—specifically, that a good raincoat protects one from the rain by means of the material made to deflect water. Understandably, if the material is not made for the rain or has lost its effectiveness, some water may seep through. Resilience is defined as how quickly one can recover from an event, a capacity that "depends not only on the kind of trauma and how extensive it was, but also on his or her genetic endowment, previous life experience and physical and emotional condition before the trauma" (English, 2008, p. 343). The opposite of resilience is learned helplessness. Learned helplessness is manifested when the behavior of an individual or group is not perceived as controlling external events and, therefore, the individuals or groups predict that other aspects of their behavior will yield no control over future events (Peterson & Seligman, 1984).

These definitions, however, apply more to a western culture than to the major factors that impact Indigenous populations. Indigeneity is a form of resilience and empowerment that reduces learned helplessness; it is resistance and cultural empowerment that is breaking through what has happened in the history of all Indigenous populations (Dei & Asgharzadeh, 2001; Kirmayer, Dandeneau, Marshall, Phillips, & Williamson, 2011). Crediting the raincoat example to Indigenous populations does not work. I would challenge it by saying that Indigenous populations must make their own form of protection against a continuous downpour of rain, not only for themselves, but for others in the community and around the world. In examining mental health and resilience in Indigenous populations, the process of healing or using different western therapeutic methods is not the best approach. Practitioners would have to consider other factors that continue to leave an impression on Indigenous past, present, and future generations of the collective community. As well, individuals should not have to adapt themselves to a certain type of healing method to match a perspective or culture that is not their own, especially with something as complicated as mental health. The complexity of mental health and resiliency, seen in both western and Indigenous perspectives, demonstrates the need for different healing methods that can be used to better understand and attain an ideal mental health state for each individual.

Implications of Western Knowledge and Theories on Indigenous Populations

From the colonial epistemology perspective, the dominant culture (western) is positioned to exercise control over other cultures and their knowledge (Kincheloe & Steinberg, 2014). Therefore, Indigenous knowledge is considered odd by the dominant culture and is described as superstitious. In recent years, there has been a desire by western cultures to explore other cultures and traditions and to articulate how they differ from the dominant culture. Some defend this as an act of cultural internationalism in which cultures will inevitably share with each other, something that is "recognized as vital both to internal cultural growth and to mutual cultural tolerance and understanding" (Howes, 1996, p. 156). However, individuals may want to keep their traditions to themselves (i.e., refrain from sharing), since they are mindful that any knowledge that they share might be used disrespectfully or be misinterpreted (Howes, 1996). Throughout my educational journey, I have been taught to use a dichotomous way of thinking to differentiate between viewpoints. An example of this can be seen in Larbalestier's (1990) description of misrepresentation of information. When individual A witnesses individual B's expression of culture, what individual A internalizes from this experience is confined to his or her own framework of knowledge. As a result, individual A may unknowingly misrepresent the significance of what was observed from individual B as a way of understanding it within his or her knowledge space.

Even if western researchers are aware of their own misunderstandings of cultural information and traditions, they may still unknowingly have a negative effect on cultural knowledge because of the influence they wield as western individuals. First, they can participate in the dilution of tradition to demoralize a culture's worldview, thereby making it less significant than the dominant culture (e.g., Larbalestier, 1990), or they can leak culturally sensitive information. Even if this is not done deliberately, it results in a loss of power when creating a dissemination of tradition (Howes, 1996). When western investigators and mental health workers come into communities to help Indigenous people (re)gain their identity or to do research, it can be a process of Europeanization (Kincheloe & Steinberg, 2014). Investigating Europeanization from a historical perspective, Borneman and Fowler (1997) outlined the process of studying mental health, which began at the end of World War II, as "redefining forms of identification with territory and people" (p. 488). Yet Kincheloe and Steinberg (2014) define Europeanization as a way for Western "intellectuals [to] conceptualize Indigenous knowledge in contexts far removed from its production" (p. 11). Both explanations offer the distinction that even though one may see Europeanization as a form of self-identification, others view it to understand something that makes sense to the population without regard to the source. Conversely, Europeanization continues to make progress in understanding the reasons and meanings of Indigenous people. An example is classifying Indigenous ways of knowing into "ethno," to be ethnic, when it is simply a different form of knowledge that does not need to be reclassified under a western rubric.

As the dominant knowledge imposes itself on other knowledge domains, either knowingly or unknowingly, individuals from the other cultures could question their knowledge formation and where their knowledge comes from. Fanon (1967) expressed the structural way in which the colonizers objectively made individuals recognize differences within their own cultural context and that of others, which ultimately led to a subjective reflection on non-western individuals' knowledge as negative and false. An example can be seen in Battiste's (2008) work examining education within the Indigenous community. Elders who were once primary sources of history and transmitters of knowledge and healing are now viewed as untrustworthy sources of information. They are thus forced to change their ways of passing on knowledge to meet the demands of the dominant society over the community. Even though tradition and knowledge should be interpreted in ways that make sense to the individual, having western ways of knowing influences Indigenous knowledge and creates a new level of Europeanization as culture becomes lost or altered to match the new generation.

The comparison and contrast of western and Indigenous populations' views on human development and mental health have demonstrated some of the many differences between the populations. When working with individuals with diverse cultural identities, most methods of healing or forms of therapy are from a western framework of knowledge in mental health. Applying healing or forms of therapy to individuals who are not a part of the western population has implications of not healing within a context that is natural to the individual and develops communication concerns between the mind, the body, and a possible diagnosis in mental health (Kirmayer & Valaskakis, 2009).

One study conducted by Gfellner and Armstrong (2012) explored the relationship between ethnic identity, ego development, and strengths with Canadian First Nations adolescents. Three questionnaires were used, one of which was a bicultural identity measure examining respondents' identification and status with their First Nations culture and the majority-western culture. One finding was that participants who defined themselves as having a "traditional identity" had higher *wisdom* (ego strength) scores than any of the other groups (Gfellner & Armstrong, 2012). *Wisdom* was defined as the outcome of integrity involving acceptance of the past rather than grieving or remorse (Markstrom, Sabino, Turner, & Berman, 1997). Even though this study maintains a focus on the research outcomes, the definitions being used are from western theories and concepts of identity development. Assuming that these definitions are applicable to all adolescent populations does not allow the First Nations participants to answer freely; rather, it merely allows them to indicate what best describes them through a western lens. However, Gfellner and Armstrong (2012) focused on participants who identified themselves as bicultural (traditional and western) and found them to have lower scores on identity development. This aligns with previous literature illustrating that residing in communities with a strong ethnic identity serves as a protective factor for First Nations students' identity development.

Smokowski, Evans, Cotter, and Webber (2013) found that ethnic identity, optimism about the future, and self-esteem are contributing factors to different mental health issues in the Lumbee Indigenous population. A major result suggested that future optimism and ethnic identity are protective factors for members of the Lumbee Indigenous population with mental health issues. They also found ethnic identity to have a significant relationship with optimism about the future for all adolescents (Smokowski et al., 2013). The researchers were limited by the measures that were used. Gathering data through western surveys and rating scales limited the main source of significant relationships to statistics. That is, there was a lack of qualitative information. Statistics provide a clear representation of a relationship, while qualitative information can provide more reasons as to why statistical relationships become significant. Regardless, their main finding of the protective nature of ethnic identity and future optimism carries extreme importance and should be explored further. Individuals should be encouraged to understand and explore that aspect of their identity for their own mental health. Still, definitions of *ethnic identity* need to be distinguished for each of the different ethnicities, with unique acknowledgment to external factors that might be preventing them from exploring their identities.

As an individual desirous of undertaking research, I understand the value of these studies, since they comprise an area of research not commonly explored. However, as I go along in my academic career and develop research awareness, I am beginning to question whether some existing articles really encompass the truth of what is being displayed and reported. Studies frequently conclude by drawing inferences about possible solutions to the topic being studied. These solutions are often very general and cannot be targeted to a specific community, given that different communities will always have different ways of healing (Reinschmidt, Attakai, Kahn, Whitewater, & Teufel-Shone, 2016). As I become more familiar with the literature on certain topics, I want to deconstruct and decolonize my knowledge and create space for multiple ideologies in my analysis of any piece of academic work.

Decolonize and Indigenize the Classroom

I remember learning about the different historical political plans of groups of individuals in Canadian society in a politics course. These included people from Quebec and the Indigenous peoples of Canada. The professor wrote two words on the board—"accommodation" and "assimilation"—and began to explain the difference between the treatment of the Quebecois and the Indigenous. After centuries of rivalry, Quebec became its own distinct place in Canada, and French became one of Canada's official languages. Unfortunately, the same cannot be said about the Indigenous population of Canada. Our class discussion centered on residential schools and the forced assimilation of Indigenous children into western society. The professor was shocked that the class had so little knowledge about the different historical events involving the Indigenous community. This example demonstrates how, at the time, the education system was not set up to discuss or identify certain historical events that show the truth of western interaction with the Indigenous. Recently, the Ontario Ministry of Education published a supporting curriculum document for elementary and high school students that incorporates age-appropriate activities, lessons, and historical events pertaining to the Indigenous population of Canada (Ontario Ministry of Education, 2016). The document uses multiple perspectives from elders, knowledge keepers, community leaders, and educators to make sure that more voices are incorporated into the curriculum. This document not only creates a new pathway for learning in western education but also utilizes Indigenous ways of knowing and knowledge to learn about math, science, and the arts.

This chapter has not only been a form of self-reflection for me. More important, it is about the resistance within the western education system to introduce and recognize Indigenous knowledge when working with students. For me, an individual who received a western-centered education, learning about Indigenous knowledge has been a way to reconstruct my own ideas of what I believe to be true about education. However, by not learning or participating in different knowledge forms throughout my education, I find myself trying to create a space in which to grow with this new knowledge that I have acquired, and attempting to highlight for others the caveats in defaulting to western ideologies when looking at culturally sensitive issues. Educating individuals to be open to different types of knowledge is a powerful tool, as these individuals will then educate their communities who, in turn, will educate the nation (Dei, 2008).

The meaning of decolonization from the colonizer body

As mentioned previously, I locate myself as a white female and am therefore not phenotypically representing an Indigenous body. What is important to consider is how an educator (western or Indigenous) can decolonize the educational setting for young learners without misrepresenting Indigenous knowledges and history. As an individual who is familiar with the importance of early education, I strongly believe that decolonization should begin in the elementary school setting, as this is the period during which students are building their first philosophies around culture, stereotypes, and attitudes.

Decolonization is not a disruption; rather, it is a restrengthening of Indigenous populations and a reconnection to their relationships with Land, ceremony, and relatives (Alfred & Corntassel, 2005). It is a liberation from an oppressive power and a building of a new relationship between the Indigenous and non-Indigenous populations with "mutual respect, sharing, and recognition of the inherent rights of [Indigenous] peoples to follow their traditional ways" (Sunseri, 2000, p. 146). This process of decolonization is not something that can be accomplished overnight. It takes years, since there is a need to return space that was taken away in both knowledge and physical Land space, thereby allowing zones of freedom and refuge (Alfred & Corntassel, 2005). This includes steps such as regaining control over things that were taken away from Indigenous populations, as well as providing anti-colonial education that includes the knowledge and traditions of their nations (Simpson, 2004). Thus, empowered by education and knowledge, the truths will come to light, the stereotypes surrounding Indigenous populations will be demolished, and the way in which individuals view Indigenous knowledge will change.

First it is important to consider where educators receive their own knowledge. Since most academic institutions are "westernized," educators are taught through a colonial lens (Ogunniyi, 2007). Their teachings and documents come from a single perspective. Educators should be provided with opportunities to understand the ways in which the very foundation of "education" is rooted in the western knowledge system. Acknowledging that reality will allow a space for teachers to explore other ideologies and knowledges and to become comfortable addressing these different knowledges in the classroom. Educators must acknowledge that classrooms are a set of:

> Complex matrices of interactions, codes, and signifiers in which both students and teachers are interlaced. Just as a complex and critical pedagogy asserts that there is no single, privileged way to see the world, there is no one way of representing the world artistically, no one way of teaching science, no one way of writing history. Once teachers escape the entrapment of the positivist guardians of Western tradition and their monocultural, one-truth way of seeing, they come to value and thus pursue new frames of reference in regard to their students, classrooms, and workplaces. (Kincheloe & Steinberg, 2014, p. 141)

Colonization was, and still is, the power narrative of the history of Indigenous populations controlled by the western population (Alfred & Corntassel, 2005), as well as the devaluing of Indigenous knowledge and the dismissal of values of cultural beliefs and practices (Wane, 2006). In history textbooks in Canada, colonization is not represented to students as the harsh concept that it is. Instead, it is narrated as a story of how we, the western body, stumbled upon this great Land, Canada, and needed to show Indigenous bodies that they could live a "better" life because they were not "advanced" like the western population. There is a new voice of technology and news media that is merely the beginning of the recognition and reconciliation for Indigenous people in Canada. It is hoped that this recognition and reconciliation will lead to a rewriting of history, but the shift will not take place on western terms. This process of decolonizing the education system with proper information, knowledge, and teaching must come from a power exchange of western knowledge to Indigenous knowledge and decolonizing methods. Once there is a recognition of this reconciliation shift, it will necessarily become one of the first places to begin decolonization.

Some may argue that there cannot be a full decolonizing approach in the education system, as it would be too drastic for the system and other institutions involved. Nevertheless, the colonial influence was a drastic shift in knowledge power for Indigenous populations to experience, and yet it has been occurring for centuries. This approach to education can be further expanded to decolonizing higher academia, as demonstrated by Bishop (1998), who created the "Maori approach" to research, which ultimately gave control to the people in the community when regeneration research was being completed.

However, this led Lopez (1998) to express concern about Bishop's (1998) method of using a colonial way of research in which the "power of control" would be yielded to another group of people. If research is going to be undertaken in the community, one way it could be completed is by using *radical Indigenism*. Radical Indigenism is defined by a Cherokee sociologist as scholarship that is grounded in community goals that allow the process of regeneration (Garroutte, 2003). If western academia would allow different forms of research for regeneration, this would be a starting point for properly educating others about Indigenous history, traditions, and cultures of Indigenous individuals.

Kincheloe and Steinberg (2014) suggest that once there is a better understanding of Indigenous knowledges and history, one approach to beginning anti-colonial education might be through transformative learning to "foster empowerment and justice in a variety of cultural contexts" (p. 137). Dei (2002) describes transformative learning as the education that "should be able to resist oppression and domination by strengthening the individual self and the collective souls to deal with the continued reproduction of colonial and re-colonial relations in the academy" (p. 122). This way of learning is meant to be a guide to challenging colonial ways of thinking by resisting oppression and strengthening the individual holistically (Akena, 2012). As I understand it, this form of learning must be undertaken with full classroom participation, which in turn would become a form of empowerment for everyone—but particularly for those who have been colonized. It is a method of learning that uses different knowledges that are not recognized by western knowledge. This could come in the form of a classroom based on a collectivist cultural perspective, in which there are stated strategies for helping others in the community to reach goals set by the class, students, and educators. Another example could be the use of the environment, Indigenous knowledge methods, and other resources to learn about science (Cronje, Beer, & Ankiewicz, 2015).

Alfred and Corntassel (2005) describe mantras of Indigenous movement, some of which could be used in transformative learning in the classroom. First, language is a primary tool for recovering knowledge (Bader, 2001; Dei, 2008; Simpson, 2004), yet not all educators will speak the language necessary to gain this knowledge. Educators can encourage students to ask questions of their families, provide culturally appropriate resources about the students' language, and bring new knowledge that resonates with students into the classroom. Suggesting that students question their family members allows them to explore the knowledge from their families first. Educators are not only there to guide but also to provide support and become leaders if they recognize that students are unable to have their knowledge and language addressed in the classroom. Second, using the Land as a resource of lost knowledge, even teaching students that knowledge can come from a variety of sources is a big step forward in creating a space for Land knowledge. Third (and most important) is developing meaningful learning-teaching relationships that foster Indigenous human development and identity.

The trialectic space as defined by Dei (2012) as a body, mind, and soul connection can serve as a way to decolonize. Body is the lived experience, soul is the spirituality of the individual, and mind is the ability to locate and use multiple knowledge frameworks to create social change. Yet teaching spirituality is a complex responsibility. The use of cultural resources, such as an elder or other member who can provide understanding of spirituality, can be very important in this stage. Educators can also create a space in their classrooms to provide students with opportunities, activities, and the ability to explore for themselves what spirituality means to them. Developing spirituality is about not attaching yourself to anything that is part a group, and instead accepting the fluidity and holistic aspect of different human knowledges about how spirituality is expressed. All methods that demonstrate a holistic view of the child must be considered in teaching about the world with different knowledges that allow space to be created within the mind.

How to Indigenize now and in the future

In order to recover Indigenous knowledge, there must be a "deconstruction of the colonial thinking and its relationship to Indigenous knowledges" (Simpson, 2004, p. 381). Kincheloe and Steinberg (2014) summarized the importance of a multilogical context of Indigenous knowledge and education that "does not involve 'saving' Indigenous people but helping construct conditions that allow for Indigenous self-sufficiency while learning from the vast storehouse of Indigenous knowledges that provide compelling insights into all domains ofhuman endeavor" (p. 2). Educating students is just as important as educating the educators and the school system (Ogunniyi, 2007), which will promptly influence the surrounding communities and other social institutions that partake in decolonizing efforts.

Part of the multilogical context can include not only concepts that are being taught in the classroom but also other concepts such as using culture, history, Land, resistance, unity, and spirituality (Anderson, 2000; Dei, 2008, 2012; Fanon, 1963; Kincheloe & Steinberg, 2014; Shahjahan, 2004). The foundations of resistance outlined by Fanon (1963) and Anderson (2000) include the building of interpersonal relationships with the family and communities under colonial powers, the rediscovery or use of Indigenous language, the connection to Land, and storytelling. Resistance also involves Indigenous communities coming together to help one another when western influences try to separate and individualize them (Fanon, 1963). By working together, different knowledges can contribute to the removal of binaries when claiming certain knowledge (Bishop, 1998) that was once separated by western influence. Using resistance in education will allow students to challenge different academic and social concepts in a way that helps them to better understand and develop their identities.

Conclusion

As products of a colonial education system, the researchers whose work I have been able to read in my exploration of my education and knowledge systems have provided me with a revelation. I have created a new space within my knowledge to be confident enough to question my prior education. I have learned that having knowledge from another point of view is not a matter of a simple exchange of ideas. Rather, it is a give and take that requires *responsibility, respect,* and *acknowledgment* of its origin. I believe in education as a path to new ideas, something that introduces critical thinking and can initiate social change. Hence, educators are the main leaders in decolonizing and Indigenizing the classroom.

Educators play an important role in influencing the next generation by shaping the development of students in the classroom setting and educating them about the world. They also have a responsibility to be attentive to any learning issues, mental health behaviors, and concerns that could impact students in current and future learning environments. Given that educators are not currently taught in Indigenous ways of knowing, this does not mean that they are exempt from such responsibility. In fact, educators have a duty to seek out resources in their communities to help students develop holistically and to better understand the communities they serve. Alternatively, educators must be acknowledged for the work that they do to develop the next generation of diverse learners. They need to have the proper resources and guidance in their teacher education and continued professional development. This emphasizes the importance of education and the different knowledge resources it can borrow from in educating others. As resources change to fit the deconstruction of colonial thinking, a message of change would be communicated to other social institutions, creating a proverbial domino effect.

In this chapter, *mental health* has been defined as something that ranges from normal, daily behaviors, all the way to severe mental illness that affects one's ability to carry out a "normal" routine. To some extent, human and identity development can be put together as overall development of the individual. In cases where mental health and identity development differ from both western and Indigenous perspectives, educators must decide how to incorporate both individual empowerment and health into the knowledge environment from which the individual comes. In particular, in knowing that mental health influences identity development, it is important for educators to be aware of the differences within identity and developmental theories that would further influence students.

Reflecting on the different theories presented in this chapter that are influenced by western knowledge, there is a need for honest recognition that Indigenous knowledge and individuals are not always afforded the opportunity to theorize their identity the way western knowledge has. Also, different Indigenous perspectives have been denied the opportunity to intellectualize in a manner similar to that of western analysis. Since Indigenous knowledge is considered a new category of knowledge from the western perspective, it will be studied to match western concepts in order to continue the power that the colonial influence has over Indigenous ways of knowing. However, if the opportunity were to be presented to develop these areas, it would have to be done according to the terms of each community's respective way of developing knowledge.

As a colonial body, I want to challenge western influence on individuals by ultimately educating them on the truth of what should be known about other knowledges and histories. Exposing consistent colonizing behaviors will allow individuals to question where different parts of western knowledge truly originated. Yet to this day I am still seeking a way to decolonize my behaviors, views, and perspectives and to be more aware of where the influence on my knowledge stems from. The first step in removing the power of western knowledge is to deconstruct what knowledge is, and this can be done through education. Since education and knowledge are closely linked to form opinions and identity development, it is important to recognize that all humans have the right to discover other ways of knowing in order to further develop their environments. Using decolonizing methods and other forms of knowledge in the classroom can be truly empowering, as it does not understate the importance of ownership within one's experience.

References

Agrawal, A. (1995). Indigenous and scientific knowledge: Some critical comments. *Indigenous Knowledges and Development Monitor (IKDM), 3*(3).

Akena, F. (2012). Critical analysis of the production of western knowledge and its implications for Indigenous knowledges and decolonization. *Journal of Black Studies, 43*(6), 599–619. doi:10.1177/0021934712440448

Alfred, T., & Corntassel, J. (2005). Being indigenous: Resurgences against contemporary colonialism. *Government and Opposition, 40*(4), 597–614. doi:10.1111/j.1477-7053.2005.00166.x

Anderson, K. (2000). *A recognition of being: Reconstructing Native womanhood.* Toronto, ON: Sumach Press.

Archibald, L. (2006). *Final report of the Aboriginal Healing Foundation: Promising healing practices in aboriginal communities* (Vol. 3). Ottawa, ON: Aboriginal Healing Foundation.

Bader, V. (2001). Culture and identity. *Ethnicities, 1*(2), 251–273. doi:10.1177/146879680100100206

Battiste, M. (2008) Research ethics for protecting Indigenous knowledge and heritage: Institutional and researcher responsibilities. In N.K. Denzin, Y.S. Lincoln & L.T. Smith (Eds.), *Handbook of critical Indigenous methodologies* (pp. 497–510). Los Angeles, CA: Sage Publications.

Bishop, R. (1998). Freeing ourselves from neo-colonial domination in research: A Maori approach to creating knowledge. *International Journal of Qualitative Studies in Education, 11*(2), 199–219. doi: 10.1080/095183998236674

Boisot, M.H. (1998). *Knowledge assets: Securing competitive advantage in the information economy.* New York, NY: Oxford University Press.

Borneman, J., & Fowler, N. (1997). Europeanization. *Annual Review of Anthropology, 26*, 487–514.

Bronfenbrenner, U. (1975). Reality and research in the ecology of human development. *American Philosophical Society, 119*, 439–469.

Bronfenbrenner, U. (1995). Developmental ecology through space and time: A future perspective. In P. Moen, G.H. Elder, & J.K. Luscher (Eds.), *Examining lives in context: Perspectives on the ecology of human development* (pp. 619–647). Washington, DC: American Psychological Association.

Bronfenbrenner, U. (2005). *Making human beings human: Bioecological perspectives on human development.* Thousand Oaks, CA: Sage Publications.

Bronfenbrenner, U., & Ceci, S.J. (1994). Nature–nurture reconceptualized in developmental perspective: A bioecological model. *Psychological Review, 101*(4), 568–586. doi:10.1037//0033-295X.101.4.568

Bronfenbrenner, U., & Morris, P.A. (1998). The ecology of developmental processes. In W. Damon & R.M. Lerner (Eds.), *Handbook of child psychology, Vol. 1: Theoretical models of human development* (pp. 993–1028). New York, NY: Wiley.

Brook, A. (2013). What is education? Re-reading metaphysics in search of foundations. *New Blackfriars, 94*(1049), 32–49. doi:10.1111/j.1741-2005.2012.01503.x

Cajete, G. (1994). *Look to the mountain: An ecology of indigenous education*. Skyland, NC: Kivaki Press.

Cronje, A., Beer, J.D., & Ankiewicz, P. (2015). The development and use of an instrument to investigate science teachers' views on Indigenous knowledges. *African Journal of Research in Mathematics, Science and Technology Education, 19*(3), 319–332. doi:10.1080/10288457.2015.1108567

Cross, W.E., Jr. (1991). *Shades of Black: Diversity in African-American identity*. Philadelphia, PA: Temple University Press.

Dei, G.J.S. (2002). Spiritual knowing and transformative learning. In E.V. O'Sullivan, A. Morrell, & M. O'Connor (Eds.), *Expanding the boundaries of transformative learning: Essays on theory and praxis* (pp. 121–132). New York, NY: Palgrave.

Dei, G.J.S. (2008). Indigenous knowledges studies and the next generation: Pedagogical possibilities for anti-colonial education. *Australian Journal of Indigenous Education, 37*. http://dx.doi.org/10.1375/S1326011100000326

Dei, G.J.S. (2012). "Suahunu," the trialectic space. *Journal of Black* Studies, 43(8), 823–846. doi:10.1177/0021934712463065

Dei, G.J.S., & Asgharzadeh, A. (2001). The power of social theory: Towards an anti-colonial discursive framework. *Journal of Educational Thought, 35*(3), 297–323.

Dei, G.J.S., James, I.M., Karumanchery, L.L., James-Wilson, S., & Zine, J. (2000). *Removing the margins: The challenges and possibilities of inclusive schooling*. Toronto, ON: Canadian Scholars' Press.

English, F. (2008). What motivates resilience after trauma? *Transactional Analysis Journal, 38*(4), 343–351. doi:10.1177/036215370803800409

Erikson, E.H. (1965). *Childhood and society*. Harmondsworth, UK: Penguin Books.

Erikson, E.H. (1968). Identity and identity diffusion. In C. Gordon & K.J. Gergen (Eds.), *The self in social interaction, Vol. 1: Classic and contemporary perspectives* (pp. 197–205). New York, NY: Wiley.

Fanon, F. (1963). *The wretched of the Earth*. New York, NY: Grove Press.

Fanon, F. (1967). *Black skin, white masks*. Boston, MA: Grove Press.

Forte, J.A. (2009). Teaching human development: Current theoretical deficits and a theory-enriched "models, metaphors, and maps" remedy. *Journal of Human Behavior in the Social Environment, 19*(7), 932–954. doi:10.1080/10911350903126817

Garroutte, E.M. (2003). *Real Indians: Identity and the survival of Native America*. Berkeley, CA: University of California Press.

George, E.W., & Reid, D.G. (2005). The power of tourism: A metamorphosis of community culture. *Journal of Tourism and Cultural Change, 3*(2), 88–107. doi:10.1080/09669580508668489

Gerrig, R.J., Zimbardo, P.G., Desmarais, S., & Ivanco, T. (2012). *Psychology and life: Canadian edition* (2nd ed.). Toronto, ON: Pearson Canada.

Gfellner, B.M., & Armstrong, H.D. (2012). Ego development, ego strengths, and ethnic identity among First Nation adolescents. *Journal of Research on Adolescence, 22*(2), 225–234. doi:10.1111/j.1532-7795.2011.00769.x

Gkotsis, G., Oellrich, A., Velupillai, S., Liakata, M., Hubbard, T.J., Dobson, R.J., & Dutta, R. (2017). Characterization of mental health conditions in social media using Informed Deep Learning. *Scientific Reports, 7*. doi:10.1038/srep45141

Glass, J. (1990). *Private terror/public life: Psychosis and the politics of community*. Ithaca, NY: Cornell University Press.

Glied, S.A., & Frank, R.G. (2008). Shuffling toward parity: Bringing mental health care under the umbrella. *New England Journal of Medicine, 359*(2), 113–115. doi:10.1056/nejmp0804447

Green, M.K. (1995). *Issues in Native American cultural identity*. New York, NY: Peter Lang.

Hanna, P., Langdon, E.J., & Vanclay, F. (2016). Indigenous rights, performativity and protest. *Land Use Policy, 50*, 490–506. doi:10.1016/j.Landusepol.2015.06.034

Hegel, G.F. (1977). *The phenomenology of spirit*. Oxford, UK: Oxford University Press.

Hoare, C. (2009). Identity and spiritual development in the papers of Erik Erikson. *Identity: An International Journal of Theory and Research, 9*(3), 183–200. doi:10.1080/15283480903344497

Howes, D. (1996). Cultural appropriation and resistance in the American southwest: Decommodifying "Indianness." In D. Howes (Ed.), *Cross-cultural consumption: Global markets, local realities* (pp. 138–160). London, UK: Routledge.

Ichikawa, J.J., & Steup, M. (Fall 2017 Edition). The Analysis of Knowledge, *The Stanford Encyclopedia of Philosophy*, Edward N. Zalta (ed.), URL =https://plato.stanford.edu/archives/fall2017/entries/knowledge-analysis/

Johnstone, M. (2001). Stigma, social justice and the rights of the mentally ill: Challenging the status quo. *Australian and New Zealand Journal of Mental Health Nursing, 10*(4), 200–209. doi:10.1046/j.1440-0979.2001.00212.x

Kilcullen, M., Swinbourne, A., & Cadet-James, Y. (2016). Aboriginal and Torres Strait Islander health and well-being: Implications for a cognitive behavioural therapy framework. *Australian Psychologist, 51*(6), 453–462. doi:10.1111/ap.12159

Kincheloe, J.L., & Steinberg, S.R. (2014). Indigenous knowledges in education: Complexities, dangers, and profound benefits. *Handbook of Critical and Indigenous Methodologies*, 135–156. doi:10.4135/9781483385686.n7

Kirmayer, L. J., Dandeneau, S., Marshall, E., Phillips, M. K., & Williamson, K. J. (2011). Rethinking resilience from indigenous perspectives. *The Canadian Journal of Psychiatry, 56*(2), 84-91.

Kirmayer, L.J., & Valaskakis, G.G. (2009). *Healing traditions: The mental health of aboriginal peoples in Canada*. Vancouver, BC: University of British Columbia Press.

Larbalestier, J. (1990). The politics of representation: Australian aboriginal women and feminism. *Anthropological Forum, 6*(2), 143–157. doi:10.1080/00664677.1990.9967404

Lau, K.M., Hou, W.K., Hall, B.J., Canetti, D., Ng, S.M., Lam, A.I., & Hobfoll, S.E. (2016). Social media and mental health in democracy movement in Hong Kong: A population-based study. *Computers in Human Behavior, 64*, 656–662. doi:10.1016/j.chb.2016.07.028

Linnekin, J. (1985). *Children of the Land: Exchange and status in a Hawaiian community*. New Brunswick, NJ: Rutgers University Press.

Lopez, C.G. (1998) Reflections on epistemology and standpoint theories: A response to "a Maori approach to creating knowledge." *International Journal of Qualitative Studies in Education, 11*(2), 225–231. doi:10.1080/095183998236692

Manuel, G., & Posluns, M. (1974a). *The fourth world: An Indian reality.* Don Mills, ON: Collier-Macmillan Canada.

Manuel, G., & Posluns, M. (1974b). The Indian world and the fourth world. *Current History, 67*(400), 263–266.

Markstrom, C.A., Sabino, V.M., Turner, B., & Berman, B.C. (1997). The psychosocial inventory of ego strengths: Development and validation of a new Eriksonian measure. *Journal of Youth and Adolescence, 26*, 705–732.

Mazama, M.A. (2002). Afrocentricity and African spirituality. *Journal of Black Studies, 33*(2), 218–234.

McAdams, D.P. (2013). The psychological self as actor, agent, and author. *Perspectives on Psychological Science, 8*(3), 272–295. doi:10.1177/1745691612464657

McClellan, C., Ali, M.M., Mutter, R., Kroutil, L., & Landwehr, J. (2016). Using social media to monitor mental health discussions—Evidence from Twitter. *Journal of the American Medical Informatics Association.* doi:10.1093/jamia/ocw133

Mclean, K.C., & Syed, M. (2015). Personal, master, and alternative narratives: An integrative framework for understanding identity development in context. *Human Development, 58*(6), 318–349. doi:10.1159/000445817

Mihesuah, D.A. (1998). American Indian identities: Issues of individual choices and development. *American Indian Culture and Research Journal, 22*(2), 193–226. doi:10.17953/aicr.22.2.9341w76528071x3j

Nagel, T., Hinton, R., & Griffin, C. (2012). Yarning about indigenous mental health: Translation of a recovery paradigm to practice. *Advances in Mental Health, 10*(3), 216–223.

O'Grady, L. (2012). What is knowledge and when should it be implemented? *Journal of Evaluation in Clinical Practice, 18*(5), 951–953. doi:10.1111/j.1365-2753.2012.01899.x

Ogunniyi, M.B. (2007). Teachers' stances and practical arguments regarding a science Indigenous knowledges curriculum: Part 1. *International Journal of Science Education, 29*(8), 963–986.

Ontario Ministry of Education. (2016). *First Nations, Métis, and Inuit connections: Scope and sequence of expectations.* Retrieved from http://www.edu.gov.on.ca/eng/curriculum/elementary/elementaryFNMI.pdf

Overton, S.L., & Medina, S.L. (2008). The stigma of mental illness. *Journal of Counseling & Development, 86*(2), 143–151. doi:10.1002/j.1556-6678.2008.tb00491.x

Peek, H.S., Richards, M., Muir, O., Chan, S.R., Caton, M., & Macmillan, C. (2015). Blogging and social media for mental health education and advocacy: A review for psychiatrists. *Current Psychiatry Reports, 17*(11). doi:10.1007/s11920-015-0629-2

Peterson, C., & Seligman, M.E. (1984). Causal explanations as a risk factor for depression: Theory and evidence. *Psychological Review, 91*(3), 347–374. doi:http://dx.doi.org/10.1037/0033-295X.91.3.347

Purcell, T. (1998). Indigenous knowledges and applied anthropology: Questions of definition and direction. *Human Organization, 57*(3), 258–272. doi:10.17730/humo.57.3.qg0427ht23111694

Reinschmidt, K.M., Attakai, A., Kahn, C.B., Whitewater, S., & Teufel-Shone, N. (2016). Shaping a stories of resilience model from urban American Indian Elders' narratives of historical trauma and resilience. *American Indian & Alaska Native Mental Health Research: The Journal of the National Center, 23*(5), 63–85.

Root, M.P.P. (1990). Resolving "other" status: Identity development of biracial individuals. In L. Brown & M.P.P. Root (Eds.), *Diversity and complexity in feminist theory and therapy.* New York, NY: Haworth.

Schouten, F. (1996). *Tourism and cultural change. Proceedings of a Round Table: Culture, tourism, development: Crucial issues for the XXIst century* (pp. 53–56). Held at UNESCO Headquarters, Paris, France, June 20–27, 1996. Paris, France: Secretariat of the World Decade for Cultural Development, UNESCO.

Shahjahan, R. (2004). Centering spirituality in the academy. *Journal of Transformative Education, 2*(4), 294–312. doi:10.1177/1541344604268330

Simpson, L.R. (2004). Anticolonial strategies for the recovery and maintenance of Indigenous knowledges. *American Indian Quarterly, 28*(3), 373–384. doi:10.1353/aiq.2004.0107

Smokowski, P.R., Evans, C.B., Cotter, K.L., & Webber, K.C. (2013). Ethnic identity and mental health in American Indian youth: Examining mediation pathways through self-esteem and future optimism. *Journal of Youth and Adolescence, 43*(3), 343–355. doi:10.1007/s10964-013-9992-7

Sunseri, L. (2000). Moving beyond the feminism versus nationalism dichotomy: An anti-colonial feminist perspective on aboriginal liberation struggles. *Canadian Woman Studies, 20*(2), 143–148.

Taylor, C. (1994). The politics of recognition. In A. Guttman (Ed.), *Re-examining the politics of recognition*. Princeton, NJ: Princeton University Press.

Throsby, D., & Petetskaya, E. (2016). Sustainability concepts in indigenous and non-indigenous cultures. *International Journal of Cultural Property, 23*(2), 119–140. doi:10.1017/S0940739116000084

Triandis, H.C., Bontempo, R., Villareal, M.J., Asai, M., & Lucca, N. (1988). Individualism and collectivism: Cross-cultural perspectives on self-ingroup relationships. *Journal of Personality and Social Psychology, 54*(2), 323–338.

Tudge, J.R.H., Mokrova, I., Hatfield, B.E., & Karnik, R.B. (2009). Uses and misuses of Bronfenbrenner's bioecological theory of human development. *Journal of Family Theory & Review, 1*, 198–210. doi:10.1111/j.1756-2589.2009.00026.x

Walsh, R. (2011). Lifestyle and mental health. *American Psychologist, 66*(7), 579–592. doi:10.1037/a0021769

Wane, N. (2002). African women and spirituality: Connections between thought and action. In E. O'Sullivan, A. Morrell, & M.A. O'Connor (Eds.), *Expanding the boundaries of transformative learning: Essays on theory and praxis* (135–150). New York, NY: Palgrave Macmillan.

Wane, N. (2006). Is decolonization possible? In G.J.S. Dei & A. Kempf (Eds.), *Anti-colonialism and education: The politics of resistance* (pp. 87–106). Rotterdam, Netherlands: Sense Publishers.

Watkins, D., Adebowale, A., Fleming, J., Maznah, I., Lefner, K., Regmi, M., & Wondimu, H. (1998). Cultural dimensions, gender, and the nature of self-concept: A fourteen-country study. *International Journal of Psychology, 33*(1), 17–31. doi:10.1080/002075998400583

Welzel, C., Inglehart, R., & Kligemann, H. (2003). The theory of human development: A cross-cultural analysis. *European Journal of Political Research, 42*(3), 341–379. doi:10.1111/1475-6765.00086

Wesley-Esquimaux, C.C., & Smolewski, M. (2004). *Historic trauma and aboriginal healing*. Retrieved from http://www.ahf.ca/downloads/historic-trauma.pdf

CHAPTER 5

Decolonizing the Geography Classroom: A Call to Action for Educators to Reimagine Pedagogy of Place

Jessica Peden

Introduction

Colonial schooling has inflicted erasure and violence and has created a divide between students and knowledge of place. This has caused a disconnect between learners and the role they play in the place they occupy in the natural world. This is particularly true if we look at the geography curriculum within settler colonial states such as Ontario. Geography has historically been used as a tool of the colonizer, and those within the discipline need to take responsibility for and engage in efforts to disrupt this narrative (Sunberg, 2014). This work serves to interrogate the current implications that the geography curriculum has on the relationship between people, the Earth, and spirituality. Earth-based spirituality connects learners to Earth systems through an anti-colonial geographic lens, inviting a conversation about the balance of water, air, Land, animals, and all Earth systems. Teaching geography every day within the walls of a settler colonial classroom is counterintuitive and does not facilitate the creation of a lasting relationship with the natural world. In order to mend the relationship between people and the Earth and to create anti-colonial spaces in education, Earth-based spirituality should be woven into the curriculum and taken up in the geography classroom.

For the purposes of this chapter, Earth-based spirituality can be conceptualized as a place outside the classroom where students and educators are able to connect with the natural environment, gain a deeper sense of self, and reflect on the roles they play in the health of their communities. Earth-based spirituality also promotes a sense of connectivity to the natural spaces. I wish to argue beyond the concept of learning about the natural environment and toward a sense of shared goals and responsibilities in preserving and honoring natural places. This connectivity is important for all people living on Turtle Island and has a direct impact on decolonization efforts. Jeff Corntassel (2012) explains the importance of reclamation for Indigenous people when he writes that

> being Indigenous today means struggling to reclaim and regenerate one's relational, place-based existence by challenging the ongoing destructive forces of colonization. Whether through ceremony or through other ways the Indigenous peoples (re)connect to the natural world, processes of resurgence are often contentious and reflect the spiritual, cultural, economic, social and political scope of the struggle. (p. 88)

Corntassel argues that colonialism systematically disconnects Indigenous people from Land, culture, and community, leading to an erosion of respect and collective responsibility of place (p. 88). If educators encourage and teach their students the importance of the connections among people, community, and the places that they occupy, it will act as a site of resurgence for Indigenous people and a site of resistance to colonization. By encouraging all students, both Indigenous and non-Indigenous, knowledge and respect for efforts to reclaim place-based existence will be further strengthened.

Feeling connected to natural space is a deeply personal concept. However, I believe that connectivity and relationship building with the Earth are important parts of feeling grounded and having a sense of purpose. As a geography educator, I would like my students to forge a positive relationship with the environment. The quiet, reflective, and grounding atmosphere that is experienced when one is immersed in the natural world cannot be replicated within the walls of the classroom. Spirituality is self-driven and deeply rooted in the ways that we know and understand the world (Dei, 2016). Providing students with an opportunity to connect inward and seek balance within their spirits, while educating them on the importance of balance in the Earth's systems, is where Earth-based spirituality can thrive in the geography classroom. Further, encouraging students to build this relationship is an important step toward supporting ongoing mental health. The adoption of Earth-based spirituality in classroom pedagogy will allow for the creation of anti-colonial spaces that serve to reconcile the connection with the Earth and reject the colonial narrative of dominance over the Earth and its people.

Educational institutions across Canada have shown an increasing commitment to reconciliatory efforts in recent years, brought forth in part by the Calls to Action outlined in the Truth and Reconciliation Committee's (TRC) final report (2015). However, progress in reforming the way Indigeneity is taken up in educational spaces has been slow, and there is a clear lack of meaningful implementation of the TRC's Calls to Action in classroom spaces. Educational reforms have not extended beyond efforts of inclusivity or multiculturalism. In my own experience as a geography educator in a secondary school classroom, it has been difficult to educate students in a colonial space. Educational reform focuses on multiculturalism and inclusivity. The geography curriculum encourages students to learn *about* rather than *from* marginalized voices. I have found it challenging to fulfill the Ontario curriculum expectations while creating anti-colonial spaces where multiple forms of knowledge hold equal currency.

It is important to understand that geography is a discipline that has played a crucial role in reinforcing a colonial logic of domination over Indigenous peoples and our reciprocal relationship with the Earth. Geography reinforces colonial notions of domination, white supremacy, and eurocentric knowledge systems (Aikenhead & Elliott, 2010, p. 322). Geography has relied on nondualistic humanist thinking, made popular in the Enlightenment era, that served to eliminate ontological frameworks in other knowledge systems (Sunberg, 2014). This universalized notion of knowledge created tension among dominant knowledge holders. In the Canadian context, this binary consisted of white settlers, on the one hand, and Indigenous peoples and nonhuman entities in the natural environment, on the other (Sunberg, 2014). Humanist geography reinforces a single narrative of civilized-versus-primitive knowledge. This foundation has remained intact in the geography discipline as a subject and is continually reinforced in classroom curricula in Ontario.

The Geography Curriculum: Critique and Current Limitations

The geography curriculum in Ontario conceptualizes the natural world as a commodity, teaching students that the Earth inherently belongs to them—a dangerous worldview that is reinforced throughout the secondary-level curriculum. This problematic outlook begins in grade 9 with the *Managing Canada's Resources and Industries* curricular thread. The goal of this curriculum strand is to "analyse the impact of resource policy, resource management, and consumer choices on resource sustainability in Canada" (Ontario Curriculum, 2013, p. 70). Further, in the subheading of this thread, educators are asked to explore the following questions with students: "What criteria should we set for extraction and development of Canada's natural resources? Which resources and industries would you consider to be most valuable to Canada?" (p. 70).

This curriculum's theme of extraction and commodification of natural resources is very problematic for two important reasons. First, it is educating students to believe that the Earth should be viewed as an economic commodity. The human and environmental cost of extraction is missing from the conversation. It teaches students to assert their ownership over something that is shared and reinforces colonial attitudes of domination.

Second, there is no mention of the Indigenous peoples in the analysis of resource extraction. This exclusion of Indigenous people from that particular discussion teaches students how to think about the natural world as a resource. With this colonial lens, students are learning that all Land and resources belong to them. Excluding Indigenous voices from this conversation is an act of violence against the Indigenous bodies that will be directly affected by the dispossession of Land, and has health implications for those communities as a result of resource extraction.

In one section, the curriculum asks students to

> analyse environmental, economic, social, and/or political implications of different ideas and beliefs about the value of Canada's natural environment, and explain how these ideas/beliefs affect the use and protection of Canada's natural assets. (Ontario Curriculum, 2013, p. 75)

This is a hugely ambiguous point that never explicitly requires the educator to bring in voices of Indigenous people. Further, this approach to Indigenous voices reinforces the colonial narrative that Indigenous knowledge counteracts progress and stands in the way of economic growth and progress, particularly in the use of the word *assets*. Included later in this section on the curriculum is a scenario that educators may want to take up with students in the classroom. The scenario reads:

> Who do you think owns a resource, such as water or air that crosses political borders? What view do First Nations people take of the ownership of such resources? What implications would the development of the rich mineral resource of northern Ontario's ring of fire region have for Ontario's economy? For the environment? For First Nations communities in the area? (p. 79)

The preceding question creates a binary between economic progress and the Indigenous bodies that live on the Land. With a lack of foundational knowledge regarding the history of treaties and the ongoing colonial project in the Canadian state, it is impossible for students to unpack and critically engage with differing worldviews. This discussion leads students to justify the continued dispossession of Indigenous people of safe and healthy Land, water, and air. Educators essentially present students with a scenario wherein Indigenous rights are pitted against the health of the economy. This element of the curriculum suggests that colonial capitalist gains are impeded by Indigenous bodies, and reinforces the civilized-versus-primitive narrative that has served the geography discipline in colonialism. When the natural world is viewed only through a capitalist lens, it allows the reciprocal connection between the health of the Earth and the health of the people to be lost. This is felt deeply by Indigenous bodies, which are typically on the front lines of resource extraction, and it has caused loss of Land, health crises, poor water and air quality, and lack of food sources due to animal-habitat loss.

The Ontario geography curriculum reinforces dominant colonial knowledges and disregards the lived experience and knowledge of the Land of the Indigenous people of Turtle Island. The geography curriculum is taught to students through a neoliberal capitalist lens, defining the world in terms of what is valuable, controllable, extractable, and commodified. An analysis of the Ontario geography curriculum reveals that the foundation of the settler colonial state is clearly perpetuated through education. According to Tuck and Yang (2012), the settler "sees himself as holding dominion over the earth and its flora and fauna, as the anthropocentric normal, and as more developed, more human, more deserving than other groups of species" (p. 6). The reproduction of this settler colonial assertion of dominance over Indigenous bodies, as well as plants and animals, is normalized in our education system and continues to deny the validity or existence of other ways of being and knowing in relation to the Land.

This study serves to disrupt the reproduction of settler colonial dominance in education by critically engaging with the geography curriculum in order to initiate a conversation about the spaces that can be created wherein meaningful anti-colonial education can take place. It serves to reconceptualize the meaning of geography education by (re)positioning people in relation to the natural world, rather than in control of it. Reimagining the geography curriculum means that we have to make space for connectivity and multiplicity in our ways of knowing and understanding the natural place we occupy. In order to adopt an anti-colonial framework for learning in the geography classroom, settler educators must actively reject the mechanisms that serve to further colonize knowledge, bodies, and the Earth. This does not mean that geography teachers must appropriate traditional Land-based knowledge from Indigenous peoples. Rather, they can create anti-colonial spaces by rejecting the settler notion that only one knowledge should exist in the classroom, and facilitate a connection between learner, Land, and spirituality. Disrupting the colonial geography classroom means that teachers are facilitating a space where students can view themselves as spiritual beings, and as part of the natural world, through experiential learning and hearing Indigenous knowledges. The challenges in creating decolonizing pedagogy in geography are twofold: appropriately integrating Indigenous knowledge into classroom material and providing professional development to support teachers (Aikenhead & Elliott, 2010, p. 322).

I believe that inspiring geography teachers to reject the notions of the hegemonic dominant narrative and adopting a multiplicity of nature-based spirituality knowledge systems will have the following effects:

1. It will create a space wherein Indigenous knowledge takes its place beside western notions of knowledge in the geography classroom.
2. It will help us to step away from overly academic assessment strategies that harbor individualism and competition and move toward community building, spirituality, and connectivity. Allowing students time to connect, reflect, and still be in their natural environments can benefit their spirit and sense of self.

3. It will facilitate a lasting, healthy relationship among students, Land, animals, and Mother Earth.

Locating Myself in My Work

It is important that I ground myself in my scholarship. I identify as a white female settler and Canadian educator. I consider myself a feminist, environmentalist, and anti-colonial educator, and I aim to ground my scholarship within these frameworks. I am positioned both politically and personally within the topics I present in my work. As a woman, I come to this topic with a vested interest in learning how to support my students as they confront issues of power and privilege. I care deeply about preserving the environment, and I believe that creating collective care, responsibility, and access to the Earth can have a positive impact on the health of a community. I would like to continue to resist the political actions that my Ancestors engaged in and allow my students to see the benefits of living in harmony with the Earth. I am a fourth-generation Canadian on my maternal side and fifth-generation Canadian on my paternal side. I have benefited from colonialism and hold power as a dominant body. I believe that it is my responsibility to disrupt colonial narratives as they relate to politics, economics, health, and education by listening to marginalized voices and creating anti-colonial spaces in my community. As a dominant body and settler, I come to this topic with a sense of great humility, eager to listen and to gain knowledge. As a secondary school geography and history teacher, I have the unique opportunity to counter dominant hegemonic structures within education. The onus of educating settlers should not be placed on Indigenous peoples. Settler educators should view this work as a call to action. Every person living on Turtle Island needs to play a role in order to heal our connection to people, the Land, and our relationships. Education is a collective responsibility that needs to be taken up throughout elementary and secondary schooling, at home, and within communities. I am hopeful that this study will outline some of the tools and tactics that I believe should be utilized in the geography classroom.

My intention is to problematize settler colonial views of education by encouraging students to reflect, create community, and redefine their relationships with the natural world. The students of the school in which I teach are predominantly first- or second-generation Canadians whose Ancestors emigrated from Southeast Asia. Many of my students do not fully grasp the identity of settler in the Canadian context. However, most of them have lived experiences with the impact of colonialism within the context of the Southeast Asian diaspora. Allowing students to explore their own positionality as it relates to the Indigenous peoples of Turtle Island allows for a broad conversation about colonialism and incites activism.

As a settler, I am also unlearning the aspects of my culture that have caused violence. The concept of self-reflectivity in issues of complacency or benefit from colonialism is discussed by Martin Cannon (2012). He writes that "before it is possible to foster a collective responsibility for our complicity in social inequality, we need to think differently about privilege and oppression, seeing the myriad... ways in which we are at once invested" (pp. 32–33). This is the beginning of my own spiritual journey, which I set out on in the hope that I can make a deeper connection with nature and my school community. As a body that holds a position of privilege—and also in my position as an educator—I understand the importance of continuous self-reflexivity. Land, water, and air are sites of violence against Indigenous bodies, and the domination of western knowledge perpetuates this violence. It is my intention to redefine the way in which I can use geography as an educator in order to disrupt notions of settler colonial superiority and dominance.

Notions of Settler Colonialism, Land, and Spirituality: Contributing to the Conversation

The conversation about disrupting the dominance of western notions of knowledge in the classroom has been ongoing for some time. Many scholars make specific mention of the prospect of weaving Indigenous forms of knowledge into the geography and science ecology curriculum (Aikenhead & Elliott, 2010, p. 332). In the interests of this chapter, I conducted research on scholars who have discussed creating decolonizing classroom spaces, weaving spirituality into pedagogy, and encouraging students to connect with nature within an anti-colonial framework.

Several scholars and researchers have informed my exploration within this issue and contributed to the discussion. Informing my critical pedagogy is Gregory Cajete (2008), who outlines seven specific ways to develop Indigenous science education in the classroom. Cajete (2008) writes that "traditional American Indian systems of educating were characterized by observation, participation, assimilation, and experiential learning rather than by low-context, formal instruction characteristic of Euro-American schooling" (p. 488). Cajete's writings are specific to Indigenous teachings in Indigenous schools and are useful in thinking about alternative ways of designing pedagogy. He emphasizes the need for Indigenous education grounded in culture, stating that "curricular changes in Native education must stem from 'cultural standards' firmly grounded in Native thought and orientation" (p. 488). For the purposes of this study, Cajete's discussion will act only as a starting point to my own reflection as to how the geography curriculum can be reimagined. Glen Aikenhead (1997; see also Aikenhead & Elliott, 2010) discusses the multiplicity of knowledges in classrooms and the need to decolonize science curriculum when he writes that "most students tend to experience school science as a foreign culture to varying degrees, but their teachers do not treat it that way. To be successful, these students must, without teacher assistance, learn to cross a cultural border between their own everyday culture and the culture of academic school science" (Aikenhead & Elliott, 2010, p. 323). Aikenhead's (1997) idea of cultural border crossing, in which Indigenous students have to leave their everyday world to travel to the subculture of a science classroom, is an important reminder for educators (p. 224). For students that do not belong to the dominant culture, classroom pedagogy can be a constant negotiation between borders. The inclusion of a multiplicity of knowledge systems in the geography curriculum can ease the cultural border crossings and (re) position dominant knowledge.

Robin Wall Kimmerer, a postsecondary ecology educator who speaks from an experienced pedagogical perspective, informed my analysis of where nature-based education could fit into the secondary school geography curriculum. Kimmerer (2012) outlines the crisis that scientific ecological knowledge is currently experiencing when she writes, "my students were unable to elucidate a single positive interaction between Land and people" (p. 318). In general, students could not imagine the possibility of mutualism, which is a deeply problematic indication of the future of the planet (p. 318). Kimmerer is speaking about students at a postsecondary level whom she is able to take to a wilderness center for two weeks at a time. Although her program is not realistic for a public high school, her critique about current attitudes that students hold and her experience in integrating traditional Indigenous knowledge into ecology are extremely useful to my work. Kimmerer problematizes the current approach to ecological education. Her analysis links the state of environmental degradation to the lack of education that connects students to ecology. Her experience contributed to my critique of the secondary geography curriculum. Annamarie Hatcher's article (2012) emphasizes the importance of equal representation of knowledges in ecology pedagogy; her framework is borrowed from Mi'Kmaw Elder Albert Marshall's analogy of "Two-Eyed Seeing" (Hatcher, 2012, p. 346). She writes: "Two-Eyed Seeing is a mechanism to cross cultural borders . . . with this guiding principle, Indigenous culture takes a place beside Western, not as an add-on" (p. 346). (The Two-Eyed Seeing analogy will be maintained throughout this chapter.) Finally, in the area of critical geography pedagogy, Anne R. Hickling-Hudson and Roberta Ahlquist's essay (2003) provides a thorough critique of the role that curriculum plays in the reproduction of a single culture by ignoring the multiplicity of identities present in the classroom.

Although many of these authors make mention of the impact that colonial education has had on marginalized bodies (high absenteeism, poor performance in literacy and numeracy, and high dropout rates, according to Hickling-Hudson & Ahlquist, 2003), many of them do not explicitly link this to the impact that colonial education has had—and continues to have—on the spirit. Conceptualizing spirituality and attempting to weave it into the classroom can be a daunting task. However, a number of scholars informed my analysis of spirituality and the decolonizing impact that supporting spirituality can have.

George Dei's discussion of the "Suahunu" (borrowed from the Akan people of Ghana), referred to in his article (2012) as the trialectic space, makes this link. Dei explains that the trialectic space "challenges conventional ways of knowing to acknowledge what hitherto is assumed not to be 'knowledge' in dominant circles" (p. 824). To create a trialectic space, learners use their bodies, minds, and spirits/souls to interface in educational dialogue (p. 826). Dei writes about the society-culture-nature interface, which provided a foundation for me as I built my arguments for spirituality within this work.

Njoki Wane's (2011) work on Black feminist spirituality allows for an important discussion of identity, reflection, and groundedness within spirituality to permeate the conversation about decolonization in the classroom for marginalized bodies, as well as a keen focus on activism (p. 159). Wane interviewed five participants, all Black women living in Canada, with commonalities in their reference to Africa as a place they call home and a place that has defined their spirituality (p. 159). She writes that, "as demonstrated in the narratives of the five participants, Black women have a history of engaging in action-oriented feminism informed by spirituality and inner strength" (p. 159). Listening to the experiences and stories of the women in Wane's essay helped me to conceptualize spirituality. Understanding that spirituality and connectedness occur in different geographic locations, or spaces, is important to my attempts to support spirituality in the classroom.

Finally, Shahjahan (2005) discusses the difficulties in adopting spirituality in the academy. Although he specifically steps away from discussions of classroom education, I find his analysis useful in thinking about being a spiritual person and spiritual educator, and the responsibility that comes with this role (p. 637).

It is extremely important to include Indigenous scholars' voices in research. Amplifying Indigenous voices in education can work as a tool for decolonization. It is important that educators and scholars listen to Indigenous voices when discussing how to create anti-colonial spaces. Settler educators have historically excluded Indigenous voices. In my work and in my classroom, I understand the importance of listening and allowing students to hear stories from Indigenous people. I cannot begin to conceptualize decolonizing education without listening to the lived experiences of Indigenous people. Indigenous voices are needed in education in order to (re)center knowledge creation. I focused mainly on Indigeneity and nature and primarily gathered work from those living on Turtle Island who specifically spoke about environmental justice issues. This focus was to highlight curriculum themes that could be implemented into geography pedagogy. As an extension of my preceding critique, the grade 9 Ontario geography curriculum focuses on Canadian geography only. In order for this work to contribute to classroom pedagogy, I decided to narrow my focus. I also consulted these sources when speaking about the impact that colonization has had on the Earth, and when thinking about who or what the geography curriculum serves and how it perpetuates the colonial narrative. This has helped me to frame the conversation about inviting Indigenous principles of nature into the geography classroom and creating anti-colonial spaces. My main source of information came from the book *Speaking for Ourselves: Environmental Justice in Canada*, by Jaramogi Abebe Agyeman (formerly known as Albert Cleage, Jr.), which is a compilation of work from Indigenous scholars focusing on the Indigenous felt impacts from degradation of the Earth and the continued dispossession of Land. Agyeman (2009) also highlights sites of resurgence and resistance through reclaiming sovereignty over the health of the Land and highlights activism focused on fighting for Mother Earth. Martinez, Salmon, and Nelson (2009) informed my research in creating a lasting connection between students and the Earth. Borrowing from their article "Restoring History and Culture to Nature," I included the notion of a *kincentric* knowledge. Martinez and colleagues (2009) explain that this concept rejects the wilderness preservation/Land management model, which seeks to control and protect the way in which humans interact with animals and plants (p. 89). They provide an example of Indigenous people digging and spreading nutrients in order to help root vegetables (referred to as "Indian potatoes") to grow. Martinez et al. explain: "where federal land agencies have come in and fenced off those places to preserve them, those tracts of Indian potatoes have disappeared" (p. 90). This reciprocal relationship is lost when humans believe they need to control the environment. In contrast, the kincentric model is based on an understanding that plants, animals, and people, though all equal, have different jobs to do on Earth (Martinez et al., 2009, p. 90). This basis for ecological interaction is what I strive to embody and teach as an anti-colonial geography educator.

Informing my nature and spirituality research is the Okanagan scholar Jeanette Armstrong, who writes about Land as a basis for healing. Armstrong (2008) explains the relationality of Okanagan peoples. She writes: "We grew up loving each other on the land and loving each plant and each species.... That doesn't just happen as an intellectual process. That doesn't just happen as a process of needing to gather food and needing to sustain our bodies for health. It happens as a result of how we interact with each other" (p. 67). Armstrong calls for more love and community building, which will extend to a love of the Land and the species that inhabit it. Allowing students to hear stories from Indigenous voices and to see examples of multiple forms of knowledge and beliefs toward the environment will help to create anti-colonial spaces in the classroom.

Decolonizing the Geography Curriculum: The Two-Eyed Classroom

In speaking about decolonization, I am mindful of the warning that Tuck and Yang (2012) issue in their article "Decolonization Is Not a Metaphor." They write that "when metaphor invades decolonization, it kills the very possibility of decolonization; it (re) centres whiteness, it resettles theory, it extends innocence to the settler, it entertains a settler future" (p. 3). Further, they state that "decolonization is not a swappable term for other things we want to do to improve our societies and schools" (p. 3). In this light, I do not claim that the present chapter is a roadmap toward decolonization within a colonial system of schooling. As an educator, I would like to add my experience to the conversation and propose steps that can be taken in the geography classroom to *begin* a conversation about decolonization. However, we cannot begin that conversation without understanding the history of how geography (as a discipline) and education (as a system) play a key role in colonizing.

In order to create anti-colonial spaces in the geography classroom, students first need to understand that the teachings they receive in school are not the only knowledge that exists and that is valuable. Hatcher (2012) refers to this as the *two-eyed* approach when she writes, "Indigenous culture takes a place beside Western, not as an add-on to be brought out for multicultural festivals" (p. 346). It is important to teach students about the existence of knowledges and the creation of hierarchies in a colonial system in order to work toward building a foundation for them to understand where knowledge comes from and why certain knowledges are erased. Besides western science, there are a number of approaches that various scholars have explored to (re)center Indigenous knowledge in the geography classroom. According to Dei (2012), "the work of decolonizing is not about placing another form of knowledge at the top of a knowledge pyramid, but rather finding a way for multiple knowledges to dialogue for anti-colonial praxis" (p. 825). It is in finding how to present other knowledges without risk of misuse that can be overwhelming for some educators. Kimmerer (2012) speaks to this concern when she writes: "there are valid concerns for the risk of misappropriation of knowledge, intellectual property, and decoupling of knowledge from its attendant responsibilities" (p. 318). However, I believe that the act of telling students that knowledges exist is anti-colonial work. Furthermore, allowing students to explore the multiplicity of knowledges held by their parents, grandparents, or members of their community is important. Geography classrooms should be a site of self-exploration into where your Ancestors lived, how they lived, and the reasons they moved to Canada. This can initiate important conversations about displacement of Land and people. By speaking to elders in their family or community, students can better understand the validation of knowledges from various sources, while engaging in an act of resistance to the hegemonic power structures. Finally, in order to further the exploration of knowledges, it is important to provide academic work written by Indigenous peoples. Educators have a platform that can be used to amplify voices, and the way in which they choose to use that platform is a vital step in beginning a conversation about anti-colonial education.

As I relate decolonizing work to my positionality, I believe that as a settler I have the responsibility to continually act against and teach against structures that perpetually colonize Indigenous bodies—in particular, and from an environmental standpoint, teaching students to reject capitalist worldviews that frame the natural world in a way that promotes overuse and misuse in order to create profit. Reconnecting students to notions of balance, synergy, and the mutual benefits of a healthy planet are a vital step toward creating anti-colonial classroom spaces. Kimmerer (2012) explains this when she writes that "we stand at a rare opportunity in time where the circumstances of humanity's weight on the planet catalyze an awareness of the shortcomings of the worldview that has brought us to the brink, both cultural and ecological" (p. 318). Celebrating the resistance that Indigenous peoples have participated in, and the instances where Indigenous communities have engaged in activism to prevent exploitation of the Land should be used as positive learning experiences for students to engage with in Geography classrooms. Naomi Klein (2014) explains the importance of highlighting environmental activism among Indigenous communities when she writes "more critically, many non-Natives are also beginning to see that the ways of life that Indigenous groups are protecting have a great deal to teach about how to relate to the land in ways that are not purely extractive" (p. 370). Creating a platform for discussion about these sites of resistance will allow for the discussion of extraction, pollution, Land degradation, and environmental racism, as well as capitalism, privatization, and ongoing colonization.

Supporting Spirituality: Experiential Learning

If I were to go back and talk to my ninth-grade geography teacher and tell her that I ended up going on to pursue a career in environmental studies and became a geography teacher myself, she would be shocked, and probably think it was a joke. As in most of my classes in high school, sitting and learning from a textbook in my geography class meant that I was disengaged. Learning about precipitation, or rock formations, by viewing slides in a classroom rather than going outside and looking at the sky or picking up a rock did not work for me. I ended up with a poor grade in the class, and the only thing I remember is the day we went for a hike. I gained something from that day that I could not achieve by sitting in a classroom. I was calm, I was breathing fresh air, the forest was quiet, and I did not feel the stress of being constantly assessed or evaluated. I gained perspective and felt humbled by the simple task of hiking. Now, as I reflect on that experience, I realize that it was a spiritual one.

I have witnessed this same reaction from my own students. When I take them outside of the classroom, where they learn about the natural world while immersed in it, they experience a different energy and outlook toward the Earth. Many scholarly articles attempt to quantify the impact of nature-based spirituality. In researching this topic, I read numerous studies that presented data from participants who engaged in outdoor activities and reported feeling an increased connection to spirit. However, I have decided not to detail these findings, as I believe that any attempt to quantify spirituality is risky. Spirituality is deeply personal. Although I believe educators should initiate conversations about supporting spirituality, I do not think it is something that should be quantified in western academe. Spirituality can be supported without engaging in research; indeed, it can be done simply by talking to students and creating spaces for self-reflection.

Cultivating quiet spaces in the geography classroom where students can gain perspective will provide them with an opportunity to look inward and support their spiritual growth. It will also give them an opportunity to create community. One of the places I like to take students to is a farm, where they learn about the interconnectedness of food, Land, water, air, and people. Students work together to harvest food and to eat some of it, too. Each student uses his or her mind, body, and soul during those moments. Okanagan scholar Jeanette Armstrong (2008) speaks about this Land-based spirituality in her article "An Okanagan Worldview of Society." She writes: "The process of being with people, out there on the land, has a healing impact... it's not just the work of collecting but it's being with people, the community, and communing with each other... it is how the land communes its spirit to you: it heals people and it does this in an incredibly profound way" (p. 74). Educators who create spaces in which students can work with their hands, breathe fresh air, and be part of the Land are also allowing students to learn about themselves and connect with their spirituality.

Spiritual healing cannot be created in spaces that are strict, controlling, and competitive. These are characterized by constant assessment and evaluation, standardized testing, and compulsory courses that are not culturally relevant or interesting to the students. Geography classrooms have a unique opportunity to reject the rigidity of colonial schooling and replace it with freeing, calm, and reflective spaces found in nature. Strengthening spirituality is a basis of knowledge; however, it is not recognized by our current educational system. Dei (2012) addresses this issue when he writes that, "emotions, intuitions, and spirituality constitute knowings and are not 'anti-intellectual'" (p. 836). He emphasizes the need to find pedagogical and methodological ways to teach about spirits (p. 832). Though I agree with Dei, I also understand the risks of teaching in an alternative way in a system that demands neoliberal accountability. I believe the answer might be in the way that educators frame spirituality. Many people confuse spirituality with religion, and this confusion can invite controversial reaction. However, if a link between spirituality and mental health is made, creating spiritual-centered pedagogy could be acceptable in mainstream education. In practice, this could be as simple as taking students out of the classroom for a hike, or allowing a few minutes at the beginning of class to do a grounding exercise, envisioning a place outside of where they have felt grounded. These spiritual practices can benefit the students without inviting criticism for participating in what may mistakenly be perceived as nonacademic activities.

Improving mental health among youth is a hugely important issue and a major focus of current policy adoption. Rather than supporting mental health through blanket approaches, educators need to allow students time to look inward. If students focus on themselves in quiet spaces, they will be better equipped to ask for what they need to improve their mental health. Further, students who are connected with spirituality in their natural environments will be more inclined to develop a lasting respect and appreciation for natural places.

Cultivating a Lasting Relationship: Students and the Earth

At the core of the geography curriculum should be the ongoing encouragement for students to engage in a lasting relationship with the natural world that will have a positive impact on future generations. In order to create a space where students gain a lasting respect for their natural world, educators should look toward the way of living and the relationship with the Land that Indigenous peoples have. Martinez et al. (2009) describe this connection that Indigenous people have to the natural world when they write that "this was a relationship model, a *kincentric* model, one in which we are all equal, but we have different jobs to do here on Earth" (p. 90). They go on to write: "The words conservation and ecology, as we use them in the Western sense, don't exactly fit what Indian people did or do with the Land. It was their livelihood, which depended on reciprocity" (p. 92). Reciprocity is a difficult concept to teach, but one that will allow students to see the mutuality of benefits that come from taking care of the Land.

In practical terms, allowing students to see firsthand the gifts that the Earth provides is an important pedagogical tool in the geography curriculum. I believe that one way to achieve this relationship is through food. Allowing students to plant, maintain, and grow their own food can demonstrate a tangible way that the Earth takes care of them. Kimmerer (2012) discusses the importance of this relationship when she writes: "I do not think it is possible to engage in reciprocity without first experiencing the gifts of the Land[,] then being drawn to return a gift in kind" (p. 321). Food is a powerful mechanism, because many students feel disconnected from their food. When I teach about food, I often ask students to determine which countries their food is traveling from. We use information offered by students to talk about what impact food that has traveled long distances has, the health of the people picking our food who may be exposed to pesticides, and water usage. Many of my students are shocked to find out how destructive our current system is to the Land, people, and the planet. I have also seen some schools that add composting to this system. Organic cafeteria waste that would normally go to a landfill is composted to create soil that provides nutrients to plants, giving students the opportunity to witness the full cycle. Planting and growing food is also a way to create anti-colonial spaces that encourage students to use their minds, hearts, and hands, rather than participate in constant assessment within classroom spaces.

As noted, I do not believe that settler teachers should partake of traditional ecological knowledge to use in their classrooms. This could invite appropriation and misuse of teachings, even in the most well-meaning scenarios. Students should read about Indigenous principles from Indigenous scholars within the classroom in order to understand different knowledge systems concerning the Earth. Where possible, educators should make connections with local Indigenous nations to learn from and build community ties based on shared knowledge and goals. Further, educators need to create spaces in which students can see the value of a healthy planet. This is where authentic, long-lasting relationships with the planet will be formed. Hatcher (2012) refers to this process as transformation learning when she writes that "individuals create meaning structures for their experiences through the frames of reference created by their values, beliefs, and assumptions. In this way, the learner can learn to see through the other's eye without subsuming his/her cultural identity" (p. 353). If students can see value in synergy with people and the environment and have an example of a knowledge basis that works within the notions of reciprocity, then they may be able to adopt new understandings. This also allows students to think about the ongoing impact that their choices have on the health of Indigenous people, as well as marginalized populations that disproportionately experience the negative impacts from an unhealthy Earth. This can invite a deeper conversation about the interconnected domination of people, politics, economics, and environment that is missing from the geography curriculum.

Conclusion

I believe that the geography classroom can be a site for disrupting settler colonial narratives and dominant knowledge, creating a space in which to foster spirituality, and encouraging lasting relationships among students, self, and nature, based on love and reciprocity with the Earth. I understand that there are foreseeable issues and constraints in working toward adopting anti-colonial education in a colonial school space. There is danger in doing decolonizing work in a colonial educational institution. I have chosen to use the term *decolonizing* because geography is a discipline that looks at Land, Earth systems, and connectivity in the environment. Colonization in Canada relied on the erasure of people and knowledge from the Land and replacing them with for-profit networks, as well as eurocentric geographic and scientific knowledge systems. Tuck and Yang (2012) warn of superficially adopting the language of decolonization: "We have observed [that] a startling number of these discussions [among Settler scholars] make no mention of Indigenous peoples, our/their struggles for recognition of our/their sovereignty, or the contribution of Indigenous intellectuals and activists to theories and frameworks of decolonization" (p. 3). Therefore, in acknowledging this violence in the curriculum and in recognizing the validity of Indigenous ways of knowing and being in the natural world, anti-colonial work can be taken up in geography classroom spaces.

There are many difficulties in the implementation of this work in our current school system. Attempting to integrate local place-based Indigenous knowledge into classrooms means that educators need to make connections with local Indigenous nations. A collective vision would be needed to move forward in integrating Indigenous knowledge systems. However, the trauma of the colonial Indian Residential School system is still impacting Indigenous communities across Canada. Settler educators need to be better equipped to do this work in an authentic way. This could come with an overhaul of the curriculum and consultation with Indigenous nations. Reconciliation and relationship building between Indigenous people and settlers will take a long time, but the work needs to begin somewhere, and it is my belief that education is an important site of resistance to begin these tough conversations.

Educators must interrogate the curriculum, asking for whom and for what purpose it is serving. How do we teach students to see themselves as part of the natural world and not, in fact, in control of it? How can education be a site for anti-colonial work? What role do other disciplines within colonial schooling play in perpetuating the colonial project? How can we connect the efforts within schools across disciplines? Can schools, having been at the center of colonization with the Indian Residential School system, really contribute to reconciliation and anti-colonial efforts? These tough questions need to be taken up in school communities, Indigenous communities, teacher-training programs, and the academy.

Educators are in a position to resist the ongoing colonization of Turtle Island by disrupting the power and privilege that creates an imbalance between people—both Indigenous and settlers—and the Earth that exists today in our education system.

References

Agyeman, J. (2009). *Speaking for ourselves: Environmental justice in Canada*. Vancouver, BC: UBC Press.

Aikenhead, G.S. (1997). Toward a First Nations cross-cultural science and technology curriculum. *Science Education, 81*(2), 217–238.

Aikenhead, G.S., & Elliott, D. (2010). An emerging decolonizing science education in Canada. *Canadian Journal of Science, Mathematics and Technology Education, 10*(4), 321–338.

Armstrong, J. (2008). An Okanagan worldview of society. In M.K. Nelson (Ed.), *Original instructions: Indigenous teachings for a sustainable future* (pp. 66–74). Rochester, VT: Bear and Company.

Cajete, G. (2008). Seven orientations for the development of Indigenous science education. In *Handbook of critical and Indigenous methodologies* (pp. 487–496). Los Angeles, CA: Sage Publications.

Cannon, M. (2012). Changing the subject in teacher education: Centering Indigenous, diasporic, and settler colonial relations. *Cultural and Pedagogical Inquiry, 4*(2), 21–37.

Corntassel, J. (2012). Re-envisioning resurgence: Indigenous pathways to decolonization and sustainable self-determination. *Decolonization: Indigeneity, Education, & Society, 1*.

Dei, G.J.S. (2012). Suahunu: The trialectic space. *Journal of Black Studies, 43*(8), 823–846.

Dei, G.J.S. (2016). *Indigenous knowledges and spirituality: Theorizing global and transnational case studies*. [Lecture.] Ontario Institute for Studies in Education, November 14.

Hatcher, A. (2012). Building cultural bridges with aboriginal learners and their "classmates" for transformative environmental education. *Journal of Environmental Studies and Sciences, 2*(4), 346–356.

Hickling-Hudson, A., & Ahlquist, R. (2003). Contesting the curriculum in the schooling of Indigenous children in Australia and the USA: From Eurocentrism to culturally powerful pedagogies. *Comparative Education Review, 47*(1), 64–89.

Kimmerer, R. (2012). Searching for synergy: Integrating traditional and scientific ecological knowledge in environmental science education. *Journal of Environmental Studies and Sciences, 2*(4), 317–323.

Klein, N. (2014). *This changes everything: Capitalism vs. the climate*. Toronto, ON: Simon & Schuster.

Martinez, D., Salmon, E., & Nelson, M.K. (2009). Restoring Indigenous history and culture to nature. In *Speaking for ourselves: Environmental justice in Canada*. Vancouver: UBC Press.

Ontario, Canada. (2013). The Ontario curriculum grades 9 and 10. *Canadian and World Studies*. Retrieved from http://www.edu.gov.on.ca/eng/curriculum/secondary/canworld910curr2013.pdf

Shahjahan, R.A. (2005). Spirituality in the academy: Reclaiming from the margins and evoking a transformative way of knowing the world. *International Journal of Qualitative Studies in Education, 18*(6), 685–711.

Shahjahan, R.A. (2009). The role of spirituality in the anti-oppressive higher-education classroom. *Teaching in Higher Education, 14*(2), 121–131.

Sunberg, J. (2014). Decolonizing post-humanist geographies. *Cultural Geographies, 21*(1), 33–47.

Truth and Reconciliation Commission, Canada. (2015, July 23). *Honouring the truth, reconciling for the future*. Retrieved from https://www.law.berkeley.edu/wp-content/uploads/2015/04/Honouring_the_Truth_Reconciling_for_the_Future_July_23_2015.pdf

Tuck, Y., & Yang, K.W. (2012). Decolonization is not a metaphor. *Decolonization: Indigeneity, Education & Society, 1*(1), 1–40.

Wane, N.N. (2011). Reclaiming our spirituality: A pedagogical tool for feminism and activism. *Canadian Woman Studies, 29*(1), 159–170.

CHAPTER 6

"Indigenous Knowledges": Issues of Commodification, Privatization, and Intellectual Property Rights

Mandeep Jajj

THIS CHAPTER WILL discuss "Indigenous knowledges" in relation to issues of privatization and intellectual property rights, in the context of India. I will address how Indigenous knowledges are turned into "economic necessities" by neocolonial and capitalist societies in order to control, subjugate, and further oppress marginalized bodies. I want readers to think about the privatization and commodification of Indigenous knowledges as a new form of colonialism, a form that controls, appropriates, and claims "Indigeneity" for its own use. I question why there is a need to monopolize renewable resources that come from the Land. Why is it that nature's abundance—for example, the neem leaves and turmeric roots of India—needs to be "privatized" and "owned" by one corporation? While trying to deconstruct Indigeneity from "privatization," I want readers to critically engage with the question of "authenticity." What does it mean to claim authenticity, and how does the process of reclaiming help with imagining new decolonial features? Reclaiming cultural knowledges—knowledges of the Land—is vital in fighting the neocolonial agenda of modern society that tries to manipulate, misuse, and extract Indigeneity for capital use. My goal in this chapter is not to provide a neat and tidy categorization of Indigenous knowledges, but to trouble our already existing imaginaries of what Indigenous means, in order to understand its necessity for decolonization and for the sustenance of life.

Locating Myself

I come from a small village called Attowal located in Hoshiarpur, Punjab, India, the child of a family that has farmed for generations. According to my grandfather, to *bijha*—which in Punjabi means "seed" or "to grow"—is vital to the sustenance of life. I remember going to India during the harvest festival of Vaisakhi. I remember celebrating the harvest season and praying with my grandfather and with the village community for the harvesting season to be endless, so that food, plants, trees, and herbs, upon which life is so dependent, would never run out. Whatever was grown was shared communally. When there was an abundance of food, trucks would deliver some to neighboring villages so that everyone would have enough to eat. My time in India was wonderful. I learned of Ayurvedic knowledge from my elders and learned how to plant, grow, and use specific herbs and spices. All of what I learned was "Indigenous knowledges," knowledges of the land of India. This knowledge was not owned by anyone; rather, it was available to anyone who needed it. Its main purpose was the sustenance of life. That summer I learned how to pick plants, save, and protect seeds for the next harvesting season to come.

When my grandfather moved from India to England, and then to Canada, we would bring some of these seeds so we could harvest food in our backyards. I remember spending hours with him growing vegetables, fruits, and herbs. We would always pray before planting. We would pray for the bijha to grow, and when we received a good harvest, we would always share with our neighbors. But several years later, when my grandfather came back from India, he brought with him not a single seed. He explained how seeds were no longer to be saved, how seeds and knowledge of how to grow and produce bijha were now claimed to be "intellectual property." He explained how many farmers who had saved seeds for generations were forced to give them up to corporations—corporations that, in return, would make these farmers buy seeds that were "non-renewable," meaning the bijha was only able to produce one-time crops. This privatization of knowledge—knowledge of the seed and how it was grown—caused an epidemic of farmer suicides. I have lost many relatives to what Vandana Shiva refers to as the "The Seed Wars" (Shiva, 2005), and this is why I am writing about the privatization of Indigenous knowledges and issues of commodification today. I am writing to expose the power of western cultures to take Indigenous knowledges and claim these knowledges as their own. I am writing to expose the label of "disposability" that western corporations such as Monsanto have placed on Indian farmers' bodies. I am writing to expose these injustices.

Analysis

Alfred and Corntassel's work "Being Indigenous: Resurgences against Contemporary Colonialism" (2005) has shaped my understanding of what it means to live and be oppressed in a state of contemporary colonialism. This article exposes how a post-imperial practice, that of a "settler's imperative" (Fanon, 1963), is grounded in policies meant to control, subjugate, and oppress Indigeneity for its own use and misuse (Alfred & Corntassel, 2005). Colonizing tactics are used by structures of power in efforts to eradicate the "native subject" culturally, politically, and physically (Alfred & Corntassel, 2005). The overarching goal of the colonial state is that of dispossession: if you dispossess a people of their land, you are directly dispossessing them of their rights (Spivak, 1988). In India, especially in the case of the farmers of Punjab, this dispossession began by not allowing farmers in their own communities to use their knowledge of bijha and of the land to harvest. When you take away or attempt to control the way Indigeneity conducts life, you reduce people's existence to "non-existence" and dismiss their cultural knowledge as illegitimate. Harvesting and growing bijha is a cultural practice, and in the Punjab region, growing bijha is part of a local knowledge system. However, this knowledge system is relabeled as "non-existent" when dominant western corporations such as Monsanto attempt to control, privatize, and commercialize these very same knowledges. The goal of the dominator becomes the removal of local knowledge systems from the minds of local communities. Removing these cultural knowledges and saying that they never existed allows the dominant power to claim these cultural knowledges as their own. Alfred and Corntassel (2005) state that this "continuing colonial process pulls people away from cultural practices and community aspects of being Indigenous" (p. 599). The process of removing local knowledge systems serves to remove community bonds, cultural identities, and languages, and thereby removes Indigenous ties to the land. In my grandfather's village of Attowal, as well as other regions of Punjab and India at large, this removal of local knowledges and ties to the land has been taking place in what Vandana Shiva refers to as "the Second Coming of Columbus," with the globalizing ventures of multinational companies such as Monsanto and Union Carbide (Shiva, 2016a).

Removing cultural ties to the land fits into the colonial scheme of domination that Fanon (1963) addresses in his analysis of the colonial social forum. Fanon reveals the colonial-capitalist dichotomy to be concerned only with economic progression, progression through the means of gaining capital. Economic progression throughout history has been achieved through the dismantling and dispossession of Indigeneity. Using Fanon's analysis (1963), I was able to understand that in a postmodern context, conditions of oppression are still directly linked to this colonial capitalist agenda. Companies like Monsanto become interested in the bijha only as a means to commercialize and make a profit. These companies are in no way concerned with the future of food sustainability or security. In her research, Shiva extensively reveals the importance of bijha and how life resides in the "seed" as the means for it to grow, continuously and on its own, over and over again (Shiva, 2009). The members of my grandfather's village relied on the harvesting and collecting of seeds for generations because they understood the importance and vitality of bijha. Saving bijha meant saving "life" (Shiva, 2009). Given the importance of bijha and the Indigenous knowledges that are required to produce bijha, I question what ideas, structures, and polices make it possible for the World Trade Organization and the Indian government to make it illegal for Indigenous farmers to save their bijha. What was the purpose, and who benefited from this national trade agreement? I thought about this question while reading Alfred and Corntassel's (2005) argument on contemporary colonialism. Their work exposes how colonial systems have always gained control over groups of people for the "sake of what the colonial power has determined to be the common good" (p. 601). The idea that the "West knows best," that the West is the hub of "correct" and "civilized" knowledge, reifies the hegemonic stance against the autonomy of Indigenous knowledges (Sadar, 1999). The idea becomes that the Indian farmers have no "proper" knowledge of harvesting and saving seeds and that the civilized west needs to help save the backward Orient for the so-called "common good." The power of the West, and of the WTO, lies in its power to define: to define a supposed problem and then enforce a solution (Shiva, 2009). Sadar, in his research on international development, states that the West's power to define results in "non-western civilization to be defined out of existence" (Sadar, 1999). This definitional power is what allows the West to claim, consume, and appropriate knowledges from all those deemed "other." For the farmers in India, their existence, their Indigenous knowledge of bijha, is rendered nonexistent in an attempt to gain control and dispossess the farmers of their Land in India.

Why is the saving of seeds for harvest made illegal in India? According to Shiva, the problem that the West locates in the "seed" is the fact that it is a renewable resource. That one single seed can multiply and produce an infinite amount of seeds is seen as the "problem." In the words of Shiva, "the fact that one [bijha] gives rise to many is a problem; one should give rise to nothing, and that's how we make profits" (Shiva, 2009). The Food and Agricultural Association, a part of the United Nations, allows chemical companies such as Monsanto to move into what has come to be known as the "seed sector." This affects how farmers harvest and cultivate seeds. Shiva exposes how Monsanto follows its corporate interests and exerts influence on creating patents and intellectual property rights, which has worked in its favor. Monsanto states that "it was not fair that farmers saved seeds, that their practices were not equitable" (Shiva, 2009). Equity for Monsanto has to do with having a monopoly over the "seed world" and dictating how the seeds should be harvested. Equity for this corporation is having sole ownership of seeds and having farmers—who for generations saved seeds—repurchase these seeds from multinational corporations for their harvest. In order to control the "seed," Monsanto claimed bijha, and the intellectual knowledge that came along with cultivating bijha, as its own. The company, backed by an international trade agreement signed by the U.N., began genetically modifying seeds for the so-called "common good" of humanity, and this goodness came in the form of one-time crops (Shiva, 2009). As stated previously, this control of Indigenous knowledges caused a spike in farmer suicides, especially in my grandfather's village and in the region of Punjab generally. The Center for Human Rights and Global Justice estimates that in 2009, 17,638 farmers had committed suicide, which is one death every 30 minutes (Akolkar, 2014, p. 113). The genetically modified seeds that Monsanto was selling back to Indian farmers produced next to nothing in crop yields. Colonizing the knowledge of bijha and claiming this knowledge as the "intellectual property" of the western world causes a disconnect between the Indigenous community of Punjab and its Land. The farmers, who had saved seeds for generations, were no longer allowed to use the cultural knowledge of their Ancestors to harvest and cultivate seeds on their own Land. These strategies of encroachment, of killing the renewable nature of the seed, expose how globalization works with a "settler imperative" (Fanon, 1963), an imperative that allows multinational corporations to take and claim Indigeneity for their own capital use (Alfred & Corntassel, 2005).

Challenging the "Definitional Power" of the West

Vandana Shiva (2016a) references James Enyart, who states: "The industries and traders of world commerce have played simultaneously the role of the patients, the diagnosticians, and the prescribing physicians" (p. 82). This reference to "industries" is a direct allusion to Monsanto, Shiva argues. "If you define the problem, you find the solution, you become the judge and executive, where is democracy?" (Shiva, 2009). Monsanto made the fact that farmers saved seeds into an international problem, and then, in collaboration the World Trade Organization (WTO), which is an affiliate of the U.N., made it illegal for farmers to save seeds on an international scale. What we get here is the privatization and monopoly over the seed. Every time a seed is planted, Monsanto wants farmers to pay a royalty—literally, to pay a royalty for harvesting and cultivating food on their own land!

In the course of my research I kept asking myself how it is possible to claim something that is so biologically material, the seed, as intellectual property. Intellectual property is defined as a property and product of the mind, and Vandana Shiva in her research points out that "the seed is not an idea that just suddenly popped out of someone's head" (Shiva, 2009). The lawyers who drafted the Intellectual Trades Agreement in relation to the harvesting of seeds made the seed, by definition, "intellectually viable" as property. And it is through this definition that Monsanto gains control and becomes a hegemonic power. The seed, or bijha, something that has never been owned, something that the community of Punjab and greater India understands as vital to life, is now reduced to "private property" (Shiva, 2009). This process of commodifying nature is what Shiva refers to as "the bio-piracy of life," a new form of colonialism (Shiva, 2016a). This form of control creates an ongoing cycle of oppression in communities, where local and cultural knowledges of bijha come under attack. My grandfather's village in Attowal was confronted with the reality of having its Land, culture, and governmental authorities reconstructed by colonial societies and corporations. All of this occurred within an international legal framework, and, as Spivak states in her work, "It is just that there be law, but law is no justice" (Spivak, 1988). For me the central issue of privatization (to own and control) and commodification (to commercialize and sell) lies in the fact that it dismisses the existence of local/

Indigenous knowledge systems and, in the case of Monsanto, appropriates local knowledges, such as that of the bijha, as its own. Shiva's work tries to reclaim "Indigeneity" from the scientists and multinational corporations that are trying to define it in their own image (Shiva, 2009). The commodification of Indigenous knowledges leads to the disappearance of Indigenous knowledge systems, which creates a "monoculture of the mind" (Shiva, 1993, 2016b). When I say "monoculture of the mind," I am referring to the power of western/eurocentric societies to enforce one dominant mode of thinking and being over others. This be-all, end-all attitude creates the dominant understanding that western knowledge is the only "correct" knowledge, and therefore validates its claim through "correctness" to spread throughout the world, in what can be understood as "intellectual colonization" (Shiva, 2016a). This constant conflict between western and Indigenous knowledge systems made me question whether these knowledge systems could coexist. I personally believe that they cannot, because for Indigeneity, such as that seen in my grandfather's village, the seed and knowledge of the seed cannot be owned by anyone. It existed as local knowledge for whoever needed it; it was understood as knowledge for the continuity and sustainability of life. However, when western corporations saw the economic value in the knowledge of bijha, they immediately used international legal means to monopolize and claim the knowledge of the bijha as their own. This monopolizing process feeds into a colonial narrative that imposes a view of the world that is but an outcome and perspective of that power (Alfred & Corntassel, 2005). This privatizing process is the power that dispossessed local communities in India and continues to negate their knowledges and existence.

In order for different knowledges to coexist, we have to do away with hierarchical modes of thinking (Dei, 2008). We have to challenge the universality of the western knowledge system in all aspects of societies, a system that deems itself to be superior. In India, and in the case of bijha that I have been discussing, we have seen the disappearance of a local knowledge system through its interaction with a western structure of power. This disappearance of knowledge is political and speaks to the disposability of Indian farmers, their village communities, and, most important, their ancestral knowledges. Western knowledge systems and structures of power have a tendency to mask and possess all "other" knowledge forms. We have to do away with the imperial and neocolonial policies that undermine the value and necessity of Indigeneity, and think along the lines of multicentricity (Dei, 2008). Corporations such as Monsanto should take into account that social equity does not rely on monopoly and profit, but relies on the understanding that there are multiple ways of being and knowing in this world. Knowledges are not meant to be locked up in a box; they are intended for the use, sustainability, and continuity of life. In researching the rights of Indian farmers in growing and harvesting seeds, and how neocolonial institutions claim and take away those rights, I have come to realize that the survival of Indigenous knowledges and identity is directly linked to the land. In her work, Spivak states: "Knowledge of the subaltern, is knowledge of the physical world." In order to comprehend this, we should understand that conquering and/or attacking the knowledges of the subaltern is, in retrospect, attacking the knowledge of the physical world, knowledge that is needed for the sustenance of life. Attacking or conquering this knowledge is equivalent to attacking cultural identities and histories, because Indigeneity presumes all of these qualities to be intertwined, to be as one.

In thinking about the Indigenous farming communities of Punjab, it is important to consider how to resist the effects of contemporary colonialism. The question here is how we resist, regenerate, and reclaim Indigenous communities. How do we work toward epistemic equity, and how do we validate non-western epistemologies? How do we challenge and rethink what George Dei refers to as the "imperial dance of globalization and development"? (Dei, 2008). How do we work with Indigenous knowledges to create social change? While trying to theorize Indigenous knowledges, we must acknowledge the social and cultural dimensions of what gives Indigeneity its meaning. Indigeneity, just like culture, is vast, diverse, and always subject to change. However, one commonality I found across contexts is that the foundation of Indigeneity is intrinsically connected to Land (Simpson, 2004). Indigenous knowledges are developed locally, over many generations, and are a result of relationships between communities, their natural surroundings, and social environments (Dei, 2008). My grandfather and his village had acquired their knowledge of the Land over time, through oral traditions and over the generations. Even during my time in India, the knowledge I acquired from my elders in regard to the growing of spices and herbs was orally transmitted and gained by way of my interaction with the environment. Leanne Simpson, in her research on the recovery and maintenance of Indigenous knowledges, explores how oral traditions are dismissed as not legitimate ways of "knowing" in western societies (Simpson, 2004). Simpson looks back into history to reveal how oral systems of knowledge sustained complex, social, spiritual, and political systems long before the arrival of the Europeans (Simpson, 2004). Her analysis of oral traditions made me think in terms of protection against those who dominate, who try to claim and steal Indigeneity, if we should comply and ground cultural knowledges and traditions in written form. It made me think that if the knowledge of bijha had been written down, it could have been protected from the exploitation of Monsanto. However, this way of thinking—that is, complying with the dominant, the normative, and hence the hegemonic system—made me realize that my thinking was flawed. To write down a tradition that for generations has been oral is to make static its meanings, and from what I have learned from Leanne Simpson's argument, oral traditions are meant to be fluid. Fluidity is essential to its nature, and it is this component of fluidity that makes oral traditions diverse and multicentric to their very core. To ground Indigenous knowledges in text is what Simpson (2004) refers to as "cage knowledge." She states: "When knowledge is made into a text, it is translated from [I]ndigenous languages into English, locking its interpretation in a cognitive box, delineated by the structures of language that evolve to communicate the worldview of the colonizers" (p. 380). This teaches us that knowledge is in constant flux and that "the fluidity of interactions of different knowledges makes knowledge dynamic and durable" (Dei, 2008). I have learned that there are limitations to grounding knowledge in text, because Indigenous knowledges intend to be experiential (Castellano, 2000). I learned that Indigeneity should not have to comply with the dominant; instead, the dominant should have to learn how to work with and understand Indigeneity in all its forms.

Indigenous knowledges impel action, and because these knowledges are communal, there is space for everyone to exist within Indigeneity (Dei, 2016). However, in western societies there is a constant fear of losing privilege, and in order to secure and produce more privilege, dominant systems use globalizing ventures like those of multinational corporations to reinforce their hegemonic standing. When local knowledge—like that of bijha—appears in the field of globalization, "it is made to disappear by denying its status as a form of systematic knowledge, and by assigning it the adjectives 'primitive' and 'unscientific'" (Shiva, 1993, p. 10). Dominant systems create sets of values based on power and capital, and the knowledges that these dominant societies produce work within this same framework. This system works to legitimize knowledges of their own (western knowledges) while delegitimizing all others. The challenge here becomes that of recognition. How do we recognize other knowledge forms in societies that deem anything "other" as inferior? Shiva points out that rendering local knowledges "invisible" or declaring them to be illegitimate or "non-existent" further allows the oppressor to destroy the realities that local/Indigenous knowledge systems represent (Shiva, 2016a). The goal here becomes one of recognition and representation, for Indigeneity to work toward political recognition in order for its existence to survive and not be dismissed (Coulthard, 2007).

Recognition has to do with identity, and it is fundamental to understand that for Indigeneity, identity is tied to the Land. This tie to the Land positions Indigenous identity as coexistent, biodiverse, and interrelated, not as monolithic (Coulthard, 2007). If the Land is under threat, for Indigeneity this means that knowledge, identity, and culture are all under threat, because all are intrinsically connected. For the farmers of Punjab, the practice of saving seeds (bijha) was not just a fight to save plants and food; it was a fight to save identity, culture, and history, and the seed was the ultimate sign and symbol for securing the future in all its forms (Shiva, 2009). In their fight for recognition, these farmers made me realize that Indigenous recognition should be a globalizing mission, one that makes sure that the interests of Indigenous peoples are served. Recognition begins with removing the label and status of western knowledge, especially that of western science, as the only worldly "truth." Removing the special epistemic status that becomes associated with western science will allow for the development of a space—a "trialectic space"—where Indigenous knowledge can be embodied and therefore survive (Dei, 2012).

Recognition is a relational process, and this relationality is what troubles me. I question how Indigeneity comes to be recognized by the dominant, when the dominant is by no means interested in its existence. It was Fanon, in his anti-colonial work, who stated that "the European peoples must first decide to wake up and shake themselves, use their brains, and stop playing the stupid game of the Sleeping Beauty" (Fanon, 1963). The question remains: How does one "wake up Sleeping Beauty"? Time and history have shown that the "west" does not wish to acknowledge that its monocultures are limiting and oppressive. The task remains as to how we reintroduce "Indigeneity" to the world, to the contemporary colonial world, in which Indigeneity has a good chance of being capitalized on. In the case of the farmers in India, the dominant (Monsanto) possessed the power to create and perpetuate the existence of Indigeneity, and this power rendered Indian farmers, and their knowledge of bijha, invisible and unreal. Indigenous identities are not only shaped by recognition, but also by nonrecognition. This nonrecognition of Indian farmers proved to be harmful and imprisoning, as evidenced in the increase of farmer suicides in Punjab (Akolkar, 2014; Kincheloe & Steinberg, 2008). I believe that in order to remain true to one's own identity, one must let go of the visible world of the West and the ways in which we have come to understand it. Recognition comes from deconstructing and not participating in the prejudices and expectations that the dominant culture imposes on Indigenous bodies. The way we are socialized influences the way we view Indigeneity. The power of perception, of the gaze, looking upon, and making meaning of "others" are all used by structures of power to create norms and standards, ideas of "rightness" and "correctness" in relation to Indigeneity. In the context of the farmers of India, white/western knowledge was visible, white/western knowledge was correct, "white" was everything Indigeneity was structured not to be. With this, I have come to understand that recognition relies on understanding the "culture of power" and resisting the status quo (Dei & Doyle-Wood, 2006). Resisting is what will allow us to rethink and recreate societies in which multiple identities and knowledges can exist—exist visibly in every sense of the word.

Power lies in perception, and in order for Indigeneity to be integrated into western structures of power, safe spaces within these structures should be incorporated. When western societies attempt to create Indigenous spaces, they should avoid essentializing, romanticizing, and appropriating discourses. The production of Indigenous spaces should not involve "saving Indigenous people, but help reconstruct conditions that allow for Indigenous self-sufficiency" (Kincheloe & Steinberg, 2008). These conditions and reconstructions should deal with "being and seeing relationships to physical surroundings, the idea of Indigeneity is that knowledge involves insight into plants and animal life, that knowledge resides in the dynamics of co-existing" (Kincheloe & Steinberg, 2008). Indigenous knowledge is "inherently scattered and local in character"; it gains vitality from being deeply implicated in people's lives (Agrawal, 1995b, p. 5). The dynamic here is that the nature of Indigenous knowledge changes in character against the changing needs of people, and this is what makes Indigeneity multicentric (Agrawal, 1995b, p. 5). In its attempts at integration, the West will have to acknowledge the reality of colonization and not mention "the effects of economic globalization that will continue to challenge Indigenous peoples in [the] present day" (Kincheloe & Steinberg, 2008). Globalization in Indigenous eyes "reflects a deepening, hastening, and starching of an already existing empire" (Alfred & Corntassel, 2005, p. 614)—an empire that uses the term *globalization*, which is just another fancy word for "westernization," to reconstruct and shape the world based on western/eurocentric norms and institutions (Mehmet, 1995). For the farming communities of India, development was enforced in terms of monopoly and not sustainability. Development for my grandfather's village of Attowal was having its knowledges and Land subjected to the label of "underdeveloped," by the norms and values of western theories, which provided no equity and no social justice (Mehmet, 1995). The WTO, along with Monsanto, used the "development" rhetoric to gain control over the harvesting of "seeds," which feeds into the noneconomic development of India but furthers that of the West. Economic development in western terms only knows progression by means of capital and market notions of supply and demand (Mehmet, 1995). There was an infinite supply of bijha in India, and because this bijha or "seed" was an uncontrolled commodity, companies like Monsanto, through the rhetoric of "westernization" and "development," have come to "universalize their markets" and claim control over the infinite supply of what I call "Indigeneity." Donaldo P. Macedo and Lilia I. Bartolomé, in their work *Dancing with Bigotry* (1999), state: "The Anglo with the innocent face has yanked out our tongues," and this is exactly what western corporations did to India. Not only did they silence Indian farmers on an international scale; they also yanked away their identities, cultural practices, and knowledges, all in the name of "globalization." The suggestive power of "development" and "globalization" is what has allowed the West to emerge as the rich center of the world, all by way of exploiting Indigeneity, intellectual properties, and ecological assets. This process damages non-western cultures and further works toward eurocentricity, which is intended to be the "white" center of the world (Mehmet & Bartolomé, 1999).

In times of globalization—times in which the West has the power to create and perpetuate the identities of "others"—it is important for Indigeneity to claim "authenticity" of cultural knowledges and traditions. Richard Handler (1986) suggests that the discussion of authenticity should begin with a profound exercise in cultural history. His analysis suggests that, as a society, we should think about cultural ideas of authenticity and challenge dominant structures that try to delegitimize the authenticity of "others." The western world has a tendency to construct, capitalize, and claim the authentic knowledges of "others" as their own, and this is where issues of accountability and credibility evolve. The knowledge of bijha that Monsanto claimed as "intellectual property" was the knowledge of Indigenous farming communities in India. The knowledge of bijha allows Indigeneity to locate ultimate reality within nature, and this is what makes such knowledges truly authentic. Authenticity for Indigenous communities does not rely on possession. In relation to knowledge, authenticity is understood to be free and connected to the physical world. However, Handler (1986) suggests that western societies understand authenticity in terms of "possessive individualism," meaning it is dependent on the possession of identity, cultures, traditions, and knowledges—in effect, anything that they deem "other" (p. 3). The fact that western ideals of authenticity get reduced to the status of "private property" ties authenticity to a consumer capital agenda and, further, creates the idea that authenticity can be bought and sold, borrowed, ingested, and incorporated into our daily being, our personal experience (Handler, 1986). Privatizing or possessing authentic cultural knowledge allows us and, by us, I am referring to modern society, to appropriate what come to be known as "cultural authenticity." It is essential to understand that appropriating the cultural knowledge of "others" allows one to take elements of a culture and claim it to be a part of oneself. Having dominant/western culture appropriate the culture of the oppressed takes something integral away from that community, that something being identity (Howes, 1996).

Even though "authenticity" is a cultural construct of the modern western world, I believe that in a modern context it should be claimed. Authenticity for many marginalized communities deals with representation and the struggle for recognition. In stating this, I am assuming that authenticity can be taken up correctly, and I am suggesting that this correctness deals with accurate representation of cultural groups that have been denied access and rights to speak on behalf of their livelihood. Authenticity can be about reclaiming a voice that has been denied; it can be about telling our stories—our cultural stories—in a culturally specific, responsive, and respecting way. By claiming authenticity, Indigenous peoples can untangle themselves from the oppressive control of contemporary colonizing states. Having said this, I still think it is important to note that the concept of authenticity has been, and still is, deeply embedded in the anthropological. I think researchers and members of society should work toward acknowledging and understanding culture-specific paradigms. Finally, as researchers, we should attempt to work within our cultural specificities, replacing cultural estrangement with cultural engagement (Dei, 2012), and this engagement should in no way be appropriating.

I believe that in order to defend Indigenous cultural traditions and knowledges—like that of the bijha—against vulgarization and exploitation by the western world, it is important to claim Indigeneity whenever possible, and this claiming works towards decolonization. Decolonization is not just a theory but also a practice, one that needs to take place in order to dismantle oppressive power structures like that of Monsanto. Decolonization is designed to get rid of the preservation of hierarchies. It is about recognizing all those who have been pushed out to the margins (Coulthard, 2007). Decolonization is a relational process that deals not only with Indigenous groups reclaiming their authentic voice, but also with the dominant accepting and facing the terms of their violent and oppressive actions. In the words of Fanon, decolonization is a way to "Wake up Sleeping Beauty." It is for the dominant to understand that there is problem with the way western systems operate and capitalize on Indigeneity. Decolonization involves getting rid of the scientific label that assigns "a kind of sacredness and social immunity to western knowledge systems" (Shiva, 1993). Decolonization in the context of India, which I have been discussing, has to do with globalization and multinational corporations and their willingness to step outside of their privilege and challenge the guidelines outlined by colonial power structures (Dei, 2016). Decolonization involves getting rid of global systems of inequity, which means dismantling the "westernizing rhetoric" and implementing discourses of self-reliance, self-sufficiency, social justice, and cultural authenticity (Sadar, 1999). Decolonization is a spiritual battle, one that is fought against the political manipulation of the dominant. Decolonization is about engaging Indigeneity, which is recognizing that true power lies within our Lands (Alfred & Corntassel, 2005). For the farmers of India, this engaging was maintained through the free exchange of bijha (seeds), which was based on cooperation and reciprocity. The bijha promoted belonging and connectedness to place and identities. The seed was something that Indigenous farming communities worked on collectively to achieve. For my grandfather and his village, claiming their authentic voice against western corporations and working in solidarity to achieve agricultural security was a movement toward decolonization. Castellano, in "Updating Aboriginal Traditions of Knowledge," quotes Donaldo Macedo, who states: "It is only through the decolonization of our minds, if not our hearts that we can begin to develop the necessary political clarity to reject the enslavement of a colonial discourse that creates a false dichotomy between western and indigenous knowledges" (Castellano, 2000). With this, I was able to understand that there is room for coexistence—that is, if you make room and work toward reciprocity. However, having said this, I think it is still important to remember that irreconcilable differences exist between different knowledge systems, and this inability or unwillingness to reconcile is what makes coexistence difficult.

In deconstructing Indigeneity from privatization, the role of education is essential. I believe new futures are possible if we educate society in the importance of local cultural knowledges. The model of development as seen from global multinational corporations such as Monsanto work within this global capitalist agenda, which calls for the exploitation of Land, its resources, and its people. This neoliberal capitalist model works by teaching members of society to be "capitalist producers." We are socialized and taught to extract resources not on the basis of need but rather on the basis of profit. This modern, neoliberal idea of development is all about productivity, capital consumption, and the privatization of biodiversity. The word *sustainability* ceases to have meaning in this neoliberal framework, and so do the cultural knowledges and stories of the marginalized that have been subjected to the exploitation of this modern development project. In trying to imagine a new future, I question what would happen if the understanding of "development," which requires us to be neoliberal capitalist subjects, were no longer taught. What would happen if we were taught development in terms of Lifeplace and Lifelong learning, which involves the coexisting of different knowledges (Harris & Chisholm, 2010)? The question is how do we do this. How do we work to erase a hierarchical educational structure that teaches us within this neoliberal, neocolonial, and global capitalist framework? How do we work on implementing a new system? This new system for me is not grounded in a single theory or thought, but begins with Margaret Harris and Colin Chisholm's concept of "Lifeplace and Lifelong learning." This concept acknowledges the question of epistemic equity and, in doing so, works toward an understanding of the coexistence of different knowledges. Harris and Chisholm's work questions the dichotomy between "work-based" and "lifelong" learning, and thereby questions how we can disrupt hierarchical institutions that position traditional western education as more valuable than everyday life learning.

Lifeplace learning is meant to widen participation of marginalized knowledges. Yet in today's society we still see a hierarchy in what is considered acceptable through labels such as "informal" and "formal" knowledge. Harris and Chisholm suggest that to widen the participation and social inclusion of different knowledges, accreditation is needed in order to account for these differences. Accreditation of so-called "informal" knowledges will help challenge the academic elitism that gets attached to various knowledges, and will help eliminate the barriers surrounding what is considered "valuable learning" (Harris & Chisholm, 2010). I believe that accreditation within academia will help promote embodied knowledges, placing the value of learning on the learner. This concept of Lifeplace/Lifelong learning lends personal autonomy to the learner, and highlights that lived, material, and embodied knowledges are useful and important. In order to create a space in which "Lifelong" learning is recognized, we need to start by changing the attitudes of society, so that learning outside the western academy can be understood as knowledgeable and skillful (Harris & Chisholm, 2010).

Work-based learning is socially acceptable because it values human productivity, functionality, and performance, and is about teaching employer-desired skills to produce economic capital. I find that Lifelong learning deals more with individual consciousness and speaks to the sustainability of environments alongside capital production. The concept of Lifelong learning is revolutionary in that it allows for marginalized voices and knowledges that have been failed by formal systems to take part and be recognized in society. I believe education and learning should be about encompassing embodied and cultural knowledges. While reading Harris & Chisholm's work, I thought about Indigenous knowledge systems and how they have been denied the status of "valuable" and "creditworthy." I thought about how implementing Lifeplace/Lifelong learning in educational institutions will help bring status and value to these types of knowledges, and how by doing this, social transformation in regard to the sustainability of land and resources could be implemented. I thought about my grandfather's village and the Indigenous farming community in Punjab, and thought about how validating local community-based knowledges would help vitalize the land, rather than exploit it through western "work-based," "formal" knowledges that have been implemented by neocolonial, capitalist, multinational corporations such as Monsanto. Discovering the concept of Lifeplace and Lifelong learning has made me question what would happen if we implemented this concept on a global scale. What would this do to the modern globalized, neoliberal market economy we live in today? I believe we should be working toward implementing Lifeplace learning within the sphere of work-based learning. By doing this, dominant "formal" knowledges would diversify, allowing space for social transformation to occur through processes that value not only economic capital, but find value in life-based knowledges that value sustainability as well.

Harris and Chisholm's concept of Lifeplace/Lifelong learning is decolonial inasmuch as it works toward epistemic equity, bringing a humility of "knowing" and acknowledging the power of "not knowing" (Dei, 2016). Because Indigeneity is multicentric and based on principles of coexistence and interrelation, I believe we can have "global humanity" and still keep Indigeneity intact. By evaluating bijha and the farming communities in India, I was able to understand the importance of working within a post-structural and anti-colonial framework. This framework has allowed me to reimagine and reposition Indigeneity as a political discourse and take into account the broader issues of neocolonialism and the impacts of globalization (Dei & Doyle-Wood, 2006). Reinforcing an anti-colonial, Indigenous, and decolonial lens has allowed me to move toward a new paradigm that aims to resist oppression. For the Indigenous farming communities of India, resistance comes in terms of protecting the vitality of community-based knowledges. Resistance comes in terms of fighting against the corporate agendas of the "modern western world," which seek to privatize and commodify Indigeneity for its own use. Resistance comes in terms of reclaiming ancestral knowledges from multinational global corporations, which appropriate and claim these knowledges as their own. Knowledge, knowledge production, and sharing are meant to open doors for communities, not close them. As resisters of contemporary colonialism, we must envision new possibilities in our attempts to confront and dismantle these neocolonial/capitalist systems. As resisters, we must push multinational corporations to step outside of their privilege and challenge the guidelines outlined by colonial structures of power (Dei, 2008). We must resist and refuse to participate in practices that uphold the colonial mindset of "whiteness" as the only measure for what is to be considered "valid." As resisters to the privatization and commodification of Indigenous knowledges, it is important to remember the power of knowledge and its ability to transform communities. It is important to remember that there is always room for resilience and healing if we, as a society, make room. With this, I can conclude by saying that to understand privilege concerning dominant structures and ideologies will allow society to undermine structures of oppression, thus creating spaces for Indigeneity and Indigenous knowledges to exist in all its forms.

To CONCLUDE, the Chipko, Appiko, Penan, and Sarawak tribes of India state:

> This is the land of our forefathers, and their forefathers before them. If we don't do something now to protect the little that is left, there will be nothing for our children. Our forests are mowed down, the hills are levelled, the sacred graves of our ancestors have been desecrated, our waters and our streams are contaminated, our plant life is destroyed, and the forest animals are killed or have run away. What else can we do now but to make our protests heard, so that something can be done to help us? (Shiva, 1993, p. 22)

These Indigenous communities work toward transformation and fight to claim their "authentic voice" in the eyes of the dominant. These movements work for epistemic equity, multicentricity, and global recognition. In the words of my grandfather, "It is better to be a roadblock in the eyes of the dominant than to comply and lose yourself in their chaos." It is better to fight for Indigeneity, because fighting for it means fighting for the vitality, continuity, and sustenance of life.

References

Agrawal, A. (1995a). Dismantling the divide between Indigenous and scientific knowledge. *Development and Change, 26*, 413–439.

Agrawal, A. (1995b). Indigenous and scientific knowledge: Some critical comments. *Indigenous Knowledge and Development Monitor, 3*(3), 3–5.

Akolkar, P. (2014). Agriculture: The original global economy. In C. Goria (Ed.), *Invisible hands: Voices from the global economy*. San Francisco, CA: McSweeney's and Voice of Witness Press.

Alfred, T., & Corntassel, J. (2005). Being Indigenous: Resurgences against contemporary colonialism. *Government and Opposition: An International Journal of Comparative Politics, 40*(4), 597–614.

Castellano, M.B. (2000). Updating aboriginal traditions of knowledge. In G.J.S. Dei et al. (Eds.), *Indigenous knowledges in global contexts* (pp. 21–36). Toronto, ON: University of Toronto Press.

Coulthard, G. (2007). Subjects of empire: Indigenous peoples and the "politics of recognition" in Canada. *Contemporary Political Theory, 6*, 437–460.

Dei, G.J.S. (2008). Indigenous knowledge studies and the next generation: Pedagogical possibilities for anti-colonial education. *Australian Journal of Indigenous Education, 37*(Supp.), 5–13.

Dei, G.J.S. (2012). "Suahunu," the trialectic space. *Journal of Black Studies, 43*(8), 823–846.

Dei, G.J.S. (2016). Lecture on Indigenous knowledge: Decolonizing pedagogical implications. Personal Collection of George Dei, University of Toronto, ON.

Dei, G.J.S., & Doyle-Wood, S. (2006). "Is we who haffi ride di staam": Critical knowledge/multiple knowings: Possibilities, challenges and resistance in curriculum/cultural contexts. In Y. Kanu (Ed.), *Curriculum as cultural practice: Postcolonial imaginations* (pp. 151–180). Toronto, ON: University of Toronto Press.

Fanon, F. (1963). *The wretched of the earth*. New York, NY: Grove Press.

Handler, R. (1986). Authenticity. *Anthropology Today, 2*(1), 2–4.

Harris, M., & Chisholm, C. (2010). Beyond the workplace: Learning in the lifeplace. In M. Malloch, L. Cairns, K. Evans, & B.N. O'Connor (Eds.), *The SAGE handbook of workplace learning*. London, UK: Sage Publications.

Howes, D. (1996). Cultural appropriation and resistance in the American Southwest: Decommodifying Indianness. In D. Howes (Ed.), *Cross-cultural consumption: Global markets, local realities* (pp. 138–160). New York, NY: Routledge.

Kincheloe, J., & Steinberg, S. (2008). Indigenous knowledges in education: Complexities, dangers and profound benefits. In N. Denzin, Y. Lincoln, & L.T. Smith (Eds.), *Handbook of critical and Indigenous methodologies* (pp. 135–156). Los Angeles, CA: Sage Publications.

Macedo, D.P., & Bartolomé, L.I. (1999). *Dancing with bigotry: Beyond the politics of tolerance*. New York, NY: St. Martin's Press.

Mehmet, O. (1995). *Westernizing the Third World: The eurocentricity of economic development theories*. London, UK: Routledge.

Sadar, Z. (1999). Development and the location of eurocentrism. In R. Munck & D. O'Hearn (Eds.), *Critical development theory: Contributions to the new paradigm* (pp. 44–61). London, UK: Zed Books.

Shiva, V. (1993). *Monocultures of the mind: Perspectives on biodiversity and biotechnology*. London, UK: Zed Books.

Shiva, V. (2005). *India divided: Diversity and democracy under attack*, Chapter 4: Seed Wars and the corporate take over of seeds. New York, NY: Seven Stories Press.

Shiva, V. (2009, February 28). The future of food and seed. Keynote Address at the 2009 Organicology Conference in Portland, OR.

Shiva, V. (2016a). *Bio-piracy: The plunder of nature and knowledge*. Berkeley, CA: Northern Atlantic Books.

Shiva, V. (2016b). *Stolen harvest: The hijacking of the global food supply*. Lexington, KY: University Press of Kentucky.

Simpson, L. (2004). Anti–colonial strategies for the recovery and maintenance of Indigenous knowledge. *American Indian Quarterly, 28*(3&4), 373–384.

Spivak, G.C. (1988). Can the subaltern speak? In C. Nelson & L. Grossberg (Eds.), *Marxism and the interpretation of culture* (pp. 65–105). Urbana, IL: University of Illinois Press.

CHAPTER 7

Decolonization Through Decentralization

Rachel Buchanan

Introduction

In striving to decolonize education, this chapter will explore the power dynamics that continue to drive euro-western imperialism in African contexts and the research and education policies that inform the centralization and standardization of education. It argues that large-scale educational initiatives are inherently problematic, that a centralized governing force can never meet the educational needs of a diverse population, and that a top-down approach—even if rooted in research—can never entirely align with the ever-changing Indigenous realities of a population. It argues that the centralization and nationalization of education in African contexts perpetuates knowledge that preserves the existing colonial power relations. Whom do centralized education systems claim to serve? Whom do they serve in reality? With this in mind, the chapter asks the reader to think beyond the parameters of governmental control, to think of what education could look like in a context that does not demand to define, structure, and control it.

I come to this research as a settler and as a privileged white woman who recognizes that I contribute to the ongoing colonization of Africa. This recognition and knowledge pushes me to interrogate the structures that implicate me in their violence. I have been educated and been an educator in settings that have catered to my skin color in North America, India, Nepal, and Uganda. I have been afforded a higher status than I deserve in these settings, which suffer from imperialism.

My first teaching experience took place in Nepal. I taught at the local school as a homeroom teacher. I was 20 years old and had no teaching degree. The teachers that

I worked alongside had been to Teachers College, and yet this was not demanded of me. It was assumed, because of my North American education, that my knowledge was more legitimate. I heard this often when I was at this school. Teachers came to me asking for advice on how to teach certain lessons, for the "correct" pronunciation of English words, how to emulate North American classrooms. I was afforded legitimacy solely because of my colonial knowledge, skin color, and way of being. Since then I have had many similar experiences in countries that suffer from colonialism. In Uganda, I offered teachers training on how reading and writing can be taught with phonics in elementary school settings. I taught hundreds of schoolteachers and principals. Once again, despite my lack of experience, my skills and knowledge were afforded a legitimacy that was in many ways undeserved. I was teaching teachers with many more years' experience than I, who evidently had a better understanding of local knowledge and realities. Yet they came to my training sessions because they valued the colonial insights that I had to offer.

I have seen how the education system serves to naturalize colonial hierarchies and celebrate colonial knowledge by delegitimizing Indigenous ways of knowing and being. Foucault (1991) writes that "power produces reality; it produces domains of objects and rituals of truth" (p. 194). The westernization of thinking stems from a particular regime of power and knowledge that affirms the linear-rational, scientific way of thinking as the truth. This is done in a way that naturalizes colonial knowledge and leaves unquestioned the power dynamics from which it stems. Those in power define what is truth and disseminate bodies of knowledge that legitimize and maintain their power (see also Wynter, 2003). The school system and the emanation of knowledge from centralized sources thus act as "strategies of control" that perpetuate the submission of students and citizens (Foucault, 1991) while promoting colonial knowledge and naturalizing colonial power.

Colonization in African contexts serves to place on a pedestal the white, western "truth," against which the African way is to be positioned and assessed. It teaches that the "white world" is superior (Fanon, 1952; Wynter, 2003). Fanon (1952) writes that the "black man is *comparaison*" (p. 186; emphasis in original). His existence is constructed in relation to "the Other" (the colonizer). His inferiority is constantly reaffirmed through the centralized control of popular culture, the colonial language, racist histories, and oppressive structures that delegitimize Indigeneity (such as schooling). He comes to believe that he must "enhance his superiority" (p. 186). Proximity to whiteness allows for this enhancement.

Education should empower rather than restrain. It should lead to the flourishing of the group rather than the enrichment of only a privileged few. This chapter is my attempt to use my privilege to challenge the systems of control that I am positioned to reproduce and to advocate for the decolonization of education. The chapter understands decolonization as challenging the power structures that reproduce and maintain oppression. It understands decolonization as synonymous with decentralization. It seeks to underline the legitimacy of Indigenous being, knowing, and living.

Unity Amid the Divisiveness

I am wary of Olutayo's (2012) proposal that "development experts" should focus on "what unites rather than what disintegrates" (p. 237). I am concerned with who these "development experts" might be. Is "development" not a new form of colonization that seeks to legitimize the West as the imperial savior (Dei, 2014)? Olutayo (2012) proposes achieving a balance that appreciates both the heterogeneity and homogeneity of societies, as it is within this space that the truth lies and in which inequality can be simultaneously exposed and combated (p. 237). Unfortunately, colonialism does not leave room for this balance: it seeks to conceal the structural nature of existing inequalities under the guise of achieving a unifying global homogeneity (one that is "cosmopolitan" or western) and, in this way, assumes a distinctiveness to Africa that does not recognize its diversity (Dei, 2014). In this sense, current hegemonic, neoliberal global structures do not allow homogeneity and heterogeneity to coexist. Balance and unity cannot be achieved within a system that seeks the standardization and homogenization of its citizens in the name of "development" and "westernization." They cannot be achieved as long as colonialism seeks to suppress the heterogeneity of African Indigeneities. The hegemony of western knowledge must be contested, or the existing power dynamics that legitimize its dominance will continue to be reproduced. As long as these "development experts" seek to work within existing colonial frameworks, their pursuits of unity are inconsequential. They should be perceived as "extension[s] of the colonial administration from decades ago" (Sium, 2014, p. 64). Can "development experts" contribute to the unification of Africa? Or do they, by nature, contribute to its divisiveness? Is there a place for the knowledge and worldviews that developmental experts bring to decolonization?

The pursuit of homogeneity need not be dismissed entirely. Homogeneity can be useful if it is understood as functioning to unify despite differences and in the name of shared histories, relationships, and Indigeneity. In the face of colonialism, it is useful to consider an Africa that is not divided by colonial borders but that instead stands united. In his discussion of the West African subregion, Adeniran (2014) highlights the pre-colonial interconnectivity of the countries of this area by reflecting upon the traditional migratory patterns that depict the intercommunity transactions, relationships, and dependency that existed. He adds that through "subsisting cross-border contact [that] routinely obliterates differences across borders" (p. 290), these borders continue to be challenged today. He argues that "transnational simultaneity," the extant culture of cross-border mobility that predates colonial institutionalization and does not take into account colonial hindrances, is an informative step toward regional integration. "Transnational simultaneity" trivializes centralized governance and the colonial borders that it commands by naturalizing the interconnectivity and interdependence of indigenous Africans and problematizing divisive frameworks.

The colonially defined frontiers that continue to partition the continent of Africa and maintain its divisiveness must be challenged in decolonization. When European dominion in Africa foundered in the years following World War II, it was agreed by African leaders and elites that the borders drawn and imposed during colonial rule would be respected. These arbitrarily partitioned borders do not take into account the demographic, ethnographic, or topographic characteristics of the continent (Herbst, 1989). Saadia Touval writes that they reflect a "complete disregard of local needs and circumstances" (cited in Herbst, 1989), and the Organization of African Unity (OAU) agrees (Herbst, 1989). Upon independence, the delineated countries established central governing bodies to mediate international and intranational affairs and to participate as independent nations on the global stage. Importantly, these sovereign nations were defined and designed in accordance with colonial language, knowledge, structures, and relationships. Contesting this colonialism becomes difficult, as these countries have been defined by their sovereignties and have developed corresponding nationalisms and identities. To what extent can decolonization be achieved while colonial borders continue to determine the governance of Africa? What purpose do colonial borders serve? Can decolonization be achieved within colonially defined nationalisms and governing systems?

Africa continues to be threatened by internal and external colonialisms. External colonialism, as defined by Tuck and Yang (2012), "denotes the expropriation of fragments of Indigenous worlds, animals, plants, and human beings, extracting them in order to transport them to—and build the wealth, the privilege, or feed the appetites of—the colonizers, who get marked as the first world" (p. 4). They define internal colonialism as "the biopolitical and geopolitical management of people, land, flora and fauna within the 'domestic' borders of the imperial nation" (p. 4). This, they write, involves the use of particularized modes of control to ensure the ascendency of a nation and its white[1] elite (p. 5). The borders that delineate Africa therefore act as internally colonizing modes of control that maintain colonial power structures and legitimize the privilege, power, and status afforded to the African elite.

"Development experts" maintain this ascendency by seeking to reproduce the "first world" in Africa, disregarding the fact that external colonialism leaves Africa at a huge material disadvantage. By idealizing the "first world," they delegitimize African Indigenous ways of existing and legitimize internal colonialism's particularized modes of control that enable the "first world" to be reproduced. By validating and reproducing "first world" knowledge, centralized education systems in Africa maintain colonial power structures. Though centralized education proponents may argue that it enables a standardization of knowledge throughout the continent that can be helpful in unifying states against conflict, this study contends that a curriculum cannot be unifying if it serves to maintain colonial hierarchies. According to these terms, unification becomes a call for decolonization—and unity in the face of colonialism and oppression.

In thinking past colonially established borders and toward a decolonized unification of Africa, it is important to remain critical of the factors that might motivate African unity. As Dei (2014) states, the New Economic Partnership for African Development (NEPAD) has "sought to encourage good governance and regional cooperation and coordination" (p. 7). However, this pursuit seeks unity on the basis of economic flourishing (p. 7), a pursuit that cannot be dissociated from its neoliberal and capitalist motives. "Capitalism and the state are technologies of colonialism, developed over time to further colonial projects" (Tuck & Yang, 2012). Stromquist (2008) writes that global economic competition "shifts educational systems toward increasing rates of productivity but does not encourage solidarity across groups" (p. 23). What are the possibilities for regional cooperation and coordination that transcend colonial constructs? How might we decolonize structures that have been developed by colonialism?

It is difficult to contest colonial boundaries in the name of a unified Africa and to extrapolate what is meant by "African" culture without essentializing its complexities (Zeleza, 2005) or resorting to a type of colonialism that seeks to define that which is authentically African and "real" in order for it to be consumed and controlled. However, "the fact that something was socially constructed—virtually every aspect of human life since we evolved from the hominids—or invented elsewhere does not mean it is not 'real'" (Zeleza, 2005, p. 15). For this reason, as I push for us an imagining of Africa beyond its colonially defined borders, I seek the homogeneity of Pan-Africanism through a decentralization of governance that values local realities, customs, and beliefs, but that does not deny the way in which African identities have been influenced by colonialism. I believe that it is possible to achieve this by decolonizing (and thus not seeking to control) education, moving away from a centralized governing body that privileges standardization, homogenization, and westernization (Dei, 2014) and toward a reverence for Indigenous ways of thinking and being in the past, present, and future. The goal here is not to eradicate personal ties to national identities but rather to decenter the dominant colonial narrative/national educational curricula in order for populations to construct their identities in relation to their local and Indigenous ways of knowing and being, instead of through the systems of control propagated by governments. Thus, it is not a harmonization of colonial and Indigenous ways of thinking and being that is sought; rather, it is decolonization in recognition of colonialism's inability to coexist with Indigeneity.

Education to Standardize Colonization

While it is presumed that universal, standardized education will lift Africa out of its "underdeveloped" state (Samoff, 1993, pp. 181, 183), this assumption legitimizes centralized education systems that serve as tools for colonization and control. Colonization's impact on African education systems has not diminished since Independence (Brown, 2000). Curricula continue to delegitimize Indigenous African knowledge and culture in favor of pro-western subjects, ways of teaching, learning, and being, that are devoid of spirituality and harmony with the environment (Adjei, 2014; Yakubu, 1994). Many Africans have internalized a belief in the superiority of the western education system as a result of their colonizing experiences within it (Sicherman, 1995). They have come to believe in the superiority of their colonizers, their oppressors (see Fanon, 1952; Freire, 1970). It is assumed that "the West knows best" because it has achieved a level of "sophistication" that Africa, stuck in the backwardness of its traditions, has not (Dei, 2014). This belief legitimizes a relationship of dependency between the western imperial savior and Africa. It infantilizes Africa and glorifies the West and the ways in which it has developed, disregarding the fact that the West has done so not through its superior education systems and governments but through its exploitation of Africa (Dei, 1993).

The research that is used to legitimize the propagation of the euro-western, "first-world" education model adheres to a colonial understanding of "development." It assumes that Africa must "develop" and that it cannot do so without the foreign assistance required to rehabilitate its education systems (Samoff, 1993). It is perceived as reliable and scientifically accurate and thus is used to inform the implementation of educational policies that are funded through conditional loans that are received as foreign "assistance." Research is hugely problematic in policymaking because it is too broad, incomplete, and short-sighted, relying on generalizations and assumptions about the existing political, economic, and social realities of a place (Psacharopoulos, 1989; Samoff, 1993). The preferences and interests of the local people cannot be fully considered. The biases (for example, the language, the methodologies, and the criteria taken for granted) of the researchers, seeking the approval of whoever is funding them, construct the way in which research is undertaken (Samoff, 1993). Researchers cannot be dissociated from the political agenda that guides them, and yet their findings are often uncritically accepted as scientific.

Once these kinds of problematic studies become legitimized and disseminated through institutions such as the World Bank, they become "guides-to" subsequent research, as Samoff (1993) argues. Research assumes that the linear-rational way of thinking is the only accurate way to problem-solve (Shizha, 2005, p. 81). Parading itself as such, it naturalizes the way in which it marginalizes other forms of knowledge and problem-solving, denying Africans the status of "rational and historical" human beings (Hume & Hegel, cited in Shizha, 2005; see also Wynter, 2003) by delegitimizing their truths and histories through hegemonic knowledge emission. While Samoff and Psacharopoulos advocate for policymakers to focus on the documentation of cause-and-effect relationships (Psacharopoulos, cited in Samoff, 1993), I contend that this is not a solution if it preserves the power dynamics of the status quo. Research does not merit being legitimized and prioritized over other forms of knowledge simply on account of its being "scientific" (consider Dei, 1993, p. 99). As Aman Sium (2014) so poignantly writes:

> It's under the guise of research that Westerners often seek to locate, extract, and re-package Indigenous African knowledges for Western consumption. It's under the guise of research that many scholars have built their careers, attained grants, secured tenure, published, and debated the fate of Africa

> from distant university classrooms and conference tables. It's under the guise of research that the West turns its soldiers of development loose on the continent, many of whom arrive with an ideological backpack filled with racist assumptions and misconceptions. (p. 63)

Research seeks to implement static change within ever-changing social, political, and economic climates that it can neither control nor predict. Yet when implemented policies do not produce the intended result, the unpredictability of the environment is often blamed. Then, a new cause for the given problem can be established through research and be marketed as the absolute truth until all stakeholders are convinced. Countries that seek to "develop" can then take out loans with the World Bank or the International Monetary Fund and accumulate debt, as the policies implemented do not fulfill their intended purposes once again. At this point, the donor countries can simply accuse their loan recipients of poor governance, corruption, or mismanagement of funds, absolving themselves of responsibility despite their participation in implementing these problematic policies in the first place (Sachs, 1980, p. 41; Sium, 2014). In this way, the loan recipients are portrayed as barbaric and untrustworthy, while the West admonishes itself for having trusted them in the first place. Claiming that the poorest countries are to blame for their poverty allows western nations to easily deny their complicity in this poverty (Sachs, 1980, p. 44), and the same can be said for education (Shizha, 2014, p. 113). As Joel Samoff (1993) has remarked: "Just as poverty is explained by the characteristics and (in)abilities of the poor, so the explanations of problems of African education are to be found within and around African schools" (p. 211). In this way, a relationship of dependency is maintained in which African countries must rely on western support in order to "develop" and to attain the "global" standards set by the West through research and propaganda. Thus, comparisons and findings rooted in research and "made true" by modern science must be critically considered: crucially, the "value-neutral" approach that research claims—that science claims—serves to deflect political and ethical critiques (Whitt, cited in Shizha, 2014). It is thus crucial to be critical of the ways in which—and the reasons why—certain knowledges are legitimized above others in political spheres. Their dominance cannot be detached from discourses of power (Foucault, 1972).

Education/Policies for Whom?

While it was believed during the colonial occupation of Africa that eurocentric schooling would "civilize" Africans (Sicherman, 1995; Shizha, 2005), this view has continued to be held since Independence. It has simply taken on a new shape. The United Nations Educational, Scientific and Cultural Organization's (UNESCO) "Education for All" World Conferences of 1990 and 2000, which were held in Jomtien, Thailand, and

Dakar, Senegal, respectively, and sponsored by the World Bank, the United Nations Development Program, and the United Nations Children's Fund, saw educators and political leaders from around the globe commit to achieving universal, quality, basic education for all, thereby confirming education as a basic human right. The educational goals that garnered legitimacy during these conferences are laden with western values and colonial understandings about what counts as education and what counts as knowledge. For instance, it was determined that education must be conducted in institutions in order to be considered legitimate; that knowledge is quantifiable; that literacy consists of reading and writing. By committing to implementing the western education model, countries agreed to be held accountable for achieving the educational goals defined by UNESCO, whose Institute for Statistics would conduct research to ensure their progress (UNESCO, 2017). The "Education for All" conferences established that dispensing knowledge was to be the official responsibility of centralized governments, thereby delegitimizing informal, Indigenous ways of teaching and learning. Crucially, non-western nations formally accepted that "education" be defined according to colonial terms and to euro-western values and beliefs, thus delegitimizing Indigenous ways of knowing and being.

What consists of knowledge, whose knowledge counts, and how it is to be taught are thus matters of politics (Shizha, 2014). As Foucault (1972) argues, the validation of certain knowledges over others cannot be detached from the politics of power and control. In this light, the politics surrounding "Education for All" and its dissemination of a particular understanding of education must be seriously interrogated. Who benefits from defining what counts as education (and as curriculum)? Is the promotion of a particular definition of education a form of cultural imperialism? How does the centralization of education dissemination benefit them? How can we make sense of the power relations that drive compulsory schooling in post-Independence settings?

Weberian scholars have argued that compulsory schooling serves to create a body of citizens who identify with (and are loyal to) their territorial nation-state and who are respectful of the state's authority (Mundy, 2008, p. 51). In this way, compulsory education in Africa during the colonial period served to secure compliance with colonial governance and to instill in African students reverence for their colonizers. Similarly, schooling after Independence served to instill students with respect for the newly established nation-states of which they were suddenly citizens. Expanded access to schooling was popularized as both a "premise and promise" of nationalist movements (Samoff, 1993, p. 184; see also Psacharopolous, 1989; Mundy, 2008). Compulsory education serves centralized governments by enabling them to maintain power and control over their citizens and to "consolidate territorial sovereignty and enhance their legitimacy within the international community of states" (p. 52). This is revelatory of what might entice a government to strive for "Education for All": it serves to organize a population, to establish alliances with other centralized governing forces, and to maintain a relationship of dependency between the global North and South.

To achieve universal education within their states, governments must implement educational policies. These generally do not have their intended effect, however, as they are poorly implemented or not implemented at all, as Psacharopoulos (1989) explores. By means of an examination of educational policies implemented in Zambia, Uganda, Ethiopia, Kenya, Botswana, Tanzania, and Swaziland, he maintains that educational targets, whether they pertain to increased coverage (p. 181), quality improvement (p. 182), combining education with production (p. 183), curriculum diversification (p. 184), better links to employment (p. 185), or vocational education (p. 186), tend not to work for reasons related to their implementation and their incompatibility with the environments for which they are designed. A primary reason for this is that the policy was never implemented in the first place; it was too vague to be implemented (as in "the quality of education must be improved"). Also, it was only partially implemented, or it never achieved the critical mass necessary for it to make an impact and was thus rejected by locals, or its infeasibility was ignored from the beginning (p. 190). Finally, it was implemented but had no effect; it was poorly conceived or based on insufficient or inadequate information (p. 190). Educational policies are by nature limited and limiting. Their attempts to control educational outcomes highlight the fact that their understanding of education is not holistic.

These educational policies often do not account for the lived realities of the school system—for example, the scarcity of resources, teachers, or infrastructure. The promotion of access over quality and content continues to mask the inequities that persist in schools (Farag, 2013; Stromquist, 2008; Unterhalter, 2008). Simply striving to make schooling accessible, available, acceptable, and adaptable (Tomasveski's "4 As," cited in Manion & Menashy, 2013) does not contest the power inequities that persist within the system. In my experience, mandatory, universal education can have disastrous consequences when the countries implementing it do not have the necessary infrastructure to accommodate it. In Uganda, teachers lack resources. A primary school teacher might be responsible for more than 100 children in a single classroom, who are moved from grade to grade regardless of their level of achievement because there is simply not enough room for them to be kept back. The students are not learning. Their education is not free because the school must charge fees to stay afloat. School is a waste of their time and resources and is culturally and locally irrelevant to their realities and Indigenous knowledges. However, the belief in the importance of schooling has been deeply internalized by the population, and the research undertaken by the West that "proves" the benefits of schooling continues to inform educational projects. What purpose and whom do these educational policies serve if they are consistently crafted for personal or political gain, only to be discarded or unfulfilled? Who is benefiting from this research? Is this how education should be defined and determined? Who benefits from these promises if those for whom they are crafted are not experiencing their results? Who should be held accountable for the failed implementation of these educational policies—those who conduct the research for them or those who implement them? The imperialists or those who continue to allow their minds to be colonized? How should "basic," "quality," "universal" education be defined and by whom? Can "quality education" be achieved if it is implemented from a centralized source that cannot possibly account for all the complexities and diversities of its vast population (one possibly constituted according to arbitrarily defined borders)?

Universalized Education

It has become accepted that standardized education offers a universal solution to poverty. Yet this belief denies the way in which hierarchies are systematically maintained through the school system: there is a reason why the most powerful Africans continue to promote a system that is failing the masses. The schooling systems inherited by African governments after independence were and continue to be largely controlled by the elite (Shizha, 2014, p. 114), who were themselves educated within these imported European systems. The knowledge that is valued in these systems hails from euro-western cultural imperialism: "through schooling and its cultural hegemony, Africans became willing accomplices and co-constructors of [this imperialism]" (Shizha, 2005, p. 68). These school systems are thus not rooted in the African sense of self, culture, or collective (Dei, 2014, p. 168), but rather serve to reproduce the colonial mentality and hierarchies, to maintain the status quo. To attempt their dismantling challenges the authority of the most powerful elite. Thus, the students with the least power are those most alienated by the school system (Shizha, 2014), and yet it is expected that they can develop skills for wealth creation to compete with the elite (Alderuccio, 2010), whom the system is designed to benefit. To what extent can education serve to alleviate poverty if it continues to be controlled by the elite and their relations with western hegemonic forces?

As Alderuccio (2010) explains, current trends in education are concerned not only with economic (and rural) development but also with "improving the quality of education by increasing the relevance and reducing urban/rural disparities" (p. 738). The author discusses ways in which Mozambique has undertaken the task of localizing curricula in accordance with the socioeconomic and political backgrounds of locals, their aspirations, expectations, and histories (p. 736), while maintaining a focus on economic development. While she recognizes the need for a curriculum to reflect the diverse realities and interests of its students, she assumes that these can be accounted for within a well-rounded, thoughtfully designed curriculum that is responsibly and ethically implemented. I, on the other hand, am reluctant to accept this view, as I believe that a standardized curriculum cannot inherently account for the diversity of its population, and that as long as a curriculum is structured around economic development and other neoliberal pursuits, it cannot reflect the Indigenous values of its population.

The decentralization of education requires a radical dismantling of the systems that center and re-center colonial western knowledge as dominant, and that delegitimize other ways of knowing and being in the process. This chapter argues that this cannot be achieved through an "Africanization" of an inequitable, faulty system. However, the decentralization of education has become a trend in international policymaking that assumes that decentralization can be achieved within the systems that maintain current power relations. In recent publications such as *Education Decentralization in Africa: A Review of Recent Policy and Practice*, by Winkler and Gershberg (2003), and *Directions in Development: Decentralization of Education: Legal Issues*, by Florestal and Cooper (1997), the World Bank has argued in favor of the decentralization of education. In line with its economic vocabulary, it equates "decentralization" with "privatization" (Winkler & Gershberg, 2003) and suggests that the "rationale for education decentralization involves improving efficiency, effectiveness and democracy" (p. xv; see also Manion & Menashy, 2013). These authors discuss how the privatization of education is problematic when local bodies do not have the necessary funding (or the capacity to raise it) to support their schools (p. 3). The World Bank has taken the liberty of defining what "basic education" consists of, and because "the responsibility of providing basic education is firmly written into the law in nearly all countries" (Florestal & Cooper, 1997, p. vii), countries have sought to establish this "basic education" throughout their nations. Predictably, many African countries lack the infrastructure to universally implement the western education system and as a result must take out loans with the World Bank in order to accomplish this.

In the name of decentralizing education, the World Bank has formally asserted its willingness to delegate some power in the education department. Yet it remains concerned about the ways in which it might monitor the amount of formal control granted to local bodies (Winkler & Gershberg, 2003, pp. 4–5). This reveals that the World Bank has no desire to define the "decentralization" of education as the "decentralization" of its own power. It does not seek to lessen its stranglehold on Africa. Education decentralization cannot be achieved as long as the World Bank and other centralized governing forces seek to define and control education on behalf of Indigenous peoples (through research, funding, or other forms of manipulation). The World Bank's advocacy of decentralization is in many ways oxymoronic: as Manion and Menashy (2013) point out, its pursuit of social justice is limited by an "economic-instrumentalist rationale" that prioritizes human economic productivity over human rights and well-being. The World Bank defines *education* in monetary terms and thus stands in direct contrast to Indigenous values.

Conclusion

The nationalized, centralized transmission of knowledge in Africa validates colonial truths that maintain oppression and perpetuate imperialism. This chapter has interrogated technologies of colonialism and strategies of citizen control and has pointed out their pervasiveness. It has asked the reader to consider a definition of *education* that is not limited by western hegemony and truths, that does not require legitimization by colonizing systems in order to be considered valid. How might education be conceived of in decolonizing terms? Who should have the power to determine this? This chapter has not sought to answer these questions. While I may interrogate the oppressive structures that implicate me in their violence, it is not my place as a white, colonizing woman to define what the decentralization and decolonization of education in Africa looks like on behalf of Indigenous peoples. I speak against these structures while I benefit from them.

Education in Africa should not work to benefit the West or its allies, but should instead be defined locally by and for Africans. It should work not to sustain oppressive power relations or to seek the homogenization and standardization of its peoples, but to sustain and empower Africans in their Indigeneity, spirituality, and environments (Dei, 1993). As Foucault (1998) writes, "discourse transmits and produces power; it reinforces it, but also undermines and exposes it, renders it fragile and makes it possible to thwart" (pp. 100–101). While it is through colonial knowledge and power that injustices have been perpetrated, it is through a decentering and decentralization of knowledge that they can be combated.

Notes

1. Tuck and Yang (2012) remind us that "white" and "whiteness" extend beyond phenotype; see also Fanon (1952).

References

Adeniran, I.A. (2014). Engendering an endogenous framework for socio-economic development in the ECOWAS sub-region. *Critical Sociology, 40*(2), 285–294.

Adjei, P.B. (2014). Toward an ontological and epistemological understanding of indigenous African process of conflicts and disputes mediations and settlements (CADMAS). In G.J.S. Dei & P. Adjei (Eds.), *Emerging perspectives on "African development": Speaking differently* (pp. 38–62). New York, NY: Peter Lang.

Alderuccio, M.C. (2010). An investigation of global/local dynamics of curriculum transformation in Sub-Saharan Africa with special reference to the Republic of Mozambique. *Compare: A Journal of Comparative and International Education, 4*(6), 727–739.

Brown, D. (2000). Democracy, colonization and human sub-capital in Sub-Saharan Africa. *Studies in Comparative International Development, 35*(1), 20–40.

Dei, G.J.S. (1993). Sustainable development in the African context: Revisiting some theoretical and methodological issues. *African Development, 18*(2), 97–110.

Dei, G.J.S. (2014). Indigenizing the school curriculum: The case of the African university. In G. Emeagwali & G.J.S. Dei (Eds.), *African indigenous knowledge and the disciplines* (pp.165–180). Boston, MA: Sense Publishers.

Fanon, F. (1952). *Peau noire, masques blancs [Black skin, white masks]*. Paris, France: Éditions du Seuil.

Farag, A.I. (2013). Does education work? Perspectives on semi-nomadic girls' education in some selected areas of Sudan. In H. Holmarsdottir, V. Nomlomo, A.I. Farag, & Z. Desai (Eds.), *Gendered voices: Reflections on gender and education in South Africa and Sudan* (pp. 77–98). Boston, MA: Sense Publishers.

Florestal, K., & Cooper, R. (1997). *Directions in development: Decentralization of education*. Washington, DC: The World Bank.

Foucault, M. (1972). *Archeology of knowledge and the discourse on language*. New York, NY: Pantheon Books.

Foucault, M. (1991). *Discipline and punish: The birth of a prison*. London, UK: Penguin Books.

Foucault, M. (1998). *The history of sexuality: The will to knowledge*. London, UK: Penguin Books.

Freire, P. (1970). *Pedagogy of the oppressed*. New York, NY: Seabury Press.

Herbst, G. (1989). The creation and maintenance of national boundaries in Africa. *International Organization, 43*(4), 673–692.

Manion, C., & Menashy, F. (2013). The prospects and challenges of reforming the World Bank's approach to gender and education: Exploring the value of the capability policy model in the Gambia. *Journal of Human Development and Capabilities, 14*(2), 214–240.

Mundy, K. (2008). "Education for all": Africa and the comparative sociology of schooling. In K. Mundy, K. Bickmore, R. Hayhoe, M. Madden, & K. Madjiji (Eds.), *Comparative and international education: Issues for teachers*. Toronto, ON: Canadian Scholars Press.

Olutayo, A.O. (2012). "Verstehen," everyday sociology and development: Incorporating African indigenous knowledge. *Critical Sociology, 40*(2), 229–238.

Psacharopoulos, G. (1989). Why educational reforms fail: A comparative analysis. *International Review of Education, 35*(2), 179–195.

Sachs, J. (1980, August 14). Sachs on development: Helping the world's poor. *The Economist*, pp. 39–47.

Samoff, J. (1993). The reconstruction of schooling in Africa. *Comparative Education Review, 37*(2), 181–222.

Shizha, E. (2005). Reclaiming our memories: The education dilemma in postcolonial African school curricula. In A. Abdi & A. Cleghorn (Eds.), *Issues in African education: Sociological perspectives* (pp. 65–84). New York, NY: Palgrave Macmillan.

Shizha, E. (2014). Indigenous knowledge systems and the curriculum. In G. Emeagwali & G.J.S. Dei (Eds.), *African indigenous knowledge and the disciplines* (pp. 113–129). Boston, MA: Sense Publishers.

Sicherman, C. (1995). Ngugi's colonial education: The subversion of the African mind. *African Studies Review, 38*(3), 11–41.

Sium, A. (2014). Dreaming beyond the state: Centering indigenous governance as a framework for African development. In G.J.S. Dei & P. Adjei (Eds.), *Emerging perspectives on African development: Speaking differently* (pp. 63–82). New York, NY: Peter Lang.

Stromquist, N. (2008). The intersection of public policies and gender: Understanding state action in education. In M.A. Maslak (Ed.), *The structure and agency of women's education* (pp. 3–30). Albany, NY: State University of New York Press.

Tuck, E., & Yang, K.W. (2012). Decolonization is not a metaphor. *Decolonization: Indigeneity, Education & Society, 1*(1), 1–40.

UNESCO. (2017). *Education for All goals*. Retrieved from: http://www.unesco.org/new/en/education/themes/leading- the-international-agenda/education-for-all/

Unterhalter, E. (2008). *Gender, schooling and global social justice.* London, UK: Routledge.

Winkler, D.R., & Gershberg, A.I. (2003). *Education decentralization in Africa: A review of recent policy and practice.* Washington, DC: The World Bank.

Wynter, S. (2003). Unsettling the coloniality of being/power/truth/freedom: Towards the human, after man, its overrepresentation—An argument. *CR: The New Centennial Review, 3*(3), 257–337.

Yakubu, J.M. (1994). Integration of indigenous thought and practice with science and technology: A case study of Ghana. *International Journal of Science Education, 16*(3), 343–360.

Zeleza, P.T. (2005). Transnational education and African universities. *Journal of Higher Education of Africa, 3*(1), 1–28.

CHAPTER 8

The Role of English Education in Post-Colonial Egypt: Criticisms and Solutions for the Future

Hagger Said

THE YEAR IS 2006. A class of eighth-grade girls is being introduced to *Jane Eyre,* by Charlotte Brontë. We will learn about a locked-up crazy woman, a rich European man, and romance. *This book is wonderful,* we are told by our English teacher. She surveys the classroom, her face bright in anticipation. The rest of the class is unreadable, except for a select few whose grasp of the English language is stronger than that of the others. She promises us that it will be very interesting. That piques our interest. But it is not the kind of interest that keeps you awake at night, yearning for another great narrative, but almost a relief that this next book will somehow be easier to remember amid an abundance of other information that must be memorized for midterm exams.

That night, over dinner, I tell my mother that I will be reading *Jane Eyre.* She recalls the book. She tells me she read it in high school in Sudan, at the best private Catholic school in all of Khartoum (at the time). My mother does not remember having read anything but the classics in English class. English existed beyond the local, past the continent of Africa, resting in the ballrooms of Northanger Abbey and in the howling of King Lear, but never on the faces of the students in the classroom or in the local fables that were spoken to my mother by family and tribal elders.

According to George Lamming, "over three quarters of the contemporary world has been directly and profoundly affected by imperialism and colonialism" (as cited in Ashcroft, Griffiths, & Tiffin, 2006, p. 99). Historically, "educational institutions were used to [help legitimize Britain's colonial rule] and maintain its power" (Abu-Shomar, 2013c, p. 265). Abu-Shomar (2013c), Dei (2014), and Shizha (2014) argue that educational institutions in contemporary postcolonial-countries "largely [continue] to entail such ideologies" (Mulenga, 2008, in Abu-Shomar, 2013c, p. 265). In recalling my experiences as a middle school student in one of Cairo's many private schools, I am reminded of the global reach of canonical English texts. Their presence in many English classrooms in post-colonial African countries such as Egypt speaks to the on-going cultural influence of Britain in Egypt's educational system. The centralization of classical English texts in my school (in particular) and more broadly, in more private, top-tier schools—both historically through colonialism, and currently through globalization—has not only managed to invalidate and marginalize the English literary works of affluent and relevant Indigenous writers, but continues to pose a problem of cultural and linguistic relevance for Egyptian students.

School systems in Africa experience challenges that are a legacy of colonial education (Shizha, 2013). For Dei (2014), the particular challenge is social, cultural, and economic relevance. In conceptualizing the purpose of education, El-Mowafy (1983, cited in Zughoul, 1987), states:

> A university exists primarily to serve the community . . . help solve problems posed by the society of which it is a part. A department of English . . . does not exist to serve the needs of either the English language or English literatures. These needs are well looked after elsewhere. (p. 226)

Although El-Mowafy (1983) is referring to postsecondary education, English departments in secondary schools are expected to familiarize students with the classics in order to be culturally enriched in ways that aim to dignify them. Unfortunately, this results in a growing number of disengaged youth, forced to consume a body of literature alien to their experiences, reminding them that neither their culture nor experiences are worthy of academic study (Dei, 2014; Dei, James, Karumanchery, James-Wilson, & Zine, 2000).

Situating Myself: Subjective Memory and Storytelling as a Form of Knowledge

Despite political independence, "colonial legacies still perpetuate the regulation and dissemination of particular forms of knowledge" (Abu-Shomar, 2013a, p. 71). The historical relationship between the global North and South—for example, the former as receptacle of knowledge and the latter as disseminator—continues to influence *the language of instruction, curricula, and research* in academic spheres (Teferra & Greijun, 2010, p. 1, as cited in Akalu, 2016, p. 223). Historically, western academia, under the guise of *research* or *objectivity*, has been "implicated in the worst excesses of colonialism" (Smith, 1999, p. 1). According to Dei (2017), "it contributes to the continuing anti-indigenization of social spaces that suggest the possibility of objectivity of knowledge" (Dei, 2017, p. 1). Objectivity, in the western academe, has traditionally been praised for its ability to escape personal biases, cultural beliefs, feelings, and attitudes, eliminating the subjective from its field of study. Examples of this include "whites routinely traveling to Africa … to study them [objectively] … and [returning] with blended and sometimes mutilated narratives, which immediately receive acclaim among their peers in the west" (Baffoe, Asimeng-Boateng, & Ogbuagu, 2014, p. 28).

As justification for the superiority of western knowledges, Smith (1999) and Achebe (1975, in Okpewho, 2003) make a case for countering the colonizers' knowledge. Adopting the subjective as a form of knowledge, while "appropriating the language of the colonizer" (Smith, 1999, p. 36), is a form of resistance against "westocentric" (Dei, 2017, p.1) epistemologies. Thus, I approach my research subjectively, centering myself in how I make sense of my experiences in a post-colonial education system in Egypt.

Smith (1999), Baffoe et al. (2014), and Absolon and Willett (2005) are critical of the neutrality of western objectivity in research. For Absolon and Willett (2005), "objectivity does not exist in research since all research is conducted and observed through human epistemological lenses" (p. 97). Due to its historical use as justification for the superiority of western knowledges, Smith (1999) and Achebe (1959) make a case for countering the colonizers' knowledge "by appropriating the language of the colonizer as the language of the colonized" (Smith, 1999, p. 36)—in other words, resisting through counter-narratives in the colonizer's own language. In choosing to resist "westocentric" (Dei, 2017, p. 1) epistemologies, I approach my research subjectively, centering myself on how I make sense of my own experiences in a post-colonial education system in Egypt.

I choose to situate myself in this manner because it allows me to account for my own positionality (Owens, 2002; Said, 1994; Tierney, 2002, as cited in Absolon & Willett, 2005, p. 97). Thus, any implicit biases, experiential limitations, or otherwise will not mask as objective. I come to this research as an African Canadian woman, an educator, a storyteller, and a resistor of eurocentric hegemony.

My interest in education, particularly English education in a post-colonial country like Egypt, stems from my own experiences as a student in a private school in Cairo. In my ongoing push for social justice, I use storytelling and oral communication as a form of knowledge. According to Abu-Shomar (2016), "narrative and storytelling, is an emancipatory approach" (p. 303) "associated with … the growing frustration over the problem of the "disappearing individual in social research" (Whittemore et al., 1986, cited in Abu-Shomar, 2016, p. 303). Narratives, via storytelling, for marginalized groups, is a way to understand the lived experience of the storyteller (Smith, 1999), highlight their agency, and limit the power of qualitative data and textual research in the creation of much of our globally recognized forms of knowledge.

Pedagogical Framework

My goal is to critique the limitations of a highly eurocentric curriculum through alternative pedagogical frameworks in order to highlight the growing disparity between what is taught in schools and its relevance and benefit to the lives of students. I draw on two pedagogical frameworks: first, *culturally relevant pedagogy*, and second, *Afrocentricity*. When combined, they serve to center the African by making education relevant and meaningful. Culturally relevant teaching, popularized by American pedagogical theorist Dr. Gloria Ladson-Billings, is a framework that takes into consideration the cultural and diverse contexts in which learning takes place (Ladson-Billings, 2011). "Instead of perpetuating the lineage of European scholarship and practice, [culturally relevant pedagogy, in centering on] Indigenous education [will reflect] the lived experience and life situation of... students" (Dei, 2014, p. 171). Afrocentric education, in celebrating the African identity, is a form of resistance that equips the learner with the necessary tools to recognize and critique limitations of eurocentric education (Dei, 2014). These pedagogical frameworks will allow me to examine, with a critical eye, the effects of a heavily eurocentric curriculum in a post-colonial country such as Egypt and propose solutions for addressing issues stemming from the ongoing centralization, celebration, and reproduction of canonical texts in non-white, non-western spaces.

English Literature: A Tool of the Colonizer

One of the most poignant and powerful indicators of colonialism is the gradual centralization of the colonizer's language and literature in the social and academic spheres of the colonized. For scholars such as Ashcroft, Griffiths, and Tiffin (2006), Hamdi (2003), and Shizha (2014), "there is a clear link between colonial domination and the emphasis on teaching English literature" (Hamdi, 2003, p. 100).

Historically, the study of English has "always been a densely political and cultural phenomenon" centered on the classics (Ashcroft et al., 2006, p. 2). The classics, a body of literature forming much of the English canon had two purposes, "educate the common man in civilized English" (Johnston, 2001, para. 5) and "improve morality and instill ethical and cultural history" (Brauer & Clark, 2008, p. 296). "[The] teaching of English literature in the colonies must be understood as part of the many ways in which Western colonial powers such as Britain asserted their cultural and moral superiority while at the same time devaluing indigenous cultural products" (McLeod, 2000, p.140, cited in Abu-Shomar, 2013c, p. 287).

Although Eaglestone (2000) explores the role of English literature in colonial India, his critique of its purpose as a civilizing force can be applied to colonial Africa as well. He states:

> The literature of England was seen as a *mould* of the English way of life, morals, taste and the English way of doing things: why not teach Indians how to be more English by teaching them English literature? Studying English literature was seen as a way of "civilizing" the native population. (p. 11)

Like Ngũgĩ wa Thiong'o, "I…read simplified versions of Dickens" (wa Thiong'o, 1994, p. 12) as well as several Shakespearean plays. My exposure to these canonical works at a young age meant that I was culturally enriched and able to converse with like-minded, Anglo-educated Egyptians of a higher socioeconomic class. After all, what better way to indicate your level of education than to speak English and familiarize yourself with the classics?

Knowledge of the canon as indicative of higher learning also exists in countries such as Canada. "Despite a more inclusive English curriculum, the hallmark of a secondary English education—particularly at the advanced levels—continues to be a eurocentric and Anglocentric curriculum" (Applebee, 1974, cited in Skerrett, 2010, p. 37). English teachers harken to "check off" (Nicol, 2008, p. 23) "higher status literature" (Au, 2009, p. 2) in order to prepare high school students for postsecondary study. In other words, "AP classes need to read the classics" (Au, 2009, p. 3) while "students in regular classes can read 'thug literature'" or "urban novels" (p. 3).

For Abu-Shomar (2016), English departments in the Middle East are still heavily reliant on the Anglo-American literary canon, thriving off their strictly exclusive English and American literature curricula (p. 300). "Any attempts to bring about change in such syllabuses, and opening the canon are often unsuccessful" (Abu-Shomar, 2013a, p. 80). "Amidst [an already] rigorous American and English literary canon…middle eastern educational institutions religiously adopt 'best works' represented by the classics of English literature" (Abu-Shomar, 2012, cited in Abu-Shomar, 2013c, p. 288; see also Balzer, 2006; Hall, 2005; Zughoul, 2003), thus posing a problem of relevance (Dei, 2014) and of class by reproducing and centering narratives that have historically been used to culturally and linguistically colonize and civilize indigenous and minority populations.

Alienation, Erasure, or Assimilation: Results of a Homogenized Reading List

In "the constant onslaught of a globalised western educational [and] cultural hegemony, Arab identity and culture are in great danger of being placed under complete erasure" (Hamdi, 2003, p. 99). For Dei et al. (2000), extensive practice of eurocentrism results in subtle and overt forms of oppression for those who cannot identify with the status quo. It either "erases the social, cultural, historical and political realities of non-white, non-western groups in society" (p. 171) or "positions them as different" (McLaren, 1998, p. 20). Students unable to see themselves reflected in the curriculum experience feelings of erasure (Maher & Tetreault, 2001) due to their inability to see their identities and realities reflected back at them—for example, the feeling of looking into a mirror and seeing "nothing" (Adrienne Rich, cited in Maher & Tetreault, 2001, p. 20).

Cultural Assimilation

During my middle school years (in Egypt), I was not exposed to any non-white authors in my English class that could allow me to see English literature as anything but inherently British. "I've been reading Shakespeare since age ten," I boast to my peers in high school and can recall the first classical text I ever read, *The Tempest,* and after that *A Midsummer Night's Dream,* and after that *The Taming of the Shrew.* It was only late into my undergraduate program (in Canada) that I begin to rethink my understanding of English literature.

Shakespeare's plays are recognized globally (Colarusso, 2009) and studied in many universities and schools throughout Britain and the post-colonial world (Johnston, 2001), making him perhaps the greatest writer known to man (Bloom, 1994). Salomone and Davis (1997) write:

> Of all the world's writers, none has received more attention than Shakespeare. Only the Bible is available in more languages. No other writer has had a larger body of critical works generated about his writings. (p. xi)

The belief in Shakespeare's adaptability to all generations and cultural experiences (Gibson, 1998) is an example of how western narratives are heavily normalized and universalized. After all, his plays are "recognizable and familiar, if not in students' real life experience, then in 'felt' knowledge" (Gibson, 1998, p. 2). Gibson (1998) believes that "students of all ages can recognize and identify with such relationships" (p. 2) as those in *Romeo and Juliet* and *A Midsummer Night's Dream.* The centralization of Shakespearean texts in my middle school years (in Egypt) represented, in some way or another, what my teachers considered to be "the best uses of the language to date, and therefore an appropriate model for students to revere, if not to aspire to" (Hall, 2005, p. 11). "With the belief that the classics [hold] everlasting aesthetic, rhetorical, and moral values" (Abu-Shomar, 2013a, p. 72), "the principle of universality in Western literature... denies the cultural identity of... oppressed nations" (Sadiq, 2007, cited in Abu-Shomar, 2013a, p. 72) "by muting the voices of those on the margins from being heard" (Abu-Shomar, 2016, p. 286).

According to Abdi and Cleghorn (2005), "colonial education did more than corrupt the thinking and sensibilities of the Africans; it filled their minds with abnormal complexes, which de-Africanized and alienated them from their socio-cultural milieu" (p. 69). Mukherjee (1982, cited in Zughoul, 1987) argues that "the constant reading of books that relate to another society's culture with very little exposure to one's own" (p. 233) reaches a point where "the student begins to assume what they read is the norm in contrast to their own culture, which gradually starts to become foreign" (in Zughoul, 1987, p. 233). For example, consider the Egyptian student reading *Romeo and Juliet,* a story about young people who fall in love and rebel by running away from their parents. Celebrated as youthful passion in the West, the Egyptian student, in his or her internalization of western culture, may begin to view this understanding of love as more *progressive* and *humane* thanks to the lengths to which the play has historically been used to humanize and universalize youthful expressions of love. The Egyptian might begin to criticize traditional courting practices in Egypt as being too constricting and oppressive, not because of the possible consequences of a more traditionally arranged marriage, but because it is not what western culture deems normal. Hence, the cultural dilemma is created when non-western students have internalized ideas about the world that will more than likely place them at odds with their own society.

Shizha (2005), in his article "Reclaiming Our Memories: The Education Dilemma in Postcolonial African School Curricula," asks: if we have already dichotomized east and west, good and bad, modern and traditional, why should we expect African youth to engage with Indigenous lifestyles and thinking when "all they see and hear on television and the internet is Western ways of life"? (p. 72). Egyptian children, in their increasing desire for "European art, language and culture" (Asante, 1991, p. 172) over Egyptian "art, language and culture" (p. 172), may begin to believe that "anything of European origin is inherently better than anything produced by or issuing from their own people" (p. 172). From what I recall, these sentiments have often been said by teachers and students alike, truly in their belief that *west is best.*

English Language as an Indicator of Good Schooling

In Sub-Saharan Africa, "curriculum content and pedagogy continues to be taught in a foreign culture...worldview (and) language that inhibits the learning experiences of students" (Shizha, 2013, p. 7). Shizha (2013) points the finger at education policymakers and African leaders who, in their "internalized western philosophical tenets" (p. 7), conduct almost all education in the same way in which they were taught themselves, through "foreign languages" (Abdi, 2014, p. 72).

The same can be said for privatized schools in Egypt. English is "still badly needed in the Arab world for the purposes of communicating with the world, education, acquiring technology, and development at large" (Zughoul, 2003, p.2, cited in Asqalan, Hijazi, & Al Natour, 2016, p. 381). "In fact, interest in teaching English language in Arab countries has been increasing" (Asqalan, Hijazi, & Al Natour, 2016, p. 381). "Most Arab countries [including Egypt] introduce English as a compulsory study subject at schools" (p. 381). The more money you pay for your private education, the greater the chances of being educated in a language other than Arabic. In an effort to compete in globalized labor markets and attract western investment, private Egyptian universities run their websites in English, give their universities foreign names—for example, German University or Futures University—and secondary schools rely more and more on English as a form of communication, even among their Egyptian peers.

I think of Ngũgĩ wa Thiong'o (1994) when my older relatives compare educational backgrounds. There is a visible sense of pride in those who went to private, more foreign-sounding schools that had better facilities, the latest textbooks (in comparison to other schools), a cleaner environment, uniforms, and had students who spoke better English and considered themselves better taught. "English [became] the measure of intelligence... and learning (wa Thiong'o, 1994, p. 11). These attitudes trickled down to my parents' generation. My mother's American University of Cairo education was seen as clearly better than my father's Cairo University education. Canadian universities also recognized her degree before they recognized my father's. These ideologies linked to schooling continue to manifest themselves in a simple example of a family get-together where children and the post-secondary institutions they've attended are pitted against one other. I am constantly reminded of how privileged I am to be able to complete a master's degree at a nationally and globally recognized university. I am reminded how *limited* my cousins' possibilities are for the future as they complete undergraduate degrees in post-colonial countries, in contrast to my globally recognized one.

The English Language as a Tool for Social and Economic Mobility in Canada, Egypt, and Beyond

I overhear my parents arguing about the pronunciation of the word *water*. You must hide the *t* and stress the *r*, my father says. My mother refuses to accept this and reminds him that her way is the correct way. I quietly watch their playful banter. My father calls me over to judge between them and I take both sides. This annoys my father, who believes that some ways of pronouncing words are more correct than others. *You have to pronounce it the way the native English speakers do. Like the way Hagger does.*

My father believes there is a single correct way to speak English. Speak like them, he reminds us. My father's advice stems from his experiences as an immigrant and the kinds of social hardships that come with an English accent, a reminder that you are different. Hence, we were raised to *speak properly* and *enunciate* words and sentences correctly, while at the same time discouraged from speaking what society refers to as *ghetto talk*, a form of colloquial English steeped in socioeconomic and racialized dimensions of language and power, resulting in potentially negative consequences for already-marginalized Black Muslim youth.

Likewise, for the Egyptian, the English language is used as a means of upward mobility. For Zughoul (1987), "[the Egyptian's] incentives for the study of English are not intrinsic nor do they stem from his admiration of Western languages and culture to a point where he would like to be accepted as a member of these communities" (p. 225), but are used to access better jobs in burgeoning fields that compete on a global scale. However, in this desire to scale up the socioeconomic ladder, the belief that English is necessary for economic success can lead to a forced appreciation of a globalized language and a slow but gradual immersion into the language and culture of native English speakers, not realising that this immersion may bring about feelings of inferiority and gradual disconnect between one's local culture and language.

Solutions: Hopes for a More Culturally Relevant and Afrocentric Curriculum

Considering the power of language and the damage colonial languages have done in post-colonial, non-western, non-English environments, I am critical of the present and future role of English education and, in particular, English literature as a form of cultural and linguistic enrichment in the lives of Egyptian students. As I explore with a critical eye the consequences of a centralized British canon in Egyptian private schools, I am reminded of how limited and potentially alienating such a narrow selection of books has made me feel. For Jawad (1983), "it was justifiable to stick to English in the teaching of English literature... because the British were in full control" (cited in Zughoul, 1987, p. 233). Now, in a post-colonial African country like Egypt, "why should non native speakers bother to study English literature at all?" (Munro, 1983, cited in Zughoul, 1987, p. 226).

James Baldwin, a prominent writer and Black homosexual, writing in *The London Observer*, considered whether or not English could "bear the burden of [his] experience" (cited in Okpewho, 2003, p. 65). I ask myself where this kind of English fits into the social and cultural needs of a bustling North African country like Egypt—so foreign to the linguistic and sociocultural experiences of native Egyptians and yet so readily consumed by its people? I consider Achebe (1964) in these circumstances.

> Is it right that a man should abandon his mother tongue for someone else's? It looks like a dreadful betrayal and produces a guilty feeling. But for me there is no other choice. I have been given the language and I intend to use it. (p. 7)

In reimagining future possibilities, I believe that we must work with what we have and imagine what can take place. Considering the current universalization of the English language, I believe restricting its use to an external means of communication (with non-Arabic speakers) can be the first step to limiting the power of a once colonizing language. Acquired mainly through schooling, a shift in current educational practices would need to take place. While Ngũgĩ would advise us to shed English and recentralize one's local language, Achebe (1964) in wa Thiong'o (1994) considers the impact of the English language and proposes adopting said language as a way to speak back against the limitations of an Anglocentric English. For example, with regards to English literature, we can begin to adopt Afrocentric literature as a way to centralize and celebrate local and national writers. Afrocentric literature will allow African students to see themselves and their experiences reflected in the literature and instill a sense of cultural pride in their own African heritage, rather than their proximity to whiteness.

An immediate example of Afrocentric literature would be Achebe's *Things Fall Apart* (1959) because it centralizes the African. The English language used is distinctly Afrocentric. In recalling my middle school experiences in Egypt, I would have loved to read a simplified version of Al-Hakim's play *Fate of a Cockroach* (1966) and seen it performed in Arabic and English. It would have instilled in me a great appreciation for Egyptian literature. This play would also have been a wonderful example of a culturally relevant text.

Afrocentric literature and education, in celebrating the African identity becomes a "site of resistance… [equipping] the learner to ask questions about omissions, negations, devaluations, and absences from texts, pedagogies [and] instruction (Dei, 2014, p. 171). With English reduced to a means of communication, I believe we can create a new English, an Afrocentric English, one that is culturally relevant to the local, regional, and national North African community in Egypt. By losing its power through a culturally relevant and Afrocentric framework, English can slowly be pulled from the center to the margins, until its power is severally limited, and finally, no longer required for active participation in any facet of Egyptian life.

References

Abdi, A.A. (2014). Re-culturing de-cultured education for inclusive social development in Africa. In E. Shizha & A.A. Abdi (Eds.), *Indigenous discourses on knowledge and development in Africa* (pp. 63–77). London, UK: Routledge.

Abdi, A. A., & Cleghorn, A. (Eds.). (2005). *Issues in African education: Sociological perspectives.* New York: Palgrave Macmillan.

Absolon, K., & Willett, C. (2005). Putting ourselves forward: Location in aboriginal research. In L. Brown & S. Strega (Eds.), *Research as resistance: Critical, indigenous and anti-oppressive approaches* (pp. 97–126). Toronto, ON: Canadian Scholars' Press.

Abu-Shomar, A., and MacDonald, M. (2012). 'Dialogic Spaces': Diasporic negotiation of difference. *Journal of Post-colonial Cultures & Societies*, 3(3 & 4): 1–36.

Abu-Shomar, A. (2013a). The enduring hegemony of the English literary canon: Symptoms of the monopoly of power relations in academia. *Journal of Arts* (King Saud University), 25(3), 71–89.

Abu-Shomar, A. M. (2013b). The apparatus of ideology: A postcolonial reading of English literature; Considerations from "institutional literatures." *International Journal of Comparative Literature and Translation Studies, 1*(2), 17–32.

Abu-Shomar, A. (2013c). The Politics of Education and Critical Pedagogy: Considerations from the English Literary Tradition in 'Post-colonial' Academic Contexts. *Postcolonial Directions in Education, 2*(2), 263-313.

Abu-Shomar, A. (2016). Narrative protocols, dialogic imagination and identity contestation: A critique of a prescribed english literature curriculum. *Arab World English Journal, 7*(2), 299–315.

Achebe, C. (1959). *Things fall apart.* New York, NY: McDowell, Obolensky.

Akalu, G.A. (2016). Revitalising higher education in the age of globalisation: The African dilemma. In E. Shizha & L. Diallo (Eds.), *Africa in the age of globalisation: Perceptions, misperceptions and realities* (pp. 219–234). New York, NY: Routledge.

Al-Hakim, T. (2002). Fate of a Cockroach. In B. Jeyifo (Ed.), *Modern African Drama* (3–63). New York, NY: Norton.

Applebee, A. N. (1974). *Traditions and reform in the teaching of English: A history.* Urbana, IL: National Council of Teachers of English.

Asante, M. K. (1987). *The Afrocentric idea.* Philadelphia, PA: Temple University Press.

Asante, M.K. (1991). The Afrocentric idea in education. *Journal of Negro Education, 60*(2), 170–180.

Ashcroft, B., Griffiths, G., & Tiffin, H. (2002). *The empire writes back: Theory and practice in post-colonial literatures* (2nd ed). New York: Routledge.

Ashcroft, B., Griffiths, G., & Tiffin, H. (Eds.). (2006). *The post-colonial studies reader* (2nd ed.). New York, NY: Routledge, Taylor & Francis Group.

Asqalan, M. M, Hijazi, D., & Al Natour, A. (2016). Teaching large classess: What are the beliefs of Yarmouk University instructors?". *Arab World English Journal, 7*(2), 380–393.

Au, W. (Ed.). (2009). *Rethinking multicultural education: Teaching for racial and cultural justice.* Milwaukee, WI: Rethinking Schools.

Baffoe, M., Asimeng-Boateng, L., & Ogbuagu, B. (2014). Their way or no way: "Whiteness" as agent for marginalizing and silencing minority voices in academic research and publication. *European Journal of Sustainable Development, 3*(1), 13–32.

Balzer, G. (2006). Decolonizing the classroom: Reading aboriginal literature through the lenses of contemporary literary theories. PhD Thesis, University of Sakatchewan.

Bloom, H. (1994). *The Western canon: The books and xchool of the ages.* Harcourt Brace.

Brauer, L., & Clark, C.T. (2008). The trouble is English: Reframing English studies in secondary schools. *English Education, 40*(4), 293–313.

Colarusso, D.M. (2009). Teaching English in the global age: Cultural conversations. Unpublished Ph.D. dissertation, Department of Curriculum, Teaching and Learning, University of Toronto. Retrieved from http://hdl.handle.net/1807/18334

Daswani, C.J. (1982). English in India: The brown man's burden. In Narasimhaiah and Srinath (Eds.), *English: Its complementary role in India.* Mysore, India: Wesley Press.

Dei, G.J.S. (2014). Indigenizing the school curriculum. In G. Emeagwali & G.J.S. Dei (Eds.), *African indigenous knowledge and the disciplines* (pp. 165–180). Rotterdam, Netherlands: Sense Publishers.

Dei, G. J. S. (2017). Guidelines for final paper. SES1942: Modernization, Development and Education in African Contexts. University of Toronto.

Dei, G.J.S., James, I.M., Karumanchery, L.L., James-Wilson, S., & Zine, J. (2000). *Removing the margins: The challenges and possibilities of inclusive schooling.* Toronto, ON: Canadian Scholars' Press.

Eaglestone, R. (2000). *Doing English: A guide for literature students.* New York, NY: Routledge.

El-Mowafy, M. (1983). The philosophy of teaching foreign languages and literatures in Arab universities. In Dahiyyat and Ibrahim (Eds.), *Papers from the First Conference on the Problem of Teaching English Language and Literature at Arab Universities.* Amman, Jordan: University of Jordan.

Gibson, R. (1998). *Teaching Shakespeare.* Cambridge, UK: Cambridge University Press.

Hall, G. (2005). *Literature in language education: Research and practice in applied linguistics.* In C.N. Candlin & D. R. Hall. (Eds.), London, UK: Palgrave Macmillan.

Hamdi, T.K. (2003). Foreign literary studies and the identity of the postcolonial subject. *ARIEL: A Review of International English Literature, 34*(4), 99–112.

Jawad, T. (1983). "Some reconsiderations of the role played by English departments." In Dahiyyat and Ibrahim (Eds,). *Papers from the First Conference on the Problems of Teaching English Language and Literature at Arab Universities.* Amman, Jordan: University of Jordan.

Johnston, I. (2001). English language, arts, citizenship and national identity. *Canadian Social Studies, 35*(3). Retrieved from http://sites.educ.ualberta.ca/css/Css_35_3/AREnglish_language_arts.htm

Ladson-Billings, G. (2011). Asking the right questions: A research agenda for studying diversity in teacher education. In A. Ball & C. Tyson (Eds.), *Diversity in teacher education* (pp. 383–396). Lanham, MD: Rowman & Littlefield.

Leggo, C. (2001). Living in words, living in the world: Literature and identity. *English Quarterly Canada, 33*(1/2), 25–39.

Maher, F.A., & Tetreault, M.K.T. (2001). *The feminist classroom: Dynamics of gender, race, and privilege.* Lanham, MD: Rowman & Littlefield.

McLaren, P. (1998). *Life in schools: An introduction to critical pedagogy in the foundations of education* (3rd ed.). New York, NY: Addison Wesley Longman.

McLeod, J. (2000). *Beginning postcolonialism.* Manchester, UK: Manchester University Press.

Mukherjee, M. (1982). "Macauly's Imperishable Empire." In Narasimhaiah and Srinath (Eds.), *English: Its complementry role in India.* Mysore, India: The Wesley Press.

Mulenga, D. (2001). Mwalimu Julius Nyerere: A critical review of his contribution to adult education and postcolonialism. *International Journal of Lifelong Education, 20*(6), 446–470.

Munro, J. (1983). The decline and fall...and elevation of the man of letters in the teaching of English. In Dahiyyat and Ibrahim (Eds.), *Papers from the First Conference on the Problems of Teaching English Language and Literature at Arab Universities.* Amman, Jordan: University of Jordan.

Nicol, J.C. (2008). Questioning the canon: Issues surrounding the selection of literature for the high school English curriculum. *English Quarterly Canada, 38*(2), 22–28.

Okpewho, I. (Ed.). (2003). *Chinua Achebe's Things fall apart: A casebook.* New York, NY: Oxford University Press.

Ontario Ministry of Education. (2007). *The Ontario curriculum grades 9 and 10: English.* Retrieved from http://www.edu.gov.on.ca/eng/curriculum/secondary/english910currb.pdf

Ontario Ministry of Education. (2013). *Culturally responsive pedagogy: Towards equity and inclusivity in Ontario schools.* Capacity Building Series. Retrieved from http://www.edu.gov.on.ca/eng/literacynumeracy/inspire/research/CBS_ResponsivePedagogy.pdf

Owens, L. (2002). As if an Indian were really an Indian: Native voices and postcolonial theory. In G. M. Bataille (Ed.), *Native American representations: First encounters, distorted images, and literary appropriations* (pp. 11- 24). Lincoln, NE: University of Nebraska.

Said, E.W. (1994). *Culture and imperialism.* New York, NY: Vintage Books.

Salomone, R.E., & Davis, J.E. (Eds.). (1997). *Teaching Shakespeare into the twenty-first century.* Athens, OH: Ohio University Press.

Sensoy, O., & DiAngelo, R. (2011). *Is everyone really equal? An introduction to key concepts in social justice education.* Multicultural Education Series. New York, NY: Teachers College Press.

Shizha, E. (2005). Reclaiming our memories: The education dilemma in postcolonial African school curricula. In A.A. Abdi & A. Cleghorn (Eds.), *Issues in African education* (pp. 65–83). New York, NY: Palgrave Macmillan.

Shizha, E. (2013). Reclaiming our indigenous voices: The problem with postcolonial sub-saharan African school curriculum. *Journal of Indigenous Social Development*, 2(1), 1–18.

Shizha, E. (2014). Indigenous knowledge systems and the curriculum. In G. Emeagwali & G. J. S. Dei (Eds.), *African indigenous knowledge and the disciplines.* (113–129). Rotterdam, Netherlands: SensePublishers.

Skerrett, A. (2010). Of literary import: A case of cross-national similarities in the secondary English curriculum in the United States and Canada. *Research in the Teaching of English*, 45(1), 36–58.

Smith, L.T. (1999). *Decolonizing methodologies: Research and indigenous peoples.* London, UK: Zed Books.

Teferra, D., and Greijin, H. (2010). Introduction: Globalisation and African higher education. In D. Teferra and H. Greijin (Eds.), *Higher Education and globalisation challenges, threats and opportunities for Africa.* Maastricht, Netherlands: MUNDO, 1–7.

Tierney, W.G. (2002). Get real: representing reality. *International Journal of Qualitative Studies in Education*, 15(4), 385–398.

wa Thiong'o, N. (1986). *Decolonising the mind: The politics of language and literature in Africa.* London, UK: James Currey.

wa Thiong'o, N. (1994). *Decolonising the mind: The politics of language in African literature.* Nairobi, Kenya: East African Publishers.

Whittemore, R., Langness, L., & Koegel, P. (1986). The life history approach to mental retardation. In L. Langness & H. Levine (Eds.), *Culture and retardation.* Reidel Publishing Company.

Zughoul, M.R. (1987). *Restructuring the English Department in Third World universities: Alternative approaches for the teaching of English literature.* IRAL, 25(3), 221–237.

Zughoul, M. (2003). Globalisation and EFL/ESL pedagogy in the Arab World. *Journal of Language & Learning*, 1(2), 106–146.

CHAPTER 9

Education in Somalia: The Role of International Organizations in Formal Education

Shukri Hilowle

Introduction

The Somali civil war grew out of an organized rebellion and resistance to President Siad Barre and his administration. Three key forces—the Somali Armed Forces, the Somali Salvation Democratic Front, and the Somali National Movement—led the resistance. In the late 1980s, the war created such violence that millions of Somalis fled to neighboring African nations, and thousands more fled to Europe and North America. The clan warfare that began after the collapse of the Siad Barre regime also led to a complete disintegration of the state. Several staged interventions have since been attempted, with the goal of bringing stability to the region, but all have been unsuccessful.

Educational development in Somalia has been slow, and extreme poverty makes it difficult to cover the costs of education. Nomadic tribes in the country have the lowest rates of education for young children, though the rates for young boys are slightly higher in these rural nomadic communities. This chapter will employ an anti-colonial framework to examine how international organizations (IOs) and non-state actors further reinforce unequal power relations in Somalia. I will argue that IOs cannot replace the role of a functioning government in education.

The chapter will examine the effectiveness of IOs and investigate their function critically. I will be using a Weberian approach to examine the power of IOs and their pathological, dysfunctional nature (Barnett & Finnemore, 1999). In doing so, I will examine the projects and goals set out by UNESCO and the U.N. in education and development. And since education is linked with development, I will also examine the history of development projects in Somalia.

Education is fundamental to economic progress and relies on foreign aid and investment, and in Somalia this has resulted in the rapid increase in such foreign investment—from bilateral, to multilateral, to interest on the part of IOs in educational efforts (Arnove, 2013). While the focus of this study is solely on Somalia, the idea of development has placed the West and the Global South on an unequal power footing. Using Somalia as a case study allows researchers to examine how "failed" states are more vulnerable to the ongoing neocolonial IOs. This chapter will examine how education is used to transmit western cultural ideas and how this has led to cultural imperialism.

Historically, the "education for all" movement and emergence of American influence in global education stemmed from the movement toward progressive ideas and reforms during the New Deal era in the United States of the 1930s. Some scholars have criticized this movement and have examined the roots of the "education for all" initiative. Under Barre's regime, educational reform had already been underway. However, it was interrupted during the civil war, after which began a decade of neoliberal policies that eroded education and the infrastructure. This study will examine the history of education in Somalia after "decolonization" and in terms of contemporary issues found in education and the role of development.

As a researcher, my focus on education derives from my background as a Somali Muslim woman. However, my Somali identity is something I constantly have to work for, and my ties to the nation are always in question. While I speak Somali, my fluency is not at a level such that my *Somalinimo* (belonging) is irrefutable. The term "1.5 generation" Somalis refers to Somalis like myself who were born in Somalia but fled during the civil war. Prior to the war, Somalia was in the process of decolonizing after many years of colonial rule, but the persistent presence of international organizations and the complete reliance on foreign aid has continued to reinforce the unequal power relations between the West and the Global South. Has Somalia shifted into a post-colonial era? I utilize an anti-colonial framework here that critically examines the role of education in Somalia, as well as what kinds of values are instilled through education. An anti-colonial framework is used to examine sites of oppression and domination.

Historical: Somalia at a Glance

In order to achieve a deep understanding of the civil war in Somalia, it is important to examine the historical events that led to and shaped the country's ongoing violence and instability. The colonial history of Somalia officially ended with the nationalist movement. July 1, 1960, marked Somalia's Independence Day, midway through the *annus mirabilis* of African independence (Cabdisalaam, 1996). On that date the Somali Republic was created by the unification of British Somaliland and Italian Somaliland. In 1969 a coup d'état marked the end of then-president Abdirashid Ali Shermarke's period in office, and the socialist state of the Somali Democratic Republic, under the military leadership of Major General Siad Barre, was born. The 22-year period during which Siad Barre led the region was marked by widespread allegations of violence inflicted upon various clans, and this brought forth charges of extreme human rights abuses. In addition, a rigid clan hierarchy reinforced the stratification of clan power and wealth (Cabdisalaam, 1996). These tensions created hostility among various clans and were further fueled by the downward economic spiral of the 1980s. In addition, Siad Barre's forces were responsible for the massacre of religious protestors. During the late 1980s, organized resistance to the authoritarian Barre government gained momentum. Several key leaders were ousted, which completely fractured the central government and led to the fall of the Barre regime. Clan warfare erupted, involving the fight for power and control of resources by several clans and warlords. This warfare resulted in chaos that served to raise the price of food, leading in turn to widespread famine in the early 1990s and a humanitarian crisis (Cabdisalaam, 1996).

This period marked the beginning of a wide variety of short-term solutions created by international organizations and peacekeeping missions from several western nations. The United States created the Unified Task Force (UNITAF), which was referred to as the "Operation to Restore Hope," and whose purpose was to bring stability and peace to the region (Cabdisalaam, 1996). The resistance to the project on the part of warlord Mohammed Farah Aidid and his many supporters led to violence, including "Black Hawk Down," the highly documented clash between the rebel forces and U.S soldiers. The mission was widely regarded as a failure and a stain on the Clinton administration. Since the Operation to Restore Hope mission, countless other initiatives have been launched to restore the central government.

The Case of Somalia: "Failed" State

There exists very little information of a documentary nature regarding Somalia before its emergence as a nation through civil war and violence that has displaced millions. Prior to the collapse of the government, very little was known about the country. It shares borders with Ethiopia and Kenya and has a large coastline stretching along the Indian Ocean. Most of the land is desert. In areas where farming is possible, frequent crop failure and very dry weather serve to make agriculture exceedingly difficult, leading to catastrophic, widespread famines. Nearly all Somalians practice Sunni Islam; clanships also play a role in the family structure. Reliance on foreign goods and foreign aid stems from the region's inability to develop industries, and much of the economy rests on livestock and a reliance on the support of the broader Somali diaspora.

The education sector in Somalia has gone through some changes, thanks in large part to the involvement of non-state actors and international organizations. Several programs have been introduced to the region through UNICEF and UNESCO, including the Family Life Project aimed at improving education in the country. While the program has had a positive impact on Somali women, particularly in the rural areas of the country, the greater threat of political turmoil and violence erects a barrier to women in Somalia seeking to gain a proper education.

The collapse of the Siad Barre regime created a multitude of problems. Prior to the civil war, education was controlled by the central government. While there were many issues, particularly in terms of resources, the implementation of a standardized language system, in combination with a mass literacy and education campaign, sought to develop a knowledge-based economy. Schools were targeted as transmission centers of culture and Somali nationalism. The Barre regime failed in its efforts to control the different territories in Somalia, and over time any semblance of state control collapsed. While dissatisfaction grew, the end of the regime marked the beginning of political instability and civil unrest. Some have argued that statelessness has been more beneficial to Somali citizens, because, in the case of the Said Barre regime, the predatory government did more harm than good to Somalis.

A nation is considered a failed state when it is unable to exert control or provide economic and political security. Once a government loses control, the entire national system becomes weak. Somalia has been in a state of failure since 1991, the longest period of chaos since decolonization (Menkhaus, 2007). Since the collapse, several failed missions have been attempted to create peace in the region, all of them unsuccessful. Between the years 1993 and 1995, the United Nations Operations in Somalia organization (UNOSOM) launched several peacekeeping missions, an effort that has made Somalia the target of the world's most concerted external state-building initiatives. In October 2004, the Nairobi peace accords crafted an agreement to help create a transitional federal government (TFG). This project, which took two years to negotiate, was accompanied by a great deal of external pressure (Menkhaus, 2007). The TFG took seven months to relocate into Somalia, where it was met with resistance from Islamic political groups that also prompted internal issues and defections. The protracted absence of a central government has given a rise to informal systems: traditional authorities, civic groups, and business groups have all promoted "organic" examples of rule of law and public order. Menkhaus (2007) argues: "Somalia's central government must not obscure the significant success of governance-building efforts within some local Somali communities." (p. 74) In the absence of a unified, central government, localized governments have formed. (This situation is not unique to Somalia, as the failure of a central government may often lead local groups to create alternative arrangements to secure basic security.) In the case of Somaliland, the collapse of the Said Barre regime created an opportunity to create an independent state, and despite its own internal struggles to maintain power, the functioning government in the northern region of Somalia is able to provide more security for its citizens as well as a more effective educational system in relation to the southern region.

Education

While western education is favored because it is felt to impart a competitive advantage, Koranic schools provide a stable education. In nomadic regions, Koranic schools—whose success is attributable to community support and the motivation of teachers—continue to be the preferred source of education for young children. Parents pay teachers in kind, in addition to paying them in cash. Staff turnover rates are lower than in primary schools. The cost of education is also lower, because the schools use accessible materials such as "erasable wooden slates, writing sticks and ink made from milk and soot" (UNICEF, 1995). While these schools attract more support, they are very poor, often lacking in nutrition, water, and basic sanitation. UNICEF conducted a study in Somaliland that showed that gender disparity in Koranic schools was less as compared to primary education schools. Teachers in these schools are poorly trained, and almost all lack proper qualifications to ensure quality education for their students (UNICEF, 1995). The Somaliland government established the Ministry of Endowment and Islamic Affairs, which oversees the implementation of Koranic schools. In 1994, UNICEF began assisting Koranic schools in an effort to increase accessibility to education, close the gender gap in Koranic and primary schools, and improve the overall welfare of the children. The language of instruction includes both English and Arabic; moral instruction and social roles are taught, in addition to literacy in Arabic. This is problematic because traditional Somali culture is not taught at either of these schools. The students are not taught in their native language but are instead forced to erase their own culture in the service of economic competitiveness.

Historically, education has been a site for cultural imperialism, and colonial education continues to be a tool for cultural imperialism in "developing" nations. The desire to learn Arabic and English is driven by economic competition and human capital theory. Many parents send their students to learn Arabic in hopes of securing employment in highly desirable locations such as Saudi Arabia and the United Arab Emirates, and the motivation to learn English is driven by similar factors. In the Middle East and in Asia, similar preferences have fueled the expansion of English-language education. This cultural imperialism is spurred both by the West and by forces within developing nations that seek to compete in the global economy. Samoff (2001) argues:

> Colonial rule provided the setting for a particular sort of international influence in education.... Emulations, models, replicas, or overseas branches,

> these institutions often reproduced not only the curriculum, pedagogy, and hierarchical organization of their European models but even their architecture and staff and student codes of conduct. (p. 56)

Koranic schools found in Somalia adhere to religious customs found in other Muslim-majority nations. Young girls are told to wear the Hijab, and the genders are separated. While the structures of these schools follow the western and Islamic models, the overall quality of education is very poor, so some Somalis send their children to Kenya for private education.

Somalia, like many other post-colonial countries, continues to depend on western nations to develop its education sector. Samoff and Stromquist (2001) make reference to "a large number of former colonies [that have] became independent, many of them very poor and with little investment or infrastructure to support autonomous development" (p. 59). After Somalia's independence in 1960, the education sector was made up of a combination of British and Italian schooling, but there was very little progress in the education sector until the implementation of the Somali language by Siad Barre. Barre used the language issue as part of his platform to create formal education, in addition to unifying the nation. He also promoted nationalism to ensure support from all regions of Somalia and launched a mass literacy campaign that—along with the expansion of the education sector—gained him more support in the country. As a result of this campaign and mass literacy promotion, enrollment increased in the 1970s. In the 1980s, however, the education sector suffered under the neoliberal polices: only 1.5% to 2% of the annual national budget was spent on improving education (Moyi, 2012). School enrollment and the number of teachers, both of which had increased rapidly during the 1970s, now saw substantial decreases. School conditions also deteriorated, and in the late 1980s, the civil war completely destroyed the already-fragile education sector.

International Organization: Dysfunctional Behavior

International organizations, much like other bureaucracies, are limited by their structure. Barnett and Finnemore (1999) argue that, like most organizations, IOs are inefficient and dysfunctional. While the intention to implement education in Somalia, where the education sector is underdeveloped, is admirable, it is important to examine whether IOs have been successful in implementing these changes. The role of IOs, which are generally desirous of providing stability to regions such as Somalia, has been made more difficult by civil unrest. They are often seen as powerless, there only to facilitate the development of countries. Barnett and Finnemore (1999) question the supposed "powerless" argument that has been used to diminish the status of IOs. While IOs are autonomous and can be sites of authority, "Bureaucracies embody a form of authority, rational-legal authority, that modernity views as particularly legitimate and good" (p. 707). Like most bureaucracies, IOs provide rationality and reason and act as authorities on various matters. For example, in education, IOs play a role in training teachers, developing curricula, and launching programs targeted at improving education.

The expertise of IOs helps them to hold on to power in Somalia despite the interference of some Somali officials. In fact, the reconstruction of Somalia has been led by IOs, along with several non-state actors. Aimé (2008) argues: "After decolonisation, African states failed to conform to the model of modernity, yet the differences produced thereby have been blurred by the various concepts of failed, collapsed or weak states" (p. 2). IOs have been ineffective in implementing western values in these collapsed or failed states, where civil unrest makes it hard for them to execute their objectives effectively. Indeed, in many cases the effect is the opposite. For instance, the U.N.-led mission into Somalia under the Clinton administration was designed to end the civil unrest and achieve peace, but the entire mission was a failure. Clan warfare did not end, and a few years later the conditions in Somalia further deteriorated with the creation of Al-Shabab, an extremist group. The "education for all" movement has also been criticized by a number of scholars, including Mundy and Manion (2014), who have questioned whether these idealistic goals are in fact achievable. Other scholars, such as Dei and Kempf (2006) and Wane, Kempf, and Simmons (2011), have called for the decolonization of education.

The universal right to education has drawn the movement into rural Somalia, where goals and targets have been set by local governors (UNESCO, 2005). According to Moyi (2012), UNESCO reports that "Somalia has the dismal distinction of having the world's highest proportion of primary school-age children not in school." Young girls living in rural areas fare the worst, as gender conflict creates barriers to school attendance for them. The author argues that the neglect of Somalia and the ineffectiveness of IOs has resulted in low education enrollment. The statistics gathered in the Moyi (2012) article show that the central south region (Mogadishu) and the neighboring rural communities exhibit the lowest enrollment. (Not coincidentally, these regions also are the poorest in Somalia.) Northern Somalia has had a semifunctional government for the last few years, along with Puntland, another region controlled by several clans. Violence is rampant in the capital city of Mogadishu, as well as in the communities located in the south, which are more prone to violence because they are perceived as controlling the capital city. Moreover, the southern regions do not have a functioning ministry of education as do other regions of Somalia, a factor that also contributes to the discrepancy in enrollment. The table used in Moyi's (2012) article also shows that nomadic young girls and boys had the lowest rates of enrollment in both Koranic schools and primary education. Meanwhile, 82% of girls and 89% of boys in urban areas attended Koranic schools at some point in their lives (Moyi, 2012). The gender imbalance was also very high in both nomadic regions and urban centers, where men were more likely to have received education as compared to women. The overall goal of the concept of a universal right to education is idealistic: it does not take into consideration cultural barriers and local conditions. It is based on a set of ideas that have developed in western nations in the post-World War II era—specifically, that education is a right and should be free for all, that education is an essential component of development, and that parents have a right to see their children educated.

Intervention on the part of IOs in the domestic affairs of African nations—and in particular the role of "development" in Somalia—has been substantial. In addition to working as advisors, IOs are permitted to be involved in "domestic working polities." Their power rests in their ability to define and implement policies and legal frameworks. IOs justify their intervention under peacekeeping and international peace, and the nation of Somalia, which has been plagued by ongoing clan and extremist violence, is the prime candidate for intervention. IOs continue to define norms, rules, and global values—values that continue to shape and define what is legitimate behavior for states. Barnett and Finnemore (1999) argue:

> Developing states continue to be popular targets for norm diffusion by 1Os, even after they are independent. The UN and the European Union are now actively involved in police training in non-Western states because they believe Western policing practices will be more conducive to democratization processes. (p. 713)

The overall goal of these initiatives is to transform "developing nations" into western-style nations. When it comes to diffusion of norms, many organizations—including both the World Bank and the IMF—are explicit in their role of fostering developing nations. "Modern" values are also instilled in developing nations, with the overall mandate being to spread western values and ideas of governance—including democracy and the expansion of the private sector—and to transform those nations into legitimate world players.

Anti-colonialists such as Frantz Fanon (1963) have challenged this notion of development and the European ideals that have come down from the Enlightenment era. The notion of progress and modernity has fueled the involvement of donor nations in the task of helping nations like Somalia to modernize. Huntington (1979, cited in Fägerlind & Saha, 1989) states that

> the process of modernization can be characterized as revolutionary (a dramatic shift from tradition to modern), complex (multiple causes), systematic, global (affecting all societies), phased (advanced through stages), homogenizing (convergence), irreversible and progressive. (p. 15)

Somalia is considered the least developed nation in Africa, as many years of civil war have left most the country in complete poverty. Development is based on a single set of western values that minimize the traditions of Indigenous cultures. A more critical approach to development would serve to question its social inequalities, structural barriers, and power relations while simultaneously expanding the definition of development. The contemporary concept of development uses the West as the model against which all nations are measured; it also disregards the continuous oppression that contributes to unstable conditions.

Most nations in the Global South are dependent on the West for foreign aid, thereby adhering to a dependency model that explains how history has shaped the current predicament of Somalia. Years of colonial rule, including the British in Northern Somaliland, the French in Djibouti, and the Italians in the south have shaped current societal structures. Fanon argues that wealth redistribution can address the unequal power relations that have enabled western nations to control resources and wealth. Marxist theorists argue that education serves to reinforce the status quo rather than challenge it. The cultural norms transmitted through education do not challenge existing conditions, nor do they address the ways in which colonial history has played a role in shaping current economic conditions. In Somalia under the Siad Barre regime, those conditions fueled the overthrow of his administration. As noted earlier, this occurred in the 1980s—the period that witnessed the growth of neoliberalism, which only served to create further disincentives to economic growth. Neoliberalism has had an impact on the education sector of Somalia as well, especially in the Global South. While it promotes a free-market approach and the overall expansion of the private sector, it also has a direct impact on the role of the state. Some African nations, including Somalia, have dealt with predatory governments, and while this has been a source of civil unrest, the overall role of the state has been threatened through neoliberal development policies.

The Role of International Organizations

The role of IOs in Somalia has been twofold: first, it has been a response to civil war and ongoing violence, and second, it has attempted to launch the reconstruction of the nation. The collapse of the state in 1991 led to a period of violence that resulted in severe disruption to the education sector. All organized systems of learning were completely severed during this period of civil unrest. Mass looting of supplies, combined with the fear of violence, forced educators to flee for their own safety. Clan-based violence also contributed to the unsafe conditions and created barriers to cohesion. Ali A. Abdi (1998) argues: "In this social disintegration, schools, technical training centres and university facilities became among the first casualties of the senseless mass destruction of the country's infrastructure" (p. 2). The outbreak of famine also greatly affected young children, who were the most vulnerable. At the height of the war in the early 1990s, a famine killed an estimated 3,000 children and triggered the influx into the country of IOs. Many of the missions carried out by those organizations were limited in scope and failed to place any blame for this social disorder on the legacy of colonialism. When viewed outside the context of these events, Somalia is seen as a "failed state" that requires support and intervention.

Rescue missions are almost always limited in scope, because such efforts are focused on violence rather than the conditions that produced the civil unrest in the first place. Years of economic downturn resulted in the complete economic breakdown of the nation, but reconstruction cannot occur in the absence of a critical examination of what caused the economic downturn in the 1980s.

Despite the failed peacekeeping attempts in the region, IOs continue to "promote rising living standards in poorer countries" (Helleiner, 2010, p. 27). The existence of IOs can be traced back to the creation of public international unions during the late nineteenth and early twentieth centuries. Some of these unions focused largely on tariffs, infrastructure, communication, and various regulations, while others focused on peacekeeping and conflict resolution. The establishment of the League of Nations was a turning point in international relations, creating, as it did, cooperation in an international, institutional framework. International development was still not a primary focus during the establishment phase of the League of Nations, though certain regions were handed over to victors following the war. These territories were seen as unfit for self-governance and "inhabited by peoples not yet able to stand by themselves under the strenuous conditions of the modern world" (Helleiner, 2010, p. 29). Similar language is used to describe failed nations, which are deemed unfit to rule and unable to "stand by themselves." Moreover, it is within the power of wealthy nations to undertake control and responsibility; colonial ideas of progress and superiority influence the role of the West as the colonial administrator.

IOs are often seen as experts who have authority over social and economic welfare, and the League used experts to oversee "modernization in areas such as health education, transportation, and the organization of rural cooperatives" (Helleiner, 2010 p. 30). The U.N. was founded on similar ideals: to ensure peace and to promote international economic, social, and humanitarian cooperation.

The U.S. role in policymaking was substantial during the early stages of international development, and the nation was a pioneer in international development. The universal idea of "freedom from want" depends on a commitment to the idea that all people deserve economic security. This idea was essential to the New Deal, whose founder, Franklin D. Roosevelt, believed that economic security would create political stability internationally (Helleiner, 2010). A fund and bank were developed to help poorer countries raise their living standards. The United States continued to play a leading role in the development of nations, often motivated by its fear of other influences, including the Germans in Latin America and the Soviet Union during the Cold War. Influenced both by New Deal ideologies and capitalism, the establishment of banks equipped to make large development loans was designed to help bring stability to several regions. (One such example was the Clinton administration's 1992 intervention in the civil war in Somalia in an effort to bring peace to the area.) Much earlier, however, during the 1960s, the United States began its involvement in the region. Its relationship with Somalia was similar to that of Latin American countries, having been based on the goal of bringing economic, social, and political stability to the region. While the principal concern was to improve living standards, at least some of the interest in this region on the part of the United States stemmed from its desire to gain power and influence.

The establishment of the U.N. and the Bretton Woods agreement marked the beginning of the aid regime to poorer nations. The process of development included "support for debt restructuring, the control of capital flight, infant industry protection, and commodity price stabilization" (Helleiner, 2010, p. 41) and provided the template for contemporary North and South relations surrounding economic growth. Initially the central role of IOs was to assist poorer nations in their development and struggle against poverty and inequality; later on, they became involved in peacekeeping missions, education, healthcare, and environmental projects. Helleiner (2010) argues that Latin America's relations with the United States in the 1930s and 1940s were essential to this development. Policymakers were motivated by several factors, including power, influence, and ideology—including the guarantee of social justice. However, the economic benefits were a determining factor in international development projects. Anti-colonial theorists have argued that this was a continuation of colonialism driven by paternalistic and economic interests in post-colonial nations. Despite the focus on economic development, the rich-poor gap has doubled since the 1960s (Klees, 2010). Children living in extreme poverty continue to suffer from inadequate healthcare and malnutrition; in addition, 75 million children living in poorer countries do not attend primary school. It is estimated that 1.4 billion survive on US$1.25 a day, and hunger is widespread in many poor nations. Critics of development aid have argued that the extreme poverty of many nations stems directly from development aid policies:

> [H]as more than US $1 trillion in development assistance over the last several decades made African people better off? No. In fact, across the globe the recipients of this aid are worse off; much worse off. Aid has helped make the poor poorer, and growth slower. Yet aid remains a centerpiece of today's development policy and one of the biggest ideas of our time. (Klees, 2010, p. 11)

Multilateral and bilateral aid reinforces the unequal power relationship between the North and the South. The role of multilateral organizations in education—for example, the World Bank—has also been met with criticism. Klees (2010) has argued that neoliberal ideas and policies continue to contribute to ongoing issues in education, and some have argued that what is needed is less money and more focus on how to spend and allocate the funds. The conditions in primary schools are inadequate; in fact, over 75 million children do not attend primary schools at all.

The history of development in East Germany and South Korea has been vastly different from that of African nations. After the end of World War II, the Marshall Plan was created to help rebuild the European infrastructure. The fact that Europe had already gone through industrialization and had a substantial educated workforce made reconstruction much easier there. Klees (2010) argues that more money was allocated in these regions than in all of Africa, where the majority of aid goes toward education, healthcare, infrastructure, and other essentials.

Conclusion

The ongoing violence in Somalia makes it increasingly difficult for any long-term solutions to be effective. While IOs provide short-term solutions, they are unable to create lasting improvements in education. Though the "education for all" movement is based on idealistic views of the world, in unstable regions like Somalia, the primary focus should be on addressing the political turmoil. The failed central government of Somalia led to the devastation of education, and since then, given unstable conditions, IOs have been ineffective in reviving education. Ongoing violence perpetrated by extremist groups, along with clan warfare, poses multiple challenges for the future of Somalia. The continual interference of IOs serves to question the country's ability to self-govern, and the ongoing dependence on aid and support from international bodies undermines the legacy of anti-colonial history in the region.

Despite the inability of IOs to create a functioning central government, Somalia, through UNICEF and UNESCO, continues to be one of the nations that receives the most aid, a factor that plays a key role in education. The implementation of western education stands in contrast to traditional Indigenous Somali education, values, and beliefs. Direct competition from Islamic schools also poses a threat to the establishment of western-style education. The combination of ongoing violence, burgeoning extremism, and failed attempts at peacekeeping in the region—including the failed AMISOM mission—complicates the implementation of the "education for all" initiative that came out of the New Deal era in the United States. A workable, functioning central state is more effective in securing human rights and education for all. The case of Somalia illustrates the complications of statelessness, the extent to which a predatory government can wreak havoc on a nation, and the ineffectiveness of IOs in addressing these long-term problems.

References

Abdi, A.A. (1998). Education in Somalia: History, destruction, and calls for reconstruction. *Comparative Education, 34*(3), 327–340. doi:10.1080/03050069828171

Aimé, E.G. (2008). *Fragile states and neoliberalism in Sub-Saharan Africa.* African Studies Group, 1–7. Retrieved from http://fride.org/download/COM_Neoliberalism_subsaharan_ENG_jun08.pdf

Arnove, R.F. (2013). *Comparative education: The dialectic of the global and the local.* Lanham, MD: Rowman & Littlefield.

Barnett, M., & Finnemore, M. (1999). The politics, power and pathologies of international organisations. *International Organization, 53*(4), 699–732.

Cabdisalaam, M.C. (1996). *The collapse of the Somali state: The impact of the colonial legacy.* London, UK: HAAN Publishing.

Dei, G.J., & Kempf, A. (2006). *Anti-colonialism and education: The politics of resistance.* Rotterdam, Netherlands: Sense Publishers.

Fägerlind, I., & Saha, L.J. (1997). *Education and national development: A comparative perspective.* Oxford, UK: Butterworth Heinemann.

Fanon, F. (1963). *The wretched of the earth.* New York: Grove Press.

Helleiner, E. (2010). Global governance meets development: A brief history of innovation in world politics. In J. Clapp & R. Wilkinson (Eds.), *Global governance, poverty and inequality* (pp. 1–45). London, UK: Routledge.

Klees, S. (2010). Aid, development and education. *Current Issues in Comparative Education, 13*(1), 7–28. Retrieved from http://www.tc.columbia.edu/cice/Issues/13.01/PDFs/13_01_Editorial_Introduction.pdf

Menkhaus, K. (2007). Governance without government in Somalia: Spoilers, state building, and the politics of coping. *International Security, 31*(3), 74–106. doi:10.1162/isec.2007.31.3.74

Moyi, P. (2012). Who goes to school? School enrollment patterns in Somalia. *International Journal of Educational Development, 32*(1), 163–171.

Mundy, K., & Manion, C. (2014). Globalization and global governance in education. In N. Stromquist & K. Monkman (Eds.), *Globalization and education: Integration and contestation across cultures* (2nd ed., pp. 39–53). Lanham, MD: Rowman & Littlefield.

Samoff, J., & Stromquist, N. (2001). Managing knowledge and storing wisdom. *Development and Change, 32*, 631–656.

UNICEF. (1995). *Koranic school project.* Retrieved from http://www.pitt.edu/~ginie/somalia/pdf/koran.pdf

Wane, N.N., Kempf, A., & Simmons, M. (2011). *The politics of cultural knowledge.* Rotterdam, Netherlands: Sense Publishers.

CHAPTER 10

Development, Research, and the Commodification of Poverty in Africa: Rethinking Research Narratives

Wambui Karanja

Introduction

Discourses on development instinctively cast the gaze on the Global South as the subject and beneficiary of the West's development and modernization efforts. In this gaze, the South is perceived as an "undeveloped third world that is impoverished, disease laden and ignorant and in need of help from the West's largesse to uplift it from its perpetual poverty and hopelessness (G.S. Dei, 2014; Sium, 2012). In the case of Africa, for example, the narrative of the continent's underdevelopment and its need for salvation through western development approaches is pervasive in the images we see of Africa and Africans in development projects, the media, and research reports. Underpinning these narratives and images is the history of colonialism and the coloniality of development, including the role of research as a tool for justifying colonial western development and modernization processes in Africa.

I base this chapter on the premise that development research has been used to commodify perceived poverty in Africa in order to enable its use for western-based development and modernization goals in Africa, and that this research is therefore implicated in perpetuating prevailing conceptualizations of Africa and Africans as impoverished. Further, African researchers, whether outside or inside the academy, have become implicated in advancing these conceptualizations. In this study, I seek to examine the complicity of African researchers in the perpetuation and continuation of African colonization through development and modernization approaches using the commodification of African poverty. I will also interrogate the West's development and modernization approaches in "helping" Africa and how research has been used as a tool for the continuing colonization of Africa and its people. I will reveal how well-intentioned African researchers and development practitioners have unconsciously contributed to and been implicated in the promotion of the West's negative and colonialist conceptualizations and constructs of Africa and Africans, thus helping to advance the negative stereotyping of Africa through research.

I come to this topic as an African woman who was born and lived in Africa for the greater part of my adult life. Now living in the West, I am not only implicated as a consumer of western education but also as the author of a published research paper that is steeped in that same colonial messaging on Africa and who is interested in decolonizing her mind and scholarship. I have also witnessed the negative consequences of colonization and its offspring on my home country's development, modernization, and, lately, globalization and have become deeply suspicious of western colonialist global economic programs and initiatives in Africa. This chapter is a pathway to my own decolonization, and I hope it will trigger interest in others to critically examine dominant research narratives on Africa and to begin interrogating those narratives in terms of their impact on Africa. The chapter will look at development research and its implications in shaping and informing the West's colonial project, perception, and narratives of Africa and by extension, other "developing" economies in the global South.

Using decolonial and anti-racist theoretical frameworks, I will attempt to provide an alternative decolonizing research approach to address issues of complicity and implication in perpetuating the colonial project. I anticipate that researchers interested in decolonizing their research will use self-reflective gazes in auditing their participation in western development research for complicity—either as researchers or participants in research—and, it is hoped, take all necessary steps to advocate for decolonization of their research projects. It is anticipated as well that future research projects on Africa and its "development" conducted by African researchers and outsiders will be rooted in a decolonizing research framework, where African and Afrocentric researchers will begin to engage in research that serves the interests of Africa and its people. Decolonizing research will be purged of prevailing western research paradigms that have continued the exploitation of African knowledges and cultural identity for western consumption.

Conceptualizing Western Development in the African Context

Interrogating development research requires that western development be understood in the context of the colonial history of—and the West's continued interest in—Africa. It begs the following questions: What is development, and who are the actors and beneficiaries of development? Why does Africa need development? What is the role of research in answering these questions? It is crucial that these questions be posed if we are to illuminate the meaning of development, its role in the recolonization of Africa, and the consequences of its implementation in Africa. Reflecting on these questions, I am reminded of the many international development "experts/consultants" I have seen in the streets and java cafes in Nairobi and on the beaches of Mombasa. I have always wondered how they seem to have unfettered access to the locals, the land, and the country's institutions. I am also reminded of the many nongovernmental organizations operating in numerous developing countries and the many young university graduates who hover around them in the hope of gaining access to employment opportunities with an international NGO.

The question of what exactly constitutes development has eluded researchers, policymakers, and academicians; indeed, no consensus has been reached regarding a uniform definition of the term (Dei & Anamuah-Mensa, 2014). The Bandung Conference of 1955, for example, defined *development* as liberatory and articulated it as a platform for liberation from colonialism and neocolonialism, while the 1949 definition offered by the Truman administration posited that development was meant to civilize the uncivilized. It aimed at developing the Global South in general and Africa in particular through imperial designs of civilizing and westernizing the non-western world (Mehmet, 1995). Irrespective of how development has been theorized, conventional development has become an instrument of external control, colonization, and recolonization of African countries into the wider global cultures of globalization, trade liberalization, and the spread of democracy (G.S. Dei, 2014; Lauer, 2007).

In his book *The Myth of Development*, Oswaldo De Rivero has argued that development and globalization institutionalized through organizations such as the World Bank, the IMF, the WTO, and multinational corporations have only served to impoverish and marginalize the Third World, leaving it powerless against rising hegemonic global power. De Rivero argues further that globalization quickly diminishes the sovereignty and autonomy of many nation-states (De Rivero, 2001). Similarly, Dei and Anamuah-Mensah have theorized the coloniality of western-style development as steeped in eurocentrism and dominant paradigms of Western thinking (Dei & Anamuah-Mensa, 2014). Conventional development, it has been argued, is rooted in the modern/traditional binary of the modern, developed West, and the backward, traditional, and ignorant Africa. By extension, development is touted as the mechanism through which Africa can be modernized like the West.

Whether Africa needs the modernization envisaged by the West is debatable. Further, the development vehicle as the civilizing platform has only served to impoverish Africa and has become a vehicle through which African wealth and resources are accessed, exploited, and taken to western-controlled international markets (G.J. Dei, 1993; G.S. Dei, 2014; Lauer, 2007; Sium, 2012). The development agenda must be critically interrogated for complicity in recolonizing Africa, and decolonizing development discourses and practices must engage this understanding of development or risk perpetuating the colonialist development agenda.

Evil Twins: Development and Poverty in Africa

> *The African nation-state is always, already failed. In the popular imagination of the west, it is never too far from its inevitable institutional death. In academic, political and media discourses, Africa is believed to be in a constant state of degradation and unraveling.*
>
> —SIUM, 2012

In eurocentric thought, Africa is conceptualized as poverty ridden and as a failed state that needs to be rescued by western development (Sium, 2012). This paradigm is the single story that permeates the minds of development agents and international development bodies, who see Africa as rife with poverty and view their role as that of helping it out of that poverty. It is a paradigm that has its origins in colonialism and eurocentric thought and that has continued to inform the West's relationship with Africa to the present day. The West's obsession with "African poverty" is pervasive. In a recent study, the World Bank, despite acknowledging the economic growth that Africa has experienced in the last decade, still finds itself unable to shed the poverty narrative. While Beegle, Christiaensen, Dabalen, and Gaddis (2016), in their Report *Poverty in a Rising Africa*, acknowledge that Africa has, since the mid-1990s, experienced economic growth at the robust pace of 4.5% per year (a more rapid pace than in the rest of the developing world, except for China), they have continued to focus on the narrative of poverty instead of focusing on the good news of Africa's economic growth. This narrative has begged the question of whether the two constructs of poverty and development can be mutually exclusive in the context of the West's development agenda for Africa. It can be argued that African "poverty" has been turned into a commodity and a tool for justifying development and modernization practices that serve the interests of the West. How, then, do we understand poverty? Does it have the same meaning globally? How did Africans conceptualize poverty before colonization? Who has discursive authority and definitional power over poverty? Is there an African and western conceptualization of poverty?

What role does a poverty narrative and agenda play in the development agenda? A World Bank Report of 2000 defined poverty as "pronounced deprivation in well-being," while earlier, in 1998, the United Nations had defined poverty as:

> fundamentally, a denial of choices and opportunities, a violation of human dignity, the lack of basic capacity to participate effectively in society, not having enough money for food, clothing and education as well as not having the land on which to grow one's food or a job to earn one's living, not having access to credit. According to the World Bank, poverty means insecurity, powerlessness and exclusion of individuals, households and communities. It means susceptibility to violence, and it often implies

> living on marginal or fragile environments, without access to clean water or sanitation (D. Gordon, 2005).

While these definitions appear to be exhaustive, they fail to contextualize or theorize why such conditions obtain, or to interrogate the implications of western colonial intrusion into the minds and spaces of those considered to be poor. Furthermore, these definitions are mediated through western-infused interpretations of poverty as defined by lack of western conveniences, where the definition of poverty is rooted in materialism and technological indicators that fail to acknowledge the social, cultural, and spiritual dimensions of human existence (G.S. Dei, 2014). It is also of note that in coming up with this definition, the World Bank sees itself not as implicated in creating the conditions that make people poor, but rather as an innocent observer willing to help through foreign aid and the funding of development programs.

Critical questions regarding, for example, the meanings of terms such as *deprivation* and *well-being,* and why choices and opportunities have been denied and by whom—are conveniently avoided, including how and by whom the violation of human dignity has occurred. In pre-colonial Africa, people lived without western commodities and conveniences. Did Africans live in perpetual poverty before colonization? How did they construct poverty, and how did they look after the less privileged members of society? These questions are crucial to an examination of the relationship between poverty and development. While Africans and the West have constructed poverty differently, it is imperative to note that the western notion of poverty is a social-economic western construct, and African poverty in development discourses is socially constructed to serve the colonizing and globalization needs of dominant societies. African poverty is necessary for development and serves as a justification for globalization and liberalization of international trade policies, one that provides unfettered access to African resources for western economic pursuits.

The symbiotic relationship between African poverty and development is sustained through research and international development economic policies and programs. This explains the West's sustained interest in and definition of Africa as impoverished and needing development and modernization. These questions can then be asked: Are development and poverty-alleviation initiatives hidden agendas whose purpose is to continue the West's colonizing influences in Africa? Can development exist without poverty? Is it possible that African poverty can be construed as a eurocentric ideology that has been constructed by the West to justify the continued colonization of Africa? Why has the west povertized Africa and universalized the narrative such that that Africa has become synonymous with poverty? Who gets to benefit from this narrative?

This account, however, has been contested by researchers who argue that that descriptions of Africa as failed, sick, and in need of western development are not only false and steeped in colonial violence but also infantilize Africa by creating dichotomies of traditional, barbaric, premodern, stuck-in-the-past, underdeveloped Africa in contrast to the attractive modern western world (G.S. Dei, 2014). The notion has also been challenged by scholars and others who see these development programs as western approaches to disguise and facilitate western interests abroad through "cruel little wars" or discursive projects that seek to unmake or remake the Third World in the western imaginary (Escobar, 1995). African poverty is intended to create dependency, to make Africans vulnerable to western development programs. These development paradigms have continually created dependency on the West and maximized the control, exploitation, injustice, and inequality in Africa and among Africans (Dei, 1993).

The racialization of poverty is another paradigm that the West has used to advance its interests in Africa. It is uncontested that development experts have flocked to Africa in droves with their poverty-alleviation programs, while failing to address the poverty in their own countries. Little is heard of international development programs universalizing and targeting western countries with their poverty research programs, though it is evident that there is extreme poverty in countries like the United States. It is estimated that, as of the beginning of 2011, 1.46 million U.S. households with about 2.8 million children were surviving on US$2 or less in income per person per day in a given month; further, almost 20% of all nonelderly households with children living in poverty (866,000 households) were living in extreme poverty (Shaefer & Edin, 2012). Neither are we bombarded with images of poverty in Appalachia or in Kentucky, the poorest states in the United States (indeed, former Virginia senator Jim Webb, a Democrat, has stated that the poorest U.S. counties are in Appalachia and are 90% white [Webb, 2014]), or in Europe, where it has been reported that poverty is prevalent (Cribb, Joyce, & Phillip, 2012). Countries such as Canada are not immune, and the research gaze only needs to be cast toward the living conditions of the original owners of Turtle Island to prove this point. In a 2011 report, it was estimated that using the international measure of poverty, Canada's 2009 overall poverty rate is 13.3% (4,337,000) (Hunter, 2011). Further, using the OECD's relative measure of child poverty, the Conference Board of Canada in 2013 cautioned that Canada's poverty rate ranks among the highest of the 17 countries they surveyed, with a child poverty rate of 15.1%—second only to the United States (Golden, 2017).

The focus on poverty as the preserve of Africa raises suspicions. If the West is interested in the alleviation of poverty, it would make sense that development, research, and poverty reduction programs would be focused on poverty alleviation at home before directing the efforts toward the global South. The question then becomes: Why the keen interest in poverty alleviation and development in the South, and especially Africa? Who is served by this narrative, and who gets to benefit from this gaze? Why are the Global South and Africa such fertile grounds for poverty and development research? While western benevolence is touted as the reason, the interactions of the West's development policies, the engagement of western development practitioners with their local research subjects, and their research results are often infused with colonial, racist overtones and conclusions that perpetuate and excuse exploitative development and modernization agendas. This focus mediates current development programs in Africa and is continued not only by western development agents, but also by local African state governments, academicians, researchers, and development practitioners who buy into and are implicated in advancing the African poverty, development, and modernization narratives of the West.

While African national governments are implicated by their participation in international organizations such as the World Bank, the WTO, and the IMF, which decide the terms of engagement between the West and Africa, for example, African leaders and their governments are also implicated locally in failing to develop regulatory frameworks to inform their engagement with these international organizations. Within a colonial framework, the ability of African governments to negotiate as equal partners in the crafting of trade and development policies is limited. This limitation allows for exploitative trade agreements and policies that advance the interests of the West at the expense of African countries. These are the policies that underpin development and research programs that see development agents unleashed into African under the guise of doing development work, the expatriates to whom Sium has referred as "benevolent expert do-gooders who are selfless and have left their comfortable lives in the West to brave the equatorial heat to bring development and help rid 'poor' Africans of disease, hunger, poverty, sexual and other forms of violence that 'they' only know how to address" (Sium, 2014). While it is not my intention to question the complicity of state governments in advancing the colonial agenda through research, it is very much my intention to illuminate elsewhere in this chapter some challenges in offering alternative decolonizing research options that privilege the interests of Africa and Africans by demonstrating how poverty, research, and development narratives have intersected to transform African "poverty" into a commodity, a kind of property that should be open to consumption by the global economy and western development markets (Asante, 2009).

Development and the Povertization of Africa

The narrative of Africa as poor has been advanced by colonialist research practices that aim to povertize Africa and Africans for western research purposes. The commodification of poverty and the povertization of Africa create marketable material for development research. A *commodity* has been defined as a marketable good, object, or service that can be demarcated, owned, transported, alienated, and traded in the marketplace (Marx, 1967). The purpose of commodification is to imbue the commodity with the capacity for it to be owned and to enhance portability and marketability. The portrayal of research as a commodity is evidenced by the plethora of development research projects taking place in Africa and requires an in-depth examination of why western researchers flock to Africa for research. What kind of research are they undertaking, and who are the beneficiaries of their research findings? Even more important, what is the purpose of that research? Why is research on poverty in Africa so enticing to western researchers? Poverty is a global phenomenon, so why is African poverty of such interest to the West? Answers to these questions are crucial to our understanding of the western neocolonialist agenda for Africa. Moreover, the perception of Africa by the West as a single state serves as a strategy to proliferate poverty in the continent to justify intrusion into any African country, even where western development in not needed. It ignores the nation-state character of African countries and is a nuanced strategy for the proliferation of the poverty discourse in Africa. Further, it is oblivious to the fact that poverty in Africa is neither all-encompassing nor experienced homogeneously across all of Africa's nation-states.

In the meantime, the West has used the power and economic imbalances between the West and African nations to issue itself carte blanche access to Africa for research purposes. This imbalance manifests itself in various ways, including limited travel visa restrictions for westerners traveling to Africa while very limited access to the West is granted to Africans willing to travel to the West. Even when such access is allowed, it is accompanied by humiliating, expensive, and microaggressive visa requirements that demonstrate that Africans are not welcome guests. White privilege and limited regulations concerning research frameworks in African countries allow unrestricted access to African resources and knowledges. How many African researchers are out there conducting research in the European countryside? Are there no poverty stories that can be told by African researchers in those areas?

The notion of research as a business has been well articulated by the International Development Research Centre (n.d.) report that has stated that since 1972, IDRC has conducted 477 research activities in Kenya worth $96.9 million Canadian dollars. How does Canada benefit from this huge investment in Kenya? What kind of research justifies such a huge investment for Canada? At the same time, the povertization of Africa is demonstrated by the characterization of Africa as being in a prolonged development crisis fueled by complex ethnic, social, and political realities, weak governments, corruption, mismanagement of resources, unregulated urbanization, soil erosion, shrinking forests, increased desert areas, wetland degradation, and the HIV epidemic, a narrative that has come to mediate any Western discourse on Africa. With such a list, it is a wonder that there is anybody alive on that continent; yet, according to a recent World Bank Report, Kenya has had a sustained growth rate of over 5% in the last 4 years. The report further states that the key drivers for this growth include a vibrant services sector, enhanced construction, currency stability, low inflation, low fuel prices, a growing middle class and rising incomes, a surge in remittances, and increased public investment in energy and transportation (Gaye, 2017).

The poverty narrative seeks to ignore any positive portrayal of Africa, as it must serve to justify the implementation of western development programs and research. Neither does the narrative critique itself on moral or ethical grounds. It proceeds to use the power and privilege of eurocentricity and western hegemony to rationalize its actions. How do western countries fail to contextualize the poverty narrative and interrogate their own complicity? How are they not able to understand that neocolonialism, modernization, and globalization have served to increase rural and urban poverty in Africa, first, by dispossessing and robbing people of their culture, language, and means of production, and second, by the exploitation of Africa's resources? Why do they choose to be willfully blind to the fact that global economic policies are hurting Africa? Why is globalization encouraged despite the plethora of research demonstrating its negative consequences in Africa? (Kossi, 2012).

The proselytization of African poverty is pervasive in the psyche of the western development researcher. I am reminded of a story I was told about a western researcher and her local research assistant, who were driving to a research site in central Kenya. They came across a group of elementary school kids walking home from school. As in many rural areas of Kenya, people do not walk around wearing shoes. It is also not a requirement that children wear shoes to school, so these kids had no shoes on, and their feet and clothes were obviously dusty from the rich, red, volcanic soil of their country. Upon seeing them, the western researcher exclaimed, "Oh my God! Look at those hungry poor kids!" The research assistant, a student at a local university, was shocked to hear the western researcher's surprising remark that the kids were hungry and poor and asked her, "Why would you say that?" Her reply was, "Look! They have no shoes!" I also remember visiting my rural home on one of my visits "back home," and my aunt, who by western notions of poverty would be considered poor, came to welcome me home and brought me a basketful of food she had harvested from her garden. I asked her whether everything was all right with her, and she answered that life was good and that, as I could see, she had brought me maize, beans, potatoes, and vegetables from her "shamba" (plot of land) and had more foodstuffs at home. The rains were also coming, and she was going to plant some more. She proceeded to tell me that her life was good and that she did not need anything else.

From my own personal experience, I recall that when I would visit my mother in our rural home, I never missed all the modern conveniences I had in the city. It was as though they were unnecessary and did not exist! The cows were milked in the morning, and in the evening the milk was consumed, sold, or given away. Telling stories around the kitchen fire was preferred over watching television, even where TV sets were available. Personally, despite growing up in rural Africa, I do not remember considering myself poor and was only made aware that I could be considered poor when, as a new immigrant family, we were offered charity by a well-meaning member of a local church who took upon herself the responsibility of "helping this poor black family!"

These stories beg the question as to whether poverty is a social construct designed to create a lust for western goods and conveniences to alienate Africans from their non-western means of sustenance. My aunt did not perceive of herself as poor, and it is doubtful those kids going home from school—who, as reported by the local research assistant, looked healthy and well-nourished—would have considered themselves poor. The argument can be made that the povertization of Africa is pervasive and necessary for development experts; it is no wonder, then, that African poverty has been universalized globally. It is no coincidence that development research initiatives in Africa appear to be undertaken and concentrated in rural areas where the majority of people do not have modern/western amenities and rely on their own rural resources and Indigenous knowledges for their sustenance. Is there a hidden agenda such that research is used to justify the povertization of people to make them believe they are poor and in need of the spoils of development and modernization to lift them out of poverty? In brief, can poverty be manufactured to justify western development?

The compelling argument is that eurocentric perceptions of poverty in Africa are more concerned with the lack of modern western conveniences. Colonization, eurocentricity, globalization, and modernization have served as tools for povertization, a necessary ingredient for access to Africa's resources. To the critical eye, the practice of development has served to destroy local cultures and traditional lifestyles and has resulted in the displacement and dislocation of people from their culture, ways of living, and means of production and self-reliance by creating an insatiable appetite for western lifestyles that are unaffordable, unsustainable, and outright incapacitating to the physical and mental psyche of African people. Another aspect of colonialism and development is their ability to corrupt people's minds into thinking they must be poor, or to povertize them into submission by diminishing their ability and capacity for self-actualization and economic independence. What role, then, does research play in furthering this povertization and development agenda?

Research, Development, and Poverty

The use of research to advance the agendas and goals of the colonial and neocolonial projects has been indisputable—indeed, some anti- and decolonization researchers and academicians have suggested that the word *research* is "probably one of the dirtiest words in the indigenous world's vocabulary" (Smith, 1999). Western researchers, like the anthropologists of pre-colonial times, operate as instruments of western hegemony, imperialism, and eurocentrism and accomplish their goals through the production of "research" that provides justification for the development of policies and international legal instruments that underpin the West's incursion into Africa through development, modernization, and globalization programs. It has been argued that the West has used research not only to usurp and exercise discursive and interpretive authority over African knowledges, but also to repackage it for western consumption (Sium, 2014).

As well, research has been implicated in the depiction of Africa as sick and "failed" and therefore in need of western development, a theory grounded and universalized through "failed-state" discourses that have suspiciously neglected to account for the role of colonization and ensuing historical, social, and political conditions that have produced that failure (Sium, 2012). National identity loss is another outcome of research in Africa. Wa Thiong'o has argued that research has been used to interpret history prejudicially to the benefit of the West, resulting in the loss of identity for African nations, thus leaving their fate to imperialist interests in the name of modernity (wa Thiong'o, 1986). Research has also been implicated in the privileging of the West's interpretation of African knowledge through an exegetic monopoly of eurocentric thought that has not only led to objectification, commodification, and decontextualization of African knowledges through research findings, but has also legitimized that interpretation through institutions such as universities, governments, and major media corporations (Sardoval, 2002). Such repackaged African knowledge is appropriated and universalized as legitimate knowledge and often used by policymakers and governments in a self-serving fashion, to the detriment of the original owners of the knowledge. The interpretation is steeped in assumptions and misconceptions emanating from embedded colonialist, eurocentric, and racist undertones cloaked in the seductive language of development and modernization, and

> it's under the guise of research that the West turns its soldiers of development loose on the continent, many of whom arrive with ideological backpacks filled with racist assumptions and misconceptions.
>
> —Sium, 2014

Sium has further argued that "the contemporary western development worker and scholar has become an extension of the colonial administrators from decades ago, modern day missionary and child of... a historical project to colonize and re-imagine Africa in the West's imperial, intellectual and now charitable imagination" (Sium, 2014). Their local partners, including research assistants, research collaborators, local governments, and NGOs and institutions of learning are implicated as well, and have become like the "good African who in post-colonial Kenya cooperated with the European colonizer, who helped the colonizer in the occupation and subjugation of his own people and country and was rewarded with being portrayed as strong, intelligent and beautiful in contrast with the resister who was characterized as ugly, weak, cowardly and scheming" (wa Thiong'o, 1986).

Western researchers, it has been postulated, come armed with development agendas in their pockets and descend on Africa under what Mamdani calls the "corrosive culture of consultancy, bearing shallow technicist prescriptions for African development with a focus on training and quantitative data collection in the hunting and gathering of raw data from which they produce consultancy reports that the West transforms into theories and development policies for Africa" (Mamdani, 2011). With povertization and infantilization of Africa agendas on hand (G.S. Dei, 2014), Sium has posited that they come in, look for authenticated experiences of poverty, despair, pain, grief, salvation, or danger (Sium, 2014), conduct research (or hire cheap African labor to do it), and return home with bagfuls of poverty stories and the occasional tribal artifact. Further, as Hountondji has postulated, research on Indigenous African culture has typically addressed the concerns of researchers (both western researchers and African researchers trained in western methodologies) and ignored the African point of view (Hountondji, 1997). Sium endorses this view by stating that

> we can think of the contemporary western development worker and scholar as an extension of the colonial administrator from decades ago. They are modern day missionaries—the sons of Conrad and daughters of Blixen ... children of a historical project to colonize and re-imagine Africa in the West's imperial, intellectual and now charitable imagination. (Sium, 2014)

Complicity and Implication of Africans in Development and Research

> *The most potent weapon in the hands of the oppressor is the mind of the oppressed.*
>
> —BIKO, 2002

Among the strategies that western researchers use to access research subjects and African local knowledges is to engage local Africans as research assistants and coresearchers as employees. As well, they gain access to local knowledge and information and data freely by flaunting money and resources to local researchers and research subjects who, through African generosity, invite them into their homes and provide them data and information—all the time unaware that they have become research subjects. There are many examples of western academicians and researchers who vacation in Africa and befriend a local who innocently provides them with access to local information and resources based on which they publish research papers with stories of poverty and deprivation. The poorer the local, the more authentic the research. Others shamelessly go in with the purpose of pillaging African resources. An example of this is a story I was told recently of a Mzungu (white man) who was roaming about one of the counties in Central Kenya, asking locals to sell him old cultural items they had in their homes. The story is that he left with a lot of Kenya's material culture, and the locals made a few thousand shillings in return. What became of the Indigenous knowledges embedded in those cultural items? Since the researcher knew that those cultural items belonged to the community and were part of the Indigenous knowledges of the locals, were these "innocent" transactions not tantamount to theft of the cultural heritage of the locals? Taking advantage of people's lack of knowledge and awareness and stealing symbols of their cultural heritage is exploitative and morally reprehensible.

The role of western education in facilitating the exploitation of African resources is well established by research (G.S. Dei, 2014; Sicherman, 1995; wa Thiong'o, 1986). As one of the tools of colonialism, western education has been implicated in advancing the colonial project by turning African researchers and academics into agents of the West through the inculcation and inheritance of a colonial education system and consciousness that has led to the internalization of the colonial world outlook (wa Thiong'o, 1986). According to Ndlove-Gatsheni, African researchers and academicians have been blinded by colonialism such that they continue to believe uncritically in the importance of development...without critically interrogating the colonial matrices embedded in those terms (Ndlovu-Gatsheni, 2012). In *Decolonizing the Mind*, wa Thiong'o has argued that the colonial "'cultural bomb'...the loss of our African culture...has served to annihilate a people's belief in...themselves such that they believe in the superiority of the colonizer and the necessity and virtue of their own colonization by embracing the ways of the colonizer as inherently superior." He has continued to caution Africans not to become the "cool, level headed servant native elite educated to prop the Empire" (wa Thiong'o, 1986).

Complicity has also been facilitated by what Dei has called the seduction of privilege, where racially minoritized bodies sometimes assume some of the trappings of whiteness to gain acceptability and credibility and mimic eurocentric ideas such that they continue to distance themselves from their marginalized and racially defined communities (Dei, 2007), a state of mind that has been referred to as a form of colonial brainwashing, the worst form of slavery (Shengold, 1989; Sicherman, 1995). This mindset continues to underpin the clamor for employment in the development industry that is so rife in cities such as Nairobi, in the belief that the best reward for one's hard-earned western education is a U.N. job. The situation holds true not only for job seekers but also for institutions of higher learning, including African universities at which research grants from international development organizations are coveted prizes. Like the rural farmers selling their cultural items, the educated academician and researcher become equally implicated in participating in colonial and neocolonial development research that takes Indigenous knowledges into the global marketplace. Likewise, researchers and scholars of the African diaspora are also implicated in development research and propagate the eurocentric ideologies from their western location, often driven by the need to remain relevant in research circles or under threat of loss of career momentum for failing to publish. Molefi Asante has asserted that sometimes African Americans believe in western cultural power so strongly that their own knowledge becomes only a part of the European's captured knowledge—often captured from themselves (Asante, 2009). Tuwihai Smith, speaking of the devastating effects of research on Indigenous peoples, has argued that colonialism is far from being a "finished business and has turned indigenous people to merely the 'researched'" (Smith, 1999).

It has been argued that colonization and neocolonization in Africa are as alive today as they were during colonial times and that modern-day researchers have just continued where early anthropologists left off (Dei & Anamuah-Mensa, 2014). It is no wonder, then, that progressive anti-colonial research discourses have emerged. In the following section, I will illuminate strategies that Afrocentric and other progressive researchers have proposed to wrestle away research on Africans from the stranglehold of western, eurocentric thought paradigms by ensuring that development research in Africa works "for" and "with" us and not "on" us (Baccar, 2012). I will then offer proposals for alternative and parallel strategies on how we can start to decolonize development research a colonial tool, considering that western research and development have continued to colonize Africa, with negative consequences for Africans and their continent.

Toward Counter-Narratives for Development Research in Africa

Theorizing Decolonization

As we construct research and development decolonization theories that will move us from "there" to" here," Dei reminds us that the worth of those theories must be measured not only by their philosophical grounding but—even more important—by their power to offer a social and political corrective. In short, our theories should bring transformative change to our daily political practices (Dei, 2000). The idea is that social theories must bring about positive change that enables self-reflection and allows us to see ourselves and how we relate to others. In the words of wa Thiong'o, theories must produce liberating discourses within which to see each other in relationship to ourselves and to others (wa Thiong'o, 1986). Decolonizing theories offer alternative pathways to reclaiming our knowledges and languages and ask that we interrogate western development and research practices for their violation of our Indigenous principles and values. These theories are counter-colonialist and offer theoretical and philosophical decolonizing perspectives. Afrocentricity, for example, provides an Afrocentric research framework that uses the principles of Afrocentricity to ground research in the viewpoint of African identity as constructed by Africans, giving them agency over research as researchers who are centered, located, and oriented instead of being in the position of the researched.

The Need for Developing Counter-Narratives

Developing counter-narratives to colonizing development research requires asking important questions about who, how, when, why, what, and for whom the research is conducted. It is also important that we critically examine how the research findings are consumed in order to identify who the actual beneficiaries are and what benefit, if any, flows to the research subject (Bishop, 1999). It is crucial that researchers be grounded in an anti-colonial or a decolonial and anti-racist framework and mindset that will allow them to engage in meaningful, respectful, and mutually responsible research that acknowledges and respects the value of local Indigenous knowledges and culture (Hart, 2010). The outcome would be a decolonizing research framework that underscores respect for the Land, the people, their knowledge, and their spiritual and cultural values, and that is relevant to and consistent with their worldview.

Engaging Indigenous Worldviews in Research and Development

According to Barker's definition, a worldview is the way in which a person tends to understand his or her relationship with social institutions, nature, objects, other people, and spirituality (Barker, 1999). Worldviews affect people's belief systems, decision making, assumptions, and modes of problem-solving. They are relational, privilege community, familial relations, respect for individualism, and advance community needs over self-interest and individualism (Simpson, 2001). For example, the Indigenous African worldview is based on the principles of Ubuntu, an African cultural view that captures the essence of what it means to be human and is based on the five principles of sharing and collectivity, importance of people and relationships over things, participatory decision making and leadership, patriotism, and reconciliation as a goal of conflict management (Venter, 2004). An example of a worldview is Molefi Asante's Afrocentric worldview, which is based on African cultural beliefs, practices, and values (Asante, 1987). Consequently, African culture has been defined as referring to the customs, beliefs, values, knowledge, habits, skills, arts, values, and a way of life of African people; and an African worldview, then, is the worldview that is informed by African culture (Barker, 1999). For research on Africa and Africans to be authentic and respectful of African culture and to be of value to the people, it is imperative that researchers honor, value, and incorporate the principles of the African worldview (Hart, 2010).

Other requirements for responsible and decolonized research practice call for researchers to be grounded in their Indigeneity and Indigenous knowledges (Smith, 1999). For development research in Africa, being grounded in one's Indigeneity and language is to be decolonizing, counter-colonialist, and anti-eurocentric in their research practices. In 1991, the World Bank defined *Indigeneity* as a close attachment to ancestral territories and to the natural resources of these areas; self-identification and identification by others as members of a distinct cultural group, having an Indigenous language that is often different from the national language; the presence of customary social and political institutions; and production that is primarily subsistence-oriented (U.N., 1983). Decolonizing research requires Indigeneity on the part of the researcher, including having an experiential knowledge of African Indigeneity grounded in culture that is relational, personal, oral, experiential, holistic, local, and conveyed in narrative or metaphorical language (Maurial, 1999).

Reclaiming/ReAffirming Indigeneity and Indigenous Knowledges

The primacy of Indigeneity and Indigenous knowledges has been buttressed by researchers and academicians. A single definition of *Indigeneity* has been elusive within the international community. For example, the U.N. has defined *Indigeneity* using an identification approach that identifies Indigenous people as tribal peoples in independent countries who are regarded as Indigenous, or people who self-identify as Indigenous, or tribal (ILO, 1989). Other definitions have recognized Indigenous peoples as individuals, communities, and nations who, having a historical continuity with pre-invasion and pre-colonial societies that developed on their territories, consider themselves distinct from other societies now prevalent in those territories. As historical occupiers of their ancestral lands, these Indigenous peoples have a keen determination to preserve, develop, and transmit to future generations their ancestral territories and identity, in accordance with their own cultural patterns, social institutions, language, and legal systems (Cobo, 1982). Key identifying features of Indigeneity have included historical occupation of land, history of being conquered, dispossession and dislocation from the land by settlers, distinctiveness from others, descendance from non-Europeans, and so forth (Gurr, 2000; Howes, 1996; Purcell, 1998; United Nations, 2004). Of note is that these western definitions of *Indigeneity* have been contested by Indigenous researchers who challenge aspects of these attributes. For example, not all Indigenous people are nondominant or were conquered (Agrawal, 1995; Alfred, 1999). Further, it has been argued that these western definitions serve to interfere with Indigenous group identities, which vary over time and place, are postmodernist and imperialistic, and serve to partition Indigenous bodies and communities by imposing political/legal fictions of cultural peoples (Anderson, 2001).

In theorizing the West's definition of *Indigeneity*, one must ask pointed questions that invoke the power embedded in definitions. The relationship between a definition and identity is crucial, as it is infused with power, as well as with power, privilege, and discursive authority over others. Standing in opposition to the Western definitions are the Indigenous peoples' conceptualizations of self, which are not only a form of resistance but also a means of challenging the power embedded in others' definition of the self. Consequently, Indigenous people self-define as people who have long understood their existence as peoples or nations, as expressed in their own languages in the axis of land, culture, and community, and have defined *Indigeneity* as the state of being Indigenous: as thinking, speaking, and acting with the conscious intent of regenerating one's own Indigeneity (Alfred & Corntassel, 2005).

Reclaiming and invoking Indigeneity is a form of Indigenous resistance that informs an Indigenist anti-colonial approach to produce oppositional counter-discourses of resistance, to bring to the fore questions of power, colonial imposition, and the imperial tendencies of knowledge to subvert a hegemonic neoliberal agenda and begin to reclaim global learning (G.S. Dei, 2014). Yet others such as Eva Marie Garroutte have recommended a "radical Indigenism" that reasserts and rebuild traditional knowledge from its roots, its fundamental principles, and argues for inclusion of spiritual and sacred elements in academic discourse (Garroute, 2003), while Sium calls for researchers to assume an anti-colonial Indigeneity (Sium, 2014). An Indigenous approach to research interrogates the power relations between the researcher and the subject and speaks to the ownership of knowledge produced by the research. It requires that African subjects of the research are aware of the research their environment, interacting with researchers from a position of strength and rootedness. Decolonization of the mind is crucial (wa Thiong'o, 1986) and must engage the principles of a person's worldview and Indigeneity to reclaim that person's identity.

Invoking Indigenous Identities

The reclamation of Indigenous identity is oppositional to counter-colonialism and requires decolonization to protect the Indigenous identity, which colonialism seeks to subvert and destroy. Dei has argued that decolonization is a political and intellectual act that begins by asking new questions to replace and reimagine alternatives to colonial thinking and practices (Dei, 2017). According to Okafor, by decolonizing our minds, we develop a critical perception of ourselves as learners, our place, history, identity, culture, and memory, and abandon all reflexes of subordination (Okafor, 1991). Further, we must pursue a decolonization of the spaces that make the research possible, the transformation of our identities and reclamation of our Indigenous roots (Zavala, 2013). Reclaiming our Indigenous identity, roots, and spaces for research requires fighting, resisting, and calling out the power and racism that are inherent in western research practices. Western researchers come with white privilege that accords them power and discursive and interpretive authority over research. They also use their resources to exert their privilege by parading research money before people and communities that their development practices have impoverished or povertized. This privilege is steeped in whiteness, something that "others" the ethnicities of Africans and becomes the norm by which other races are defined (Gilborn, 2006). Linda Tuwihai Smith has called for a modern Indigenous peoples' research project that resists the oppression found within research (Smith, 1999), while wa Thiong'o has argued that in working toward decolonization, we must consciously and critically assess how our minds have been affected by colonization (wa Thiong'o, 1986).

Problematizing Western Education

It has been posited that western education has served as an instrument of mental subversion, 'breaking down the students' mental tissues and re-constructing them along western lines, a process of systemic conditioning and de-culturation of students that was supposed to distance them from their families through cultural isolation and eventual passive submission to European culture (Sicherman, 1995).

To engage in truly decolonizing research practices, it is crucial for African scholars and academicians to decolonize their research by reacquainting themselves with their own culture and knowledge systems (Owusu-Ansah & Mji, 2013). As well, research methodologies are conducted using the western research processes that privilege the researcher and position the providers of the knowledge as subjects. The researcher, who often comes from outside the community, is in a powerful position as the provider of research resources (most often money) and as the knowing body, while the knowledge holders are positioned as passive, unknowing subjects whose role is simply to tell their stories. In the African worldview, knowledge is not for sale but is rather to be shared for the benefit of others and the community. The African worldview does not treat Indigenous knowledge as property, and thus the owners of the knowledge do not perceive the research as transactional or the payment—if any—as reimbursement for their knowledge. Rather, they see the payment as compensation for their time, during which the knowledge is given free of charge.

Indigenizing and Decolonizing Research and Development Practices

Research conducted on Indigenous communities is often undertaken by outsiders who are ignorant of the local culture and language of the people and who conduct research in a colonizing manner, unless they ground themselves in the respective community's worldview or in their own Indigeneity. Moreover, they may be required by their employers to conduct research in a colonizing manner without asking questions. I have heard of those who conduct research by asking culturally inappropriate questions, using culturally inappropriate words that transgress the cultural boundaries of language use and decorum, and who end up disrespecting the knowledge holders, who are often elders. Some researchers deliberately or through ignorance fail to educate the knowledge holders as to the purpose of their research, who stands to benefit from it, and how and whether the knowledge to be gained has a cash value. They fail to offer (or choose to withhold) any information about the business aspect of the research, often making it appear as though they are volunteers on a benevolent helping mission. So, through African generosity, they are provided facilitative services, often without paying for them. There is no doubt, then, that research is often exploitative; that it undervalues, disregards, and disrespects African people, their culture, and their knowledges; and that it continues to advance and enhance the interests of the western researcher or the colonized local researcher/development practitioner.

Rootedness and Cultural Location

> *Do we start from There and move to Here . . . a colonial process, a self-negating process or move from Here to There . . . the anti-colonial, the self-affirmative, the progressive process?*
>
> —WA THIONG'O, 1986

Decolonizing development and development research requires us to ask ourselves the fundamental question of whether we move from a colonizing *there* to *here*, or from a decolonizing *here* to *there*. The colonial project has moved us from our original and authentic positions of pre-colonial *here*, such that our colonized minds now operate from *there*. The process of finding our way back home requires the decolonization of our minds and, through that, the decolonization of our institutions and ways of living, guided by and anchored in our Indigeneity, Indigenous knowledges, and languages. In this section I will highlight decolonization approaches that have been offered by researchers. While these approaches are by no means exhaustive, they provide strategies and starting points for decolonization of research and international development programs in Africa and other colonized countries.

Cultural location should take precedence over the research topic or the data under consideration. It challenges the dominant worldview of research and the production of knowledge by asking researchers to avoid what Asante calls *technocratic rationality*, which restricts diversity in terms of research methods and inquires about the personal connection the researcher has to the people or topic being researched, locates Africa as the cultural center for the study of African experiences, and interprets research data from an African perspective (Asante, 1987). Another example of an Indigenous research framework is one developed by the Maori of New Zealand—namely, the Kaupapa Maori approach to research, a discursive research framework that ensures that the Maori actualize their self-determination and have agency as research participants. In Kaupapa Maori research, the researcher is a seeker of a way of knowing and not an expert (Bishop, 1999). The Whanau, a supervisory organizational structure, handles research and resolves outsider/insider research dilemmas (Smith, 1999). The Afrocentric and Kaupapa Maori research paradigms offer excellent examples of how research can be decolonized using an Indigenous framework and worldview. And just as research can be decolonized, development can be decolonized as well. Dei encourages the adoption of an "endogenous development paradigm" requiring that local people be involved in all stages of the development agenda, including planning, design, implementation, and evaluation, and the identification of socially responsible local facilitators who can best articulate locally defined needs and aspirations (Dei, 1993).

Challenging Western Accountability and Complicity

Colonized and marginalized people are often vested with the responsibility of "making things right," or at least addressing the wrong, and often seek strategies for addressing the harm. As the ones who know where the proverbial shoe pinches, they cannot sit idly by and do nothing about the pain of the transgressions of colonialism. They often find themselves engaged in decolonization activities that include educating the colonizer—with the colonizer becoming a silent observer or, at worst, engaged in devising new tools of recolonization. Africans and other colonized people around the world are busy putting out fires from new colonial mini-projects that keep sprouting like mushrooms in the social, economic, political, and cultural lives of the people. Rarely is there time to pause to shift the gaze to the colonizer and hold him or her accountable for the ills of colonization. More important, little time is left for demanding that colonizing practices be stopped or to debate liberatory approaches for sanctioning and holding the colonizers accountable. Indigenous-infused research continues to focus on exposing the ills of colonialism and on seeking remedies to help the colonized overcome the pain of colonialism. While acknowledging the research that has been ongoing, I propose three areas for further research that can widen the decolonization research space and address pertinent accountabilities.

Challenging Our Own Complicities in the Academy

Black African scholars, students, and researchers have a responsibility to acknowledge and challenge their own complicities, not only in their academic and research activities but also in their pursuit of other opportunities that come with the privilege of being in the academic spaces they inhabit. Dei has argued that Black African scholars are implicated by their silence and failure to articulate Indigeneity and Indigenous knowledges as necessary tools for decolonization of development or to engage in African Indigenous discourses (G.S. Dei, 2014). Furthermore, they often fail to engage opportunities and discourses that privilege and harness the power of African cultural resource knowledges (Matowanyika, 1990) and that reconceptualize African development through spiritual ontologies and epistemologies (Belay, 2011). Belay has argued the need for African scholars to rethink culture, science, and technology in development; to ask whose technology, science, and culture should drive development; and to inquire about what kind of development is being envisioned. He has cited the need to theorize development outside the confines of western conceptualizations of development, and he challenges researchers to develop a culturally sustainable development framework informed by Indigenous knowledges and science.

Apart from challenging complicity and silence on questions of social difference, Black scholars must be willing to take the risks associated with scrutinizing and challenging power and resistance that is embodied in the colonial spaces and bodies that inhabit and control the academy by challenging institutional and structural barriers embedded in the functions of the academy. Further, Black African scholars need to critically examine their pedagogy and how it engages students through a nonlinear, Indigenous philosophy of circularity, orality, and spirituality, as upheld by Indigenous knowledges, and be willing to pioneer new analytical systems for understanding Africa (Yankah, 2004). For Black African scholars, challenging their own complicity must entail engaging in anti-colonial educational pursuits that require the interrogation of western education. They must ask themselves whether the education they provide equips their learners with what they need to attain cultural empowerment, reclaim their histories, and provide lessons for negotiating and navigating their present and future lives. Does it build on their Indigenous identities and knowledges? Does it decolonize or recolonize their minds? (Dei, 2017; Smith, 1999; wa Thiong'o, 1986). These are crucial questions that must trouble not only Black African academicians and researchers, but also those allies who wish to engage in development and research in Africa.

Issues in Challenging Complicities

Engaging these questions does not come without risks. It is important to consider the power and privilege that inform the teacher and the learner, the teacher and the academy, and the academy's history and philosophy. What risks are involved in challenging powerful dominant and privileged bodies and institutions? What does a Black African scholar need to challenge these powerful entities? The adage "power is very powerful" is a real threat that must be navigated if one is to challenge power and privilege in the academy.

To the Black scholar, the western academy is a colonial space whose functions are directed through a eurocentric worldview. It is a space that can engage in colonial practices and further the colonial agenda through its research focus while allowing decolonizing discourses to take place. The challenge is in how power is negotiated in those conversations and who gets discursive authority over research decisions and resources. Precarious employment for nontenured faculty, lack of access to research dollars, and the need to continuously justify his or her relevance through mountains of research under the threat of the publish-or-perish imperative can create obstacles to challenging power and engaging in decolonizing discourses. It is no wonder, then, that the resumes of Black faculty often look like mini-manuscripts, while nonracialized faculty seem to be able to get away—and even advance—with the occasional publication.

Beyond Decolonization: Futurity and Indigenous Resurgence

The future of decolonizing discourses lies in the imagination of decolonized futures that are built on decolonized philosophies, mindsets, and structures. While decolonization is not a destination but instead a process, questions such as these must be asked: What future are we decolonizing for? What does it look like? To some, this imagination would appear to be utopian and unreachable, but this proposition is open to question. In this section, I will argue that a decolonized future is not based in a distant location, but resides within us, requiring only that we awaken our senses and faculties to the Indigenousness that resides in our psyches and collective memories. This memory is embodied in us and is part of Indigenous knowledges based on our worldview. Such knowledge resides in Indigenous traditions and customs (De La Torre, 2004) transmitted through language and speech, memory, recall, repetition, and orality that reside in elders (Howes, 1996). The dynamism of Indigenous knowledges exists in a local context and is anchored to a social group setting at a specific time (Agrawal, 1995). It stands in juxtaposition to wider realms of meaning connected to history, place, and people, and as dynamic knowledge it moves with and within us (Dei, Hall, & Rosenthal, 2000). In Africa, for example,

Indigenous knowledges are understood in the context of local proverbs, parables, fables, myths, mythologies, and folklore, and contain words of wisdom, instruction, and knowledge about societies as sources of Indigenous cultural knowing (Dei, 2008). Due to its dynamism, it changes with time and place. As subjective knowledge, it is historical and rooted in Indigenous peoples' cultural experiences, residing in undocumented observations in tangible and intangible antihegemonic forms, in contrast with western science (Dei et al., 2000). It is with this understanding of the knowledge embodied in our beings, culture, language, relationships, epistemologies, cosmologies, and ontologies that the decolonizing power of Indigenous resurgence can be unleashed.

How can it be explained that, despite hundreds of years of settler occupation, colonialism, and cultural genocide, Indigenous people have managed to survive? What underpins the collective kinship that buttresses resistance to oppression and the collective empathy we feel when transgressions are visited among us? Despite the never-ending atrocities of colonialism and neocolonialism, Indigenous people are like the proverbial Phoenix that rises from the ashes. Indigenism is inherent in us, and it is because of it that our survival has been ensured. Resurgence is about invoking this power that has been suppressed by western colonizing influences. Recently I saw a Kenyan youth wearing a T-shirt that read: "I do not need therapy. I just need to go to Kenya." As an Indigenist thinker, I was reminded of the spirit that must connect this young diasporic person with his ancestral lands. Indigenism, I would argue, is that spirit that informs resurgence and infuses it with the powers of survival and resistance.

Indigenizing the Academy and the Role of the African Academy in Development

The awareness of the power of Indigeneity and resurgence will allow for challenging colonial and oppressive sites and institutions of western power and privilege. As Black African scholars and researchers, we must begin to imagine not only in our psyches but also within the realm of physicality how we can imagine and create a decolonized future. In this section I will focus on strategies premised on the concept of *Futurity*, which allows us to imagine how decolonized institutions, minds, and bodies would look. How can we envision decolonized development and research? According to Linda Tuwihai Smith, decolonization is a social and political process aimed at undoing the multifaceted impacts of the colonial project and re-establishing strong contemporary indigenous nations and institutions based on traditional values, philosophies, and knowledge (Smith, 1999). It requires subverting hegemonic ways of thinking, imagining new futures, and designing communities informed by Indigenous philosophies (Dei, 2000).

Designing new communities informed by Indigenous philosophies calls for rethinking our educational institutions and academies. What would an African academy look like, and what role would it play in development and research? How would an African academy be Indigenized? A future in which this academy exists has been theorized by academicians and researchers, who argue that an African academy must begin by incorporating "an indigenous anti-colonial discursive practice as resistance to the historic and continuing… damage that dominant [Western-informed] narratives and practice of development have and continue to foster on the African human condition" (G.J. Dei, 2014, p. 16; Yankah, 2004). Not only must they be grounded in a philosophy that champions an African-centered development approach; they must also challenge colonizing knowledges rooted in eurocentricity that purport to know us better than we know ourselves (Prah, 1997). Scholarship in the African academy must take on the responsibility of uncovering and subverting the power hierarchies of global colonizing powers through anti-colonial perspectives, as well as the complicities in the hegemony of global development (Charania, 2011).

The African academy must also challenge western notions of modernity and the violence of development discourses on the social values and cultural norms of Africans through the West's binary of modern/traditional—with modern representing western development and traditional seen as barbaric, backward, and evil—that works to alienate Africans from their social reality (Agrawal, 1995; Appiah, 1992; Lauer, 2007). In challenging western eurocentricity, the African academy must be grounded within an Indigenous pedagogic framework that engenders an emancipatory commitment to public education in order to construct counter-hegemonic discourses and struggles that critically question and offer alternatives to liberatory learning that brings about social and personal change (Regnier, 1991). Furthermore, educators must engage in critical education that interrogates privilege, eurocentrism, research, and education curricula to engage what Dei calls the "Deep Curriculum" and the ideals of epistemological equity (Bowers, 2006; G.J. Dei, 2014; Smith, 1999). The goal of this critical education should be to awaken us to the wisdom of traditional Indigenous cultures and to the illusions of western education, media, politics, and public discourse that deny that wisdom of traditional Indigenous culture (Bowers, 2006).

African scholars have called for the creation of centers of Indigenous knowledge systems and languages devoted to African development through the exploration of Indigenous science, technology, and culture to promote African human cultural development and Indigenous resource applications (Asante, 1987; G.S. Dei, 2014; Wangoola, 2000). Such centers of Indigenous knowledge are rooted in African Indigeneity within an Afrocentric framework. As African centers of Indigenous knowledge systems or African universities, they should be distinguished from universities in Africa that are relics of a colonial education and whose goal is to subvert the African mind (wa Thiong'o, 1986). African universities should engage in discourses that question the dominant paradigms and models of development that subjugate and marginalize local voices and intellectual agencies, and should aim to educate and produce what researchers have called "our own national experts on development informed by indigenous knowledge systems for local science and industrial development (Etzkowitz & Dzisah, 2007). They should aim to decolonize development by producing what Lebakeng calls a people-centered, culturally sustainable development framework to counter the prism of market-oriented economics

(Lebakeng, 2010). Pedagogic practices should be informed by Indigenous knowledges using the community as classroom (Stites & Semali, 1991).

Finally, conventional development discourses seem to focus on gender issues and African women as the targets of development programs. They highlight the issues of women's rights to land and resources, feminize poverty, and target women with experimental reproductive, economic, health, and educational access rights. The African girl has become the poster child of the western NGOs Me to We, Plan International, and others. Women's socioeconomic, political, health, and educational rights are paramount in western research and development programs. This focus on women calls for critical interrogation concerning its implication in the colonization of African women by western education and development programs. Unfortunately, African researchers, including this writer, are implicated in advancing that narrative (Karanja, 1991; McCarney, 1991; Meinzen-Dick, Kameri-Mbote, & Markelova, 2009). This focus is realized through the feminization of poverty programs, as well as education programs that tout the benefits of privileging the education of women over that of males.

What is crucial to understand is that in pre-colonial Africa, women held powerful structural positions within the family, and this abused, poor, and disenfranchised African woman syndrome that permeates development programs in Africa came with development and modernization. The focus on African women and development is suspicious. Could it be that women are targeted because, demographically, they outnumber men and are more suitable targets for development programs in their communities? It is also imperative to examine the narrative of the abused, overworked African woman who must be saved from all forms of abuse and exploitation by her male relatives, especially her husband, and whose only salvation comes from the handouts of development programs. What is the impact of the targeting of African women by development and modernization programs?

Alternative Decolonizing Paradigms and Proposals for Further Research

In decolonizing development and research, Black African scholars and development agents must question western definitions of development and research. They should also seek to disrupt and subvert prevailing development and research practices that are anchored in manufactured African poverty and modernization narratives. Questions must be asked: What is development, and what is research? Who gets to define these terms? Whom do they serve and how are they practiced or implemented in Africa? Why does Africa provide such fertile ground for western development and research practices? Any researcher or development practitioner or agent who does not answer these questions truthfully must face his or her complicity in advancing the colonial agenda in Africa and among Africans. To begin addressing these questions, I offer proposals for further inquiry as follows.

(1) I propose further research that casts the gaze on western colonizers to investigate the extent to which they hold themselves accountable for the violence of colonialism, modernization, and development programs in Africa, and what they have done to right the wrongs they have perpetrated on those they have colonized. I argue that it is not enough to create U.N. policy statements, conventions, and legal instruments that have no built-in accountability frameworks or capacity to address the negative consequences of their decision-making and program-implementation activities. Furthermore, crafted apologies and half-hearted reconciliation programs should no longer be sufficient when the oppressor continues to devise more efficient strategies for continued colonization or recolonization. We must hold western researchers accountable and ask the question: What are you doing to hold your countries accountable for the negative consequences of their policies on developing countries? What kind of ally are you?

(2) I further propose that African researchers begin focusing on research that demonstrates the many things that Africans and Africa are doing right. Despite the brutality of colonialism, Africa and Africans continue to survive, and very little research is being conducted on these manifestations of resilience. We can leave the dirty work of povertizing Africa to western researchers while we concentrate on telling the stories of our successes. Continuing the status quo is a kind of complicity that places us in the same category as the colonizers.

(3) Our countries and governments have allowed western researchers to run roughshod over our countries in the name of research and development. Researchers and academicians should join with civil society and social justice advocates to require that our governments develop legislative frameworks for how outsiders should conduct research in our countries. Such legislative frameworks should be guided by our Indigenous worldview and knowledge.

(4) African governments should establish protocols that require any research conducted in Africa to be vetted by a college of Afrocentric scholars from the African academy. Research proposals should be vetted for compliance with African Indigenous philosophies of Afrocentrism, Ubuntu, and so on. Further, there should be monitoring processes to ensure that the research is conducted in compliance with those Afrocentric principles.

(5) Universities in Africa should be required to have Indigenous Studies departments or colleges in order to begin giving back to the community. Western education in Africa corrupts not only the best brains but is funded by taxpayers. Mandating an Indigenous department in the university should be seen as part of its corporate social responsibility.

Conclusion

The coloniality of research and development has excluded Indigenous communities from research processes and decontextualized cultural knowledge and reinforced the image of Africa as a continent in need of saving, and Africans as poverty and disease laden (Wright, 2014). To challenge this narrative, it behooves us not only to decolonize our minds, but also to critically question how we are implicated in the colonial project, and the role of the education we receive in reinforcing our complicity. We must ask what our relative complicities are in the hegemonic sway of the global, and our matching responsibilities to uncover and subvert the power hierarchies of globalism through an Indigenist anti-colonial perspective (G.S. Dei, 2014). We must invest in decolonial research protocols that require that western and other non-African researchers adhere to decolonizing research policies (Dei, 2017). It is also critical that we challenge the discursive, interpretive, and definitional monopoly that eurocentric thought has created (Battiste, 2002) and, as Tuhiwai Smith has posited, we should adopt a "local" theoretical positioning that enables the researcher to draw on her own very "specific historical, political and social context" to develop an embedded critical theory (Smith, 1999). As researchers, we must be accountable to all our relations and examine how relationships both shape our Indigenous reality and are vital to reality itself. We must make careful choices about our selection of research topics, methods of data collection, forms of analysis, and, finally, the way we present the information (Wilson, 2009). Engaging in research practices that use Indigenous pedagogy and epistemology, including sharing circles, talking, dialogues, observations, experiential learning, modeling, meditation, prayer, ceremonies, storytelling as ways of knowing and learning is critical (Stiffarm, 1998). Finally, as colonialism is an ongoing agenda, decolonizing our minds must also be a process, not a destination.

References

Agrawal, A. (1995). Indigenous and scientific knowledge: Some critical comments. *Indigenous Knowledges and Development Monitor (IKDM), 3*(3), 3–6.

Alfred, T. (1999). *Peace, power and righteousness: An Indigenous manifesto.* Don Mills, ON: Oxford University Press.

Alfred, T., & Corntassel, J. (2005). Being Indigenous: Resurgences against contemporary colonialism. *Government and Opposition: An International Journal of Comparative Politics, 40*(4), 597–614.

Anderson, K. (2001). *A recognition of being: Reconstructing native womanhood* (2nd ed.). Toronto, ON: Women's Press.

Appiah, K. (1992). *In my father's house: Africa in the philosophy of culture.* New York, NY: Oxford University Press.

Asante, M. (1987). *The Afrocentric idea.* Philadelphia, PA: Temple University Press.

Asante, M.K. (2009, May 16). *Knowledge as property: Who owns what and why.* Retrieved from http://www.asante.net/articles/#scholarly_papers

Baccar, K.E. (2012). Moving from research *on*, to research *with* and *for* Indigenous communities: A critical reflection on community-based participatory research. *Canadian Geographer, 56*(2), 195–210.

Barker, R. (1999). *The social work dictionary.* Washington, DC: NASW Press.

Battiste, M. (2002). *Indigenous knowledge and pedagogy in First Nations education: A literature review.* Ottawa, ON: National Working Group on Education, Ministry of Indian Affairs, INAC.

Beegle, K., Christiaensen, L., Dabalen, A., & Gaddis, I. (2016). *Poverty in a rising Africa.* Washington, DC: International Bank for Reconstruction and Development/The World Bank.

Belay, S. (2011, February 24). *Recapturing spiritual and cultural values into science education: The case of Ethiopia.* Paper presented at CIDEC Seminar, OISE/UT, Toronto, Ontario.

Biko, S. (2002). *I write what I like.* Chicago, IL: University of Chicago Press.

Bishop, R. (1999). *Kaupapa Maori research: An Indigenous approach to creating knowledge.* Hamilton, ON: University of Waikato, Dept. of Psychology.

Bowers, C. (2006). The language of conquest and the loss of the commons. In *Unlearning the language of conquest: Scholars expose anti-Indianism in America* (pp. 180–189). Austin, TX: University of Texas Press.

Charania, G. (2011). Grounding the global: A call for more situated practices of pedagogical and political engagement. *ACME: An International E-Journal for Critical Geographies, 10*(3), 351–371.

Cobo, M.J. (1982). *Study of the problem of discrimination against Indigenous peoples: Final report submitted by special rapporteur.* New York, NY: United Nations Economic and Social Council, Commission on Human Rights.

Cribb, J., Joyce, R., & Phillip, D. (2012, January). *Living standards, poverty and inequality in the UK.* London, UK: Institute for Fiscal Studies.

De La Torre, J. (2004). In the trenches: A critical look at the isolation of American Indian political practices in the non-empirical social science of political science. In D.A. Mihesuah & A.C. Wilson (Eds.), *Indigenizing the academy: Transforming scholarship and transforming communities* (pp. 174–190). Lincoln, NE: University of Nebraska Press.

De Rivero, O. (2001). *The myth of development.* London, UK: Zed Books.

Dei, G. (1992). *Hardship and survival in rural West Africa.* Dakar, Senegal: Codesria.

Dei, G., & Anamuah-Mensa, J. (2014). The coloniality of development: Reforming South-South co-operation and resistance. In A. Asabere-Ameyaw, J. Anamuah-Mensah, G.S. Dei, & K. Raheem (Eds.), *Indigenous African development and related issues: Towards a transdisciplinary perspective* (pp. 27–47). Rotterdam, Netherlands: Sense Publishers.

Dei, G., Hall, B.L., & Rosenthal, D.G. (2000). *Indigenous knowledge in global contexts: Multiple readings of our world.* Toronto, ON: University of Toronto Press.

Dei, G.J. (1993). Sustainable development in the African context: Revisiting some theoretical and methodological issues. *Africa Development/Afrique et Développement, 18*(2), 97–110.

Dei, G.J. (2007). *Integrative anti-racism: Keynote address at the symposium on "Multiculturalism with(out) guarantees."* Vancouver, BC: University of British Columbia.

Dei, G.J. (2008). Indigenous knowledge studies and the next generation: Pedagogical possibilities for anti-colonial education. *Australian Journal of Indigenous Education, 37*(S), 5–13.

Dei, G.J. (2014). Reflections on "African development": Situating Indigeneity and Indigenous knowledges. In E. Shizha & A.A. Abdi (Eds.), *Indigenous discourses on knowledge and development in Africa* (pp. 15–30). New York, NY: Routledge.

Dei, G.J. (2017, May 10). *Decolonizing education for inclusivity: Implications for literacy education* (keynote speech). Retrieved from https://www.uregina.ca/education/assets/docs/pdf/events/20170310-11-Decolonizing-Teacher-Education-Presentation-George-Dei.pdf

Dei, G.S. (2000). *Indigenous knowledge in global context: Multiple readings of our world.* Toronto, ON: University of Toronto Press.

Dei, G.S. (2014). Abstract: Global education from an "Indigenist" anti-colonial perspective. *Journal of Contemporary Issues in Education, 9*(2), 4–23.

Escobar, A. (1995). *The dispersion of power: Tales of food and hunger.* Princeton, NJ: Princeton University Press.

Etzkowitz, H., & Dzisah, J. (2007). The triple helix of innovation: towards a university-led development strategy for Africa. *ATDF Journal, 4*(2), 3–10.

Garroute, E.M. (2003). *Real Indians: Identity and the survival of Native America.* Berkeley, CA: University of California Press.

Gaye, D. (2017, April 12). *Kenya economic growth update.* Retrieved from http://www.worldbank.org/en/country/kenya/overview

Gilborn, D. (2006). Rethinking white supremacy: Who counts in "WhiteWorld"? *Ethnicities, 6*(3), 318–340.

Golden, A. (2017). *Child poverty in Canada.* Ottawa, ON: Conference Board of Canada.

Gordon, D. (2005). *Indicators of poverty & hunger.* New York, NY: UN Expert Group Meeting on Youth Development.

Gurr, T.R. (2000). *People versus states: Minorities at risk in the new century.* Washington, DC: United States Institute of Peace Press.

Hart, A.M. (2010). Indigenous world views, knowledge and research: The development of an Indigenous research paradigm. *Journal of Indigenous Voices in Social Work, 1*(1), 1–16.

Howes, D. (1996). Cultural appropriation and resistance in the American West: Decommodifying Indianness. In D. Howes (Ed.), *Cross-cultural consumption: Global markets, local realities* (pp. 138–160). New York, NY: Routledge.

Hunter, G. (2011). *Poverty in Canada and Saskatchewan in 2011: No closer to the truth.* Regina, SK: University of Regina, Social Policy Research Unit.

ILO. (1989). *Convention concerning Indigenous and tribal peoples in independent countries* (No. 169). Geneva: General Conference of the International Labour Organisation.

International Development and Research Centre. (n.d.). *477 research activities worth CA$96.9 million since 1972.* Retrieved from https://www.idrc.ca/en/what-we-do/regions-and-countries/sub-saharan-africa/kenya

Karanja, P. (1991). Women's land ownership rights in Kenya. *Third World Legal Studies, 10*, art. 6, 109–135.

Kossi, A. (2012). The impact of globalization on African countries' economic development. *African Journal of Business Management*, 57–76.

Lauer, H. (2007). Depreciating African political culture. *Journal of Black Studies, 38*(2), 288–307.

Lebakeng, T. (2010). Discourse on Indigenous knowledge systems, sustainable social economic development and the challenge of the academy in Africa. *Codesria Bulletin, 1*(2), 24–29.

Mamdani, M. (2011, April 21). The importance of research in a university. *Pambazuka News.* Retrieved from www.pambazuka.org/en/category/features/72782

Matowanyika, J. (1990). *Cultural heritage as a resource towards sustainable rural Africa in the 20th century.* Paper read at the Annual Conference of the Canadian Association of African Studies, Dalhousie University, Halifax, Nova Scotia.

Marx, K. (1967). *Capital.* In *The collected works of Karl Marx and Frederick Engels*, Vol. 35. New York, NY: International Publishers.

Maurial, M. (1999). Indigenous knowledge and schooling: A continuum between conflict and dialogue. In L.M. Semali & J.L. Kincheloe (Eds.), *What is Indigenous knowledge? Voices from the academy* (pp. 59–77). New York, NY: Farmer Press.

McCarney, R. (1991). Household food security and the role of land in Africa. *Third World Legal Studies Journal, 10*, 157–179.

Mehmet, O. (1995). *Westernizing the Third World: The eurocentricity of economic development theories.* New York, NY: Routledge.

Meinzen-Dick, R., Kameri-Mbote, P., & Markelova, H. (2009). *Property rights for poverty reduction.* New York, NY:

Ndlovu-Gatsheni, S.J. (2012). *Coloniality of power in development studies and the impact of global imperial designs on Africa.* Inaugural lecture, Archie Mafeje Research Institute (AMRI) and Department of Development Studies, University of South Africa.

Okafor, V. (1991). Diop and the African origin of civilization: An Afrocentric analysis [book review]. *Journal of Black Studies, 22*(2), 252–268.

Owusu-Ansah, F.E., & Mji, G. (2013). African Indigenous knowledge and research. *African Journal of Disability, 2*(1). doi:10.4102/ajod. v2i1.30

Prah, K. (1997). Accusing the victims...in my father's house: A review of Kwame Anthony Appiah's "In My Father's House." *Codesria Bulletin, 1*, 14–22.

Purcell, T.W. (1998). Indigenous knowledge and applied anthropology: Questions of definition and direction. *Human Organization*, 57(3), 258–272.

Raheem, K., Anamuah-Mensah, J., & Dei, G. (2014). Rethinking development and growth theories for Africa. In A. Asabere-Ameyaw, J. Anamuah-Mensah, G.S. Dei, & K. Raheem (Eds.), *Indigenous African development and related issues: Towards a transdisciplinary perspective* (pp. 15–26). Rotterdam, Netherlands: Sense Publishers.

Regnier, R. (1991). Nuclear advocacy and adult education: A case for counter-hegemonic struggle. *Canadian Journal for the Study of Adult Education, 5*(2), 47–62.

Sardoval, C. (2002). *Methodologies of risky scholarship.* Minneapolis, MN: University of Minnesota Press.

Shaefer, H.L., & Edin, K. (2012). *Policy brief #28: Extreme poverty in the United States 1996–2011.* Ann Arbor, MI: National Poverty Center.

Shengold, L. (1989). *Soul murder: The effect of childhood abuse and deprivation.* New York, NY: Fawcett Columbine.

Sicherman, C. (1995). Ngugi's colonial education: The subversion of the African mind. *African Studies Review, 38*(3), 11–41.

Simpson, L. (2001). Aboriginal peoples and knowledge: Decolonizing our processes. *Canadian Journal of Native Studies, 21*(1), 137–148.

Sium, A. (2012). From starving child to rebel pirate: The West's new imagery of a "failed" Somalia. *Borderlands, 11*(3). Retrieved from http://borderlands.net.au/vol11no3_2012/sium_somalia.pdf

Sium, A. (2014). Dreaming beyond the state: Centering governance as a framework for African development. In G.A. Dei (Ed.), *Centering Indigenous governance as a framework for African development* (pp. 63–82). New York, NY: Peter Lang.

Smith, L.T. (1999). *Decolonizing methodologies: Research and Indigenous peoples.* London, UK: Zed Books.

Stiffarm, L. (1998). *Aboriginal pedagogy...as we see it.* Saskatoon, SK: University of Saskatchewan Extension Press.

Stites, R., & Semali, L. (1991). Adult literacy for social equality or economic growth? Changing agendas for mass literacy in China and Tanzania. *Comparative Education Review, 35*(1), 44–75.

United Nations. (1983). *Official definitions of Indigeneity.* New York, NY: UN/WGIP.

United Nations. (2004a). *Fact sheet: Indigenous peoples, Indigenous voices.* New York, NY: United Nations Permanent Forum on Indigenous Issues.

United Nations. (2004b). *The concept of Indigenous peoples.* New York, NY: Department of Economic and Social Affairs.

wa Thiong'o, N. (1986). *Decolonizing the mind: The politics of language and African literature.* Portsmouth, NH: Heinemann.

Wangoola, P. (2000). MPAMBO: The African multiversity: A philosophy to rekindle the African spirit. In G.J.S. Dei et al. (Eds.), *Indigenous knowledges in global contexts* (pp. 265–277). Toronto, ON: University of Toronto Press.

Webb, J. (2014, November 19). *Politifact, Virginia*. Retrieved from http://www.politifact.com/virginia/statements/2014/dec/01/jim-webb/jim-webb

Wilson, C. (2000, December). Decolonizing methodologies: Research and Indgenous peoples. *Social Policy Journal of New Zealand*, 214ff.

Wilson, S. (2009). *Research is ceremony: Indigenous research methods.* Black Point, NS: Fernwood Publishing.

Wright, L.H. (2014). Transforming Canada's hegemonic global education paradigm through anti-colonial framework. In G.J.S. Dei & P.B. Adjei (Eds.), *Emerging perspectives on African development: Speaking differently* (pp. 83–97). New York, NY: Peter Lang.

Yankah, K. (2004). *Globalization and the African scholar.* [monograph]. Accra, Ghana: University of Ghana.

Zavala, M. (2013). What do we mean by decolonizing research strategies? Lessons from decolonizing, Indigenous research projects in New Zealand and Latin America. *Decolonization, Indigeneity, Education and Society*, 2(1), 55–71.

CHAPTER 11

Dreaming Our Way to New Decolonial and Educational Futurities: Charting Pathways of Hope

Kimberly L. Todd

Locating the Self

My location is rife with tensions and contradictions. I am a Canadian of Goan and Anglo Indian ancestry. I am both a settler on Turtle Island and a colonized body. Colonialism robbed me of my ancestral language, religion, culture, and Ancestors, and it is also the reason I exist; without colonization, I would not have been born. Knowing that my existence is tied to colonialism, I am always aware of the way in which it continually oppresses, extracts, and degrades knowledge forms, peoples, and the Earth. This knowledge has left me with a fragmented sense of identity, home, and place, and a deep desire to seek a sense of connection and wholeness in any way that I can, and to help others do same. Therefore, the process of decolonization offers me a way to speak and think about revival, healing, resurgence, and liberation. By undergoing the process of untethering itself from ongoing colonialism, decolonization is a domain in which I have found a home. I rely on the works of Walter Mignolo, George Dei, Leanne Simpson, Audre Lorde, and Gloria Anzaldúa, to name but a few, because their bodies of work speak to a reaffirmation of connection that is steeped in spiritual resurgence, communal activism, and a powerful renunciation of the ongoing colonial narratives. Thus, I am drawn to the unending process of decolonization and to the medium that continues to facilitate my own process of decolonizing: dreaming.

Dreams have always played a prominent role for me. For most of life I was haunted by nightmares until I began to cultivate a relationship with my dreams. That is when my worldview began to shift. Dreams have the power to instruct us about connection, transformation, and spiritual awakening by teaching us how to love. In our dreams, we can transcend the physical boundaries of our world, remember our ancestral connections to all life forms past and present, and, through this process, understand both our interconnection and interdependence with the planet. When you begin to value dreams, you begin to learn a new language, a language of the spirit that has answers to questions that colonization—through intergenerational trauma—has tried to eradicate (Jung, 1974). It is time we began valuing dreams, because they provide one of many ways to bring new decolonial futurities into our present.

Decolonial futurities reimagine worlds where the colonial skin of oppression, dehumanization, and extraction is left by the wayside. I cling to these decolonial futurities because there is a part of me that is participating in a deep remembering that is not linear, but instead cyclical. There is part of me that remembers what it is to see the world imbued with spirit and yearns for this, but I have never lived it. By spirit I mean the essence of life that connects us, that results in an interconnected and interdependent world where love operates as the binding principle that enables life to thrive, and where sentience abounds—most important, acknowledging that what we do to each other, to other life forms, and to this planet we do to ourselves, erasing the notion of our separateness. Living in a world imbued with Spirit means living this at the core of all that we do, and it is deeply relational. Decolonial futurities reimagine worlds grounded in spirit that I believe are possible, and therefore we must do the work to connect us by bridging the gap between present and future.

In my years as an elementary educator working abroad and at home, the construct of maintaining these colonial logics in the classroom was unbearable. Curricular objectives, classroom management, work ethic, and assessments all manifested the colonial logics in myriad ways. This took a toll on me mentally, emotionally, and spiritually, and I could see that it did the same to my students. I worked hard to decolonize when and where I could in the classroom by attempting to emphasize narratives that fell outside the colonial narrative, providing room for the voices of my students to be heard, allowing room for students to engage in their own spirituality, and fostering a classroom community based on trust and respect. However, my efforts always felt insufficient because the systems, structures, knowledges, and standards remained inherently colonial. These were the standards that both my students and I were measured against—what we were to aspire to—and there were and are real emotional, economic, and mental consequences for falling outside of these structures. The education system needs to be revolutionized, and in order to do this we need a vision. Educational futurities are about conjuring that vision and imagining an education system that values life, humanity, diversity, and the mind-body-soul connection of the student. Decolonization can put us on a path toward the goal of achieving an education system that sheds colonial logics.

Introduction

This chapter seeks to chart a pathway from individual to collective decolonial transformation. It begins by investigating Indigenous and decolonial futurities as a useful starting point for charting a route toward these futurities by proposing that cultivating a relationship with dreaming can enable such a path. I will return to educational futurities as the bridge between individual and collective transformation at a later point in the chapter.

I will begin by examining what Walter Mignolo (2011) terms *the colonial matrix of power* and the necessity for what he terms *decolonial options.* Utilizing the work of Indigenous and decolonial scholars, I will reflect on the role of spirituality and explore visions of new decolonial futurities. The commonalities inherent in these decolonial futurities will be laid out and tied to ways in which dreaming can facilitate these transformations, and how educational futurities can provide that bridge. Finally, educational futurities, which entail a framework for school systems built on connection, are offered to help further the decolonial process that cultivating a relationship with dreaming brings. In essence, this chapter points the way to a path of hope through dreaming. It is time for humanity to tap into its multirelational ways of communing with the world so that decolonial futurities can one day become a reality. As a starting point, the colonial matrix of power will be discussed in an effort to expose the logics and analytics of its destructive systems.

The Colonial Matrix of Power

The term *the colonial matrix of power* was first coined by Anibal Quijano and was expanded and extended in Walter Mignolo's *The Darker Side of Western Modernity: Global Futures, Decolonial Options* (2011). It explains the underlying logics through which modernity has been born. Mignolo explains the four pillars of the colonial matrix of power and how these pillars uphold the colonial matrix through hierarchies and control (2011). The first pillar comprises knowledge and subjectivity; the second pillar consists of racism, gender, and sexuality; the third is economy; and the fourth is authority (Mignolo, 2011, pp. 8–9). With these four pillars, colonialism spread throughout the world, dispossessing Indigenous people of their Land and stripping them of their languages, their cultures, their spiritualties, and their identities. As colonialists asserted control through these four pillars, colonized bodies were subjugated and oppressed. Riyad Shahjahan, in his article "Spirituality in the Academy: Reclaiming from the Margins and Evoking a Transformative Way of Knowing the World" (2005), states the following in regard to colonialism:

> Colonialism, as noted by Fanon (1963), "by a kind of perverted logic... turns to the past of the oppressed people, and distorts, disfigures, and destroys it" (p. 210). Western knowledge systems and those who materialize such

> knowledge, with a similar neo-colonial logic, have been shown to displace other ways of knowing the world (Shiva, 1995; Battiste & Henderson, 2000). (Shahjahan, 2005, pp. 693–694)

What happens when a colonized person's mind is replaced by that of the colonizers? The intergenerational trauma of this destruction reverberates into space and time, altering it in destructive ways. Thus, colonialism is about the dehumanization, degradation, and destruction of people and their identities and carries forward to the present, morphing and recreating itself through the same four pillars (Mignolo, 2011). Mignolo writes: "Let's take the example of language, knowledge, racism, authority, and economy... that transform themselves and yet remain, maintaining the logic of coloniality: the context and the content changes, but the logic remains..." (p. 19). The colonial matrix of power is demonstrated on local, national, and international scales, where systematic racism and patriarchy play out in workplaces, governments, and courts. Epistemic violence is committed daily in schools, where western knowledge reigns supreme and where national languages in settler states are always the languages of the colonizer.

Control is therefore achieved and maintained through the four previously-mentioned pillars, creating hierarchies to which all structures of modernity adhere (Mignolo, 2011). Mignolo elaborates on this concept when he writes, "They all connect through the logic that generates, reproduces, modifies, and maintains interconnected hierarchies" (p. 17). The colonial matrix of power goes back 500 years to when the Earth was spatially and physically conquered, a movement "originating in the Atlantic, then expanding and encroaching on other civilizations justified by the colonial and imperial differences" (p. 17). Thus, the colonial matrix of power is what upholds western civilization through its interconnections and intersections, which are referred to as *nodes* (p. 16). These nodes operate through hierarchies of the four pillars, shaping relations among people, institutions, governmental structures, and laws through the "colonial logics" of knowledge, gender, and sexuality, economy and authority (p. 19). Therefore, modernity is built upon and by the colonial matrix of power, ensnaring humanity. It needs to be understood and acknowledged if we are to find pathways out of its grip (Mignolo, 2011).

Colonialism and Schooling

The current education system has been considerably shaped worldwide by means of what are termed the four pillars of the colonial matrix of power, described previously. The results of the four pillars can be seen, for example, in state control of schooling, state-mandated curricula (in regard to what knowledges are validated and what knowledges are excluded), and insistence upon the use of colonial languages in schools. In the next section, I will provide a few examples of just how the current school system falls under the four pillars of the colonial matrix of power.

The first pillar of the matrix covers knowledge and subjectivity (Mignolo, 2011, pp. 8–9). Mignolo writes: "Knowledge in the colonial matrix of power was a double-edged sword: on the one hand, it was the mediation to the ontology of the world as well as a way of being in the world (subjectivity)" (p. 13). Knowledge and subjectivity are embedded in the school system with the state-mandated curriculum, which is eurocentric in nature. "Eurocentrism (as imperial knowledge whose point of origination was Europe) could be found and reproduced in the colonies and ex-colonies, as well as in locales that have not been directly colonized (routes of dispersion)" (p. 19). Eurocentrism, as such, is thus "packaged" into the curriculum through the choice of authors that read and books that are studied, the versions of history that are told, the values that are disseminated, and the languages that are employed. In the same vein, the voices, history, and literature that are excluded leave a lasting mark on students. Lisa Hart's chapter "Nourishing the Authentic Self: Teaching With Heart and Soul" in *Spirituality, Education & Society* (2011) states the following: "The curriculum is a prescriptive document based on Eurocentric knowledge that we expect all students to embrace as truth, while devaluing their own truths and lived experiences" (p. 38). Through the process of schooling, students are taught that only western eurocentric knowledge is valuable, since it positions itself as universal (Zine, 2007).

The second pillar of the colonial matrix of power addresses racism, gender, and sexuality (Mignolo, 2011, p. 8), which implicates student groups, through an exclusion of their identities and in what they learn, by masking issues of racism, gender, and sexuality. However, when this leads to student disengagement through racism, gender, and sexuality, the school system fails to address inequalities and refuses to assume any responsibility for the situation. Marie Battiste, in her book *Decolonizing Education: Nourishing the Learning Spirit* (2013), writes about education in Canada:

> The key in designing meaningful education in Canada must begin with confronting the hidden standards of racism, colonialism, and cultural and linguistic imperialism in the modern curriculum and see the theoretical incoherence with a modern theory of society.... It is a culture of nationalism imposed by the state. It is not reflective of the heritage, knowledge, or culture that the students bring to education, or their skills and shared traditions. (p. 29)

Battiste encapsulates the insidious nature of the second pillar. However, racism, gender, and sexuality, when not acknowledged, can have devastating consequences on the lives of students, who learn to internalize the dehumanization that such colonial logics seek to enact. George Dei's (2003) essay "Schooling and the Dilemma of Youth Disengagement" exposes these colonial logics. He writes: "Despite some successes, Black/African-Canadians, First Nations/Aboriginal and Portuguese students are at the forefront of student disengagement from school" (p. 244). Schools fail to adequately address the ongoing forms of oppression, whether they be racial, gender, or heteronormative in nature, even though colonial markers of difference (race, gender, and sexuality) directly influence students' success.

The third pillar of the colonial matrix of power is economy (Mignolo, 2011), and school systems enact this by aiming to produce students who are active contributors to the national economy. Riyad Shahjahan (2005) discusses economy in relation to colleges and universities and writes: "These discourses are reinforced through academic capitalism and globalization. Academic capitalism, whereby the university mimics business corporations, reinforces this positivist discourse and the concept of utilitarian knowledge" (p. 693). However, economy also plays a central role in the public school system, and this is demonstrated through the validation of some subjects over others—such as an emphasis on math, the sciences, and technology. Also, significant effects of the third pillar are seen through time allotments, funding, and the resources dedicated to such subjects. The effect of the economy can also be seen in budget cuts made to subject areas that deal with the soft sciences, arts, and/or trades, subject areas that are perceived as less economically viable. For example, M. Kathleen Thomas, Priyanka Singh, and Kristin Klopfenstein (2015) elaborate on the lack of arts education in their article "Arts Education and the High School Dropout Problem," wherein they cite the research and policy briefings related to New York City public schools from the Center for Arts Education, authored by Douglas Israel in 2011:

> Despite the transformative power that the arts can have in the lives of youth, the flow of resources into arts education is often stagnant at the best. According to the Center for Arts Education, New York City public schools eliminated or failed to replace 135 arts teachers during the 2009–2010 school year, [and] the budget for art supplies, equipment, and musical instruments was also slashed by 80%. (p. 329)

Moreover, competition is an everyday component of the school system in classrooms where assessments, testing, and grading are commonplace. Thus, when viewed under this lens, students are seen simply as cogs in the wheels of the business that is schooling, and they are required to feed the system in the global and national economy rather than operate as individuals with their own goals, ambitions, hobbies, emotions, and dreams. This leads us to the third pillar of the colonial matrix of power—the economy—which largely dictates precisely how schools are to be run, what programs or subjects of study are to receive funding, and what social and institutional values are prioritized in the school system.

The fourth pillar of the colonial matrix is authority (Mignolo, 2011), and it is demonstrated within the school system through the authority that the colonial state holds over education. After all, it is ultimately the state that determines what is to be taught, what parameters are to be used in how each subject is to be taught, and the languages employed to do the teaching (Battiste, 2013). The state upholds the principles and structures under which it was founded, and this means engaging the colonial logics that gave rise to it. In the words of Battiste, "In this way, the state has established one main stream, a culturally imperialistic stream that ignores or erodes, if not destroys, other ways of knowing or the accumulated knowledge of some groups" (p. 104). This provides fundamental challenges for educators who see firsthand the violence that invalidating other knowledge forms, languages, and histories imposes on the lives of students. Moreover, it creates substantial problems in promoting anti-colonial and decolonial frameworks for education and in validating knowledges that fall outside of eurocentric colonial standards. This will be discussed at greater length toward the close of this chapter, where a re-visioning of an education system will be enacted. The term *educational futurities* will be engaged and a framework attached to it that falls outside the four pillars of the colonial matrix of power to envision an education system that values the whole student.

Decolonial Options

Decolonization, which will be explored in this section, refers to the way in which we resist colonialism. Decolonization is about breaking free from the myriad forms of colonialism both individually and collectively. This requires an understanding of how the colonial matrix of power operates and how it permeates everyday lives, in addition to economic, political, and educational structures. Mignolo (2011) says that "Decoloniality, therefore, means both the analytic task of unveiling the logic of coloniality and the prospective task of contributing to build a world in which many worlds will coexist" (p. 54). And so, decolonization requires coexistence through diverse ways of living and thriving in the world. It also means stepping away from hegemonic forces of colonialism and finding new pathways to resurgence by un-learning, re-envisioning, and re-creating. Leanne Simpson, in her book *Dancing on Our Turtle's Back* (2011), discusses the destructiveness inherent in ongoing colonialism and the Nishnaabeg decolonial movements, which need to grow in order to help facilitate the regeneration of life. She says:

> Colonialism has only created a loss of life in terms of extinct and endangered species of animals and plants, and a drastic and traumatic decline in the quality of life for the fraction of Nishnaabeg that survived the original conquest.... Resurgence movements, then, must be movements to create more life, propel life, nurture life, motion, presence and emergence. (p. 143)

Life is at the heart of decolonization. It is about reconnecting with our multirelational ways of communing with the world by embracing the various options that emerge from this process. These options can arise through subjugated modes of epistemic thought—for example, intuition, the valuing of emotions, visions, and/or dreams. In the words of Audre Lorde in her book *Sister Outsider: Essays and Speeches* (2007):

> But as we come more into touch within our ancient, non-european consciousness of living as a situation to be experienced and interacted with, we learn more and more to cherish our feelings, and to respect those hidden sources of our power from where true knowledge and, therefore, lasting action comes. (p. 37)

Decolonization can emerge through engaging in a revival of storytelling to combat an education system that fails to fully engage in dialogical modes of teaching and learning; by re-examining conceptions of time not as something that is linear, but cyclical; and by moving away from thinking in binaries that fail to serve us. Decolonization can thrive through Indigenous knowledges and an active reconnection with them. However, decolonization also involves seeking to address the ongoing injustices that colonialism has reproduced and continues to reproduce, and, most important, working collectively to achieve these ends.

Ultimately, spirituality is at the heart of decolonization because it has the ability to break people out of their colonial epistemic barriers. It also forms the backbone of Indigenous knowledges and has the capacity to reconnect colonized peoples to their ancestral roots. It is spirituality that helps to provide the fertile soil into which new decolonial futurities can sink their roots and grow.

Spirituality's Role in New Futurities

In his work, Mignolo (2011) discusses "the spiritual option" and how it is essential to decolonization because it "decolonizes religion" (p. 62). He writes: "It is an-other spirituality, a decolonial spirituality that is not only confronting modernity but also proposing to delink from it" (p. 63). Spirituality provides the means by which to begin envisioning new decolonial futurities, because it is about strengthening connections that are dialogical. This awakening taps into the sacredness in an embodied, holistic way that releases one from the conditionings that colonialism attempted to subvert. Spirituality is inclusive of all modes of time—past, present, and future—and with all Ancestors and the very Land and creatures that have fostered one's human existence. In the words of Joe Sheridan and Roronhiakewen "He Clears the Sky" Dan Longboat (2014):

> Spiritual force is the timeless heartbeat of Indigeneity. It preserves a human identity that is symmetrical with traditional territory, while acting as a protection from environmental conceptions and practices that diminish

> and exclude the Ancestors and spirit beings that travel the universe in the spiritual realms of the temporal and spatial dimensions that belong to them. (p. 309)

Spirituality is an acknowledgment of being at the highest level, and in this dialogical process reciprocity, respect, and an openness to the process of awakening are required. It can be transformational, starting inward and radiating outward to bring about positive change. George Dei, in his essay "Suahunu: The Trialectic Space" (2012), discusses decolonial modes of education using the concept *Suahunu* as the trialectic space. These include "body-mind-soul interconnections, culture-society-nature interface, sacredness of activity, spiritually centered space, ancestralism, embodied connection, decolonization, and multicentricity" (p. 1). Dei's theoretical analysis discusses how this trialectic space, which is inherently spiritual, can provide a means of resistance against ongoing colonialism. Dei says:

> Immanently, trialectic space is transgressive and counterhegemonic to institutionalized colonial epistemes. It challenges conventional ways of knowing to acknowledge what hitherto is assumed not to be "knowledge" in dominant circles. Central to the trialectic space is the question of ontological space, innate, intuitive ways of knowing associated with long-term dwelling within particular historical spaces. The trialectic space concerns histories, epistemological ways of knowing as imbued through space, time, and memory. (p. 2)

This concept of Suahunu as trialectic space beautifully encapsulates how spirituality can provide pathways of hope in the visioning of new decolonial futurities. These spiritually based ways of knowing, which are steeped in Indigenous knowledge systems, can provide ways of tapping into cyclical time and provide glimpses of futures to come. In the next section, I will delve into the ways in which Indigenous and decolonial scholars have utilized Dei's trialetic space to harness visions of new decolonial futurities.

New Decolonial Futurities

New decolonial futurities help to provide regenerative hope amid the continual struggle against colonialism, as they enable us to envision what collective decolonial transformation will look like. I define *new decolonial futurities* as spiritual visions of futures that have successfully emerged out of the colonial matrix of power. I focus on them in order to call attention to their inherent power and spiritual capability to provide a glimpse of worlds where all species work together in harmony with the life force. These are not utopian ideals or yearnings for a time before European contact. New decolonial futurities are powerful because they also provide a glimpse into creative and life-giving processes of the universe, where life is placed above profit, where new languages morph to disrupt colonial languages, and where ancient and ongoing concepts of time are once again valued. Moreover, they are visions that speak to a collective transformation fueling the work that needs to be accomplished. Andrea Smith, in her essay "Unsettling the Privilege of Self-Reflexivity" (2013), delves into the topic of new futurities. She discusses Vine Deloria's *God is Red* remarks: "However, I think Deloria's analysis could be better understood not as a literal reading of Indigenous epistemologies but as a gesture toward a beyond the colonial order. Because of colonization, one must articulate these frameworks within colonial terms. Yet, colonialism cannot contain them either" (p. 274). Consequently, these new futurities provide ways of speaking that have not yet come into existence but are in the process of being created. They are visions that shift the colonial worldview away from a parasitical conception of life, toward a reverence for all components of the sacredness of life. Therefore, new decolonial futurities are always inherently based on valuing life, thus providing a counter-vision to the ongoing colonial present that locates consumption as its mode of existence (Mignolo, 2011).

Pathways of Hope

New futurities also provide hope that decolonial futurities are possible. They imbue a sense of momentum that while we as colonized and marginalized bodies who engage in this work of shedding our conditioning can be hopeful because these decolonial futures are in the process of becoming a reality. Thus, they fuel the motivation to work toward the continual process that is decolonization. One such example can be found in Gloria Anzaldúa's "Let Us Be the Healing of the Wound" in the *Gloria Anzaldúa Reader*:

> Like the moon rising over the scintillating blue water, let's be resilient, let's persevere and prevail with grace. Like Coyolxauhqui, let's put our dismembered psyches and patrias (homelands) together in new constructions. It is precisely during these in-between times that we must create the dream (el sueno) of the sixth world. May we allow the interweaving of all the minds and hearts and life forces to create the collective dream of the world and teach us how to live out ese sueno. May we allow spirit to sustain and guide us from the path of dissolution. May we do work that matters. Vale la pena, it's worth the pain. (cited in Keating, 2009, p. 314)

In the quotation, Anzaldúa engages us in a new decolonial futurity. Her writing sounds like a summons, almost a calling to action or a prayer that provides both healing and a sense of regeneration. By naming a world that she sees emerging, it reminds her readers that the world in which we currently live is not static—it moves, shifts, and is always in a state of flux. Anzaldúa helps to break individuals out of the restraints of a colonial mentality and conjures a deep-seated spiritual faith in the worlds that are to come and the decolonial work that is part of that process.

Developing a New Language

Andrea Smith (2013) discusses the need to create new languages when speaking about new futurities. Built into the colonial languages are restraints that keep us from an understanding of being and existing in the world that falls outside of the colonial matrix of power. Smith refers to this in the following quotation, wherein she discusses the possibility of multiple worlds and the need for a new language: "Based on this analysis then, our projects becomes less of one based on self-improvement or even collective self-improvement, and more about the creation of new worlds and futurities for which we currently have no language" (pp. 274–275). Because we lack the language, we have to delve into our cultural knowledges, our imaginal, intuitive, and embodied ways of knowing in order to weave together ways of speaking about these new futurities. A new language is necessary to understand a world that is ensouled, and how we can begin to reattune our bodies, minds, and souls to these processes, without which we cannot adequately communicate these continual and ongoing transformations. Joe Sheridan and Roronhiakewen "He Clears the Sky" Dan Longboat (2006) speak to the issue of the limiting nature of the colonized tongue: "The tongue that settlers hear as imagination is the budding of the autochthonous archetype that begins the intellectual task of restructuring or abandoning prophylactic English and is learning to think as the continent thinks" (p. 370). Creativity needs to aid the resurgence of subjugated knowledge forms, and in this birthing process new languages need to be coined to begin speaking about these coming new worlds.

Time

Another fascinating aspect of new decolonial futurities is the concept of how time is utilized. Here I will focus solely on linear and cyclical time. In decolonial futurities, time is presented as inherently cyclical, as opposed to linear (Anzaldúa, 2002; Sheridan & Longboat, 2014; Smith, 2013). Thus, we are reminded that linear time is a colonial construct and that, as Shahjahan (2014) points out, prior to the invention of the pendulum clock, time was measured cyclically through seasons, life cycles, crop rotations, and so forth (p. 490). Shahjahan elaborates on the oppressive nature of linear time, encapsulating how progress is measured in time and how notions of wasting time came into being (p. 490). Most important, Shahjahan states: "Consequently, with the introduction of the clock, time was delinked from human bodies and human bodies from nature" (p. 490). Therefore, linear time served to callously sever humanity from the natural cycle.

Cyclical time required that human beings be aware of the world around them—that they remain ever cognitive of the slow changing of the seasons, that they be attuned to the workings of their bodies, and that sun, stars, and the moon overhead be continually observed. Cyclical timekeeping required presence, awareness, and communion with nature, both internally and externally. With the invention of the clock, all that is now required is a glance that usually brings about a sense of panic, because now time is something of a scarcity. Joe Sheridan and Roronhiakewen "He Clears the Sky" Dan Longboat delve into what dominant cultures have lost by disregarding cyclical time:

> Without attempting to find a language and epistemology resonant with elemental ubiquity, colonial environmentalism applauds the 180 degrees of perception it has achieved from the 90 degrees inherited from its positivist scientific heritage. All the while, this partial perspective has missed the factuality of the 360 degrees and 720 degrees of Creation's circular and spherical realities and the language resonating with such realities. (p. 311)

As this quotation demonstrates, linear time is a refusal to engage in all aspects of the creative order, and this has come at great cost to humanity. This cost represents a further separation between matter and spirit. Therefore, the process of envisioning new decolonial futurities involves tapping into cyclical time once again, breaking individuals out of time constructed in colonial frameworks, and acknowledging that we as humans exist not in isolation but in an interconnected and interdependent world.

Reconnection With the Earth

Reconnecting with the Earth is embedded in the envisioning of new decolonial futurities, since there is an understanding that the Earth is not separate from the destiny of humanity (Berry, 1998). A thriving planet is understood to be beneficial to all of creation. Leanne Simpson (2011) writes about the cannibalistic nature of colonialism in the retelling of the Anishnaabeg creation stories. She says: "When one harms the earth, one harms oneself because we are part of that whole" (p. 70). The Earth is understood to be sentient and to give rise to awakening and transformation. One of the most powerful components of Simpson's work is her participation in envisioning a new decolonial future by remembering the Anishnaabeg creation story of Turtle Island (p. 149). She writes: "In Nishnaabeg thought, resurgence is dancing on our turtle's back; it is visioning and dancing new realities and worlds into existence" (pp. 69–70). The act of dancing is about moving with the flow and flux of the spiritual aspects of the universe that are in harmony and balance with the Earth, thus bringing about new possibilities, new ways of living in creative potential with the planet. Simpson's words are powerful, and the title of the book—*Dancing on Our Turtle's Back*—reminds one that humanity belongs to

Earth, and we exist in ever-continuing relations with Her and all other manifestations of Her creations (2011). This remembering of our belonging to the Earth will help in the process of awakening our collective consciousness, thus enabling us to work from a place of love for our planet, actualizing new decolonial futurities.

Collective Transformation

Collective transformation is one of the quintessential aspects of new decolonial futures. All envisioning of these futures coalesces around collective transformation. They speak of a shift in consciousness, in worldview, and in a balancing of processes that brings about harmony. They also discuss the work required to engage these new futurities. They do not magically arise but are rather set in motion through dedication, determination, strategizing, labor, and, most importantly, love. But the vision of collective decolonial transformation is so powerful and hopeful that these visions help to motivate the work required to achieves these worlds. Gloria Anzaldúa writes beautifully about collective transformation in her vision of new decolonial futurities found in *The Gloria Anzaldúa Reader*:

> In addition to community-building we can transform our world by imagining it differently, dreaming it passionately via all our senses, and willing it into creation.... Individually and collectively we can begin to share strategies on peaceful co-existence y desparamar (spread) conocimientos. Each of us can make a difference. By bringing psychological understanding and using spiritual approaches in political activism we can stop the destruction of our moral, compassionate humanity. Empowered, we'll be motivated to organize, achieve justice, and begin to heal the world. (cited in Keating, 2009, pp. 312–313)

Collective transformation is indeed what decolonizing work is all about. It may be a difficult, alienating, and sometimes exceedingly frustrating path, and there are sure to be moments of intense despair and hopelessness. However, when immersed in the new decolonial visions, they help dispel the alienation and encourage the seeking out of allies propelling transformation and collective action. Anzaldúa expands on this concept when she writes:

> We are the queer groups, the people that don't belong anywhere, not in the dominant world not completely within our own respective cultures. Combined we cover so many oppressions.... Not all of us have the same oppressions, but we empathize and identify with each other's oppressions.... In El Mundo Zurdo I with my own affinities and my people with theirs can live together and transform the planet. (p. 50)

These visions of decolonial futures are necessary and imaginably beautiful. They are worlds we seek to bring into existence because they reflect the love that we, as children of the Earth, are all made of. However, this collective transformation needs to be preceded by a personal transformation. It requires an initial awareness of the colonial matrix of power, an epistemic break, and, as Mignolo (2011) says, a delinking from it. An epistemic break entails a rupture in previously held beliefs, an unlearning or fracturing of cognitive barriers. Interestingly, this is where dreaming plays a crucial role by facilitating this fracture and recreating what is inherently decolonial in the coming of these new worlds. In the next section, the power of dreaming will be examined as a pathway to new decolonial futurities.

Dreaming Our Way to New Decolonial Futurities

Dreaming occurs nightly and is a largely mysterious and undervalued phenomenon. It is a biological necessity that can bring about great creativity and transformation. Dreaming in the West has largely been a subjugated knowledge form, perhaps because of its inherently powerful capacities when taken seriously. Thomas Berry, in his book *The Dream of the Earth* (1998), writes: "In this context we might say: In the beginning was the dream. Through the dream all things were made, and without the dream nothing was made that has been made" (p. 197). This quotation speaks to the intrinsic potentialities of dreams.

Cultivating a relationship with dreaming can enable and facilitate personal transformation, preparing the dreamer for new decolonial futurities. It acts to introduce the dreamer to the roads that lead to decolonial futurities. Karen Jaenke discusses the inherent power of dreaming in her chapter "Earth Dreaming" in a book edited by Craig Chalquist entitled *Rebearths* (2010): "If humans are to bring forth a new relationship to the Earth, its seeds will be in dreaming. Our dreams express the leading edge of creation" (p. 188). The process of dreaming begins by teaching the dreamer the language of spirit, working on an individual level, breaking the dreamer out of linear conceptions of time, reconnecting the dreamer with the Earth, and eventually bringing about an individual transformation that radiates outward. The following section will further explore these dreaming processes that will chart pathways of hope toward new decolonial futurities.

Developing a New Language

Dreaming is a highly symbolic operation that is manifested through imagistic processes. These imagistic processes are highly symbolic and break the dreamer out of colonial epistemic thought processes. Lee Irwin, in his book *The Dream Seekers: Native American Visionary Traditions of the Great Plains* (1994), elaborates on how this colonial epistemic break occurs: "Dreams express complex moments of encounter and manifestation that surpass the constraints of purely rational thought, because dreaming engages not only the rational aspects of mind but also deeper and more enigmatic potentials" (p. 9). Because of the importance of the symbolic content, cultivating a relationship with dreaming requires learning the symbolic language of dreams. This is a slow process that necessitates considerable attentiveness, curiosity, and intuition. Equally important, it requires the ability to retain the memory of dreams upon awakening. Slowly the dreamer learns to read her dreams and the power and meaning inherent in the symbols. The dreamer learns to watch for the symbols in waking life, and dreaming and waking lives therefore connect and merge to enhance understanding. New and ancient modes of thought are fostered that are regarded to be both spiritual and decolonial. Through this dialogical process unfolds a new symbolic language that connects the dreamer and the dream. Irwin (1994) explains this symbolic language of dreaming in the following quotation:

> The visionary language of belief and experience is part of a holistic relations between the visionary and the world of explicit phenomena—the sky, the earth, this tree, that butterfly, this rock, that feather—all of which embody varying degrees of the visionary world and help unfold the potential of a world-revealing process. It is the experienced dreamer's role to explicate that world, to show [that] the part expresses the whole and how the visionary experience is the door into the hidden order of potential and personal empowerment. (p. 25)

In short, by cultivating a relationship with dreaming, the dreamer can be propelled out of her colonial thought processes. The world is seen anew as something that is imbued with spirit, as opposed to a Cartesian perspective in which spirit and matter are segregated (Sheridan & Longboat, 2014; Tedlock, 1992). "To enter the dream world means, in this sense, to alter consciousness and enter into an implicit dreaming order—the enfolded, psychic potential of the visionary realm—that has a structural, morphological effect on consciousness" (Irwin, 1994, pp. 23–24). New language is born out of necessity and is created to express this shift in understanding in order to give voice to both the dreamscape and the waking world and the multifaceted ways in which they coalesce. Therefore, this symbolic language of dreaming lays the groundwork for new decolonial futurities by providing the dreamer with the language to dialogically create, tap into, and manifest the spiritual aspects of the universe.

Time

Dreams also provide a means of disrupting colonial linear notions of time. In a dream state, time is unconstrained, and in this way the dreamer's perception of time can move at an erratic pace, achingly slowly, backward and forward. Dream states illustrate flux and flow in a way that lived reality never can. "The dream world does not represent a static world of objects fixed in empty Euclidian space, but a dynamic world of events in a multilayered, enfolded potential." (Irwin, 1994, pp. 63–64). Therefore, dreamers can learn by cultivating a relationship with their dreams and understanding that nothing is static, which is contrary to colonial thought processes. Moreover, powerful dreams can expose the dreamer to cyclical time. In this regard, Irwin alludes to cyclical time in relation to dreaming when he writes:

> The visionary experience inevitably leads to apotheosis through which various potential abilities are transferred to the visionary. The later enactment in ritual recreation expresses that very same "sacred time" (or timelessness) in which the gift of power was bestowed. The unified topology of the dreaming and lived worlds can only be grasped if the "checkered tablecloth of Cartesian space-time" is pulled out from under the externally observed world, leaving the multidimensional, unbound, fluid contours of a non-causal, visionary space-time to expand or contract according to individual experience. (p. 63)

Therefore, dreams have the capacity to enable dreamers to experience time in a cyclical fashion. Such opportunities allow the dreamer to engage in timeframes in which the past, present, and future are inextricably interwoven, demonstrating that interconnectedness and interconnection are not merely a concept but a reality—that is, "Through dreaming... an altered awareness in which past, present, and future are manifested as the indefinite and powerful imagery of our shared spiritual and cultural history" (Irwin, 1994, p. 10). This awareness of enhanced experiences and possibilities brought on by dreaming leads to questions about colonial conditioning and linear time. These questions can cause ruptures in the carefully constructed colonial matrix of power by opening the dreamer to possibilities for new decolonial futurities that adhere to cyclical time.

Reconnection With the Earth

Dreams are relational and dialogical processes whereby the Earth reminds the dreamer of his or her belonging. This interconnectedness is demonstrated by the manner in which animals, insects, reptiles, flora, and landscapes appear in dreams. It is important to point out that there is a summoning here, a calling to remind humanity of its true belonging to Earth. In dreams, humanity participates in a deep remembering, a remembering of its origins, but also that its ancestry belongs to a planet thriving with life in a vast and creative universe. Cultivating a relationship with dreaming provides a medium through which love can be deepened. A love develops that is grown and fostered through dreaming for the individual self, the broader community, and all the species that inhabit the Earth. Jaenke (2010) states the following in regard to the dialogical process of dreaming and the Earth:

> Not only do dreams help individuals work through personal psychological issues, the dreaming soul carries and expresses a much larger agenda—as wide as the cosmos itself. Dreams labor to heal the fragmented breaks in our relationships with our deep nature, our nuclear family, our ancestors, the immediate community, and the entire web of earthly life. Dreams restore connection to what is essential. (p. 189)

Dreaming can therefore provide a pathway to decolonial futurities because it is the unbound sentience of the Earth that speaks while the dreamer sleeps. Thus, dreams strengthen the dreamer's capacity for love and empathy and imbues the dreamer with an understanding of the interconnection of all life forms. It is critical to recognize that dreams have the capacity to help repair the damage of colonialism that has continuously perpetuated narratives of disconnection, damage, and destruction. As Jaenke (2010) so eloquently puts it:

> Each night the universe addresses us personally in our dream, and we are offered the opportunity to reconnect to our essential relatedness. Dispelling the illusion of separateness.... Dreams reveal afresh each night the interior depths and hidden threads that bind together the web of life. (p. 188)

Therefore, it is critically revealing and absolutely essential to note that cultivating a relationship with dreaming is a spiritually centered, decolonial act of love, renewal, and remembrance; in addition, it is beautifully transformational. In the words of Leanne Simpson (2011), "Dreams and visions provide glimpses of decolonized spaces and transformed realities that we have collectively yet to imagine" (pp. 34–35). Dreaming is one of many mediums in which the Earth speaks to us, daring us to participate in a visionary process of bringing about new decolonial worlds.

Individual Transformation Radiating Outward

Because the dreamer has begun the critical and necessary process of cultivating a relationship with dreaming, the following elements fall into place: symbolic language is learned; cyclical understanding of time is experienced; the idea that all things exist in a state of flux is understood; and a reconnection to the Earth is reaffirmed. Altogether, the process of cultivating a relationship with dreaming leads to personal transformation. On a deep experiential level, the blinders come off and a sense of loss emerges—a sense that one has lived most of his or her life cut off from relational connections. If this thread is followed, the dreamer will realize that the cause of this loss stems from a colonial worldview that has suppressed these capacities in the dreamer. A desire emerges to flourish in this new capacity of tapping into the nightly dreams and all their possibilities. The transformational experience might be slow and steady, but once it begins, it only continues radiating outward, because dreaming and waking experiences manifest and bring about a cocreation that is witnessed by others.

> Simultaneously, it is necessary to recognize the transformative effect that dreaming has on the dreamer—the many ways in which the shared contents of dreaming have shaped the perceptions and experiences of the "everyday." All dreamers are part of an ongoing encounter or drama of cultural enactment by which culture itself is transformed. This dynamic, transformative experience, enacted through dreaming as well as through waking, represents the challenge all dreamers and visionaries set for themselves: to unite and develop a meaningful continuity between the dreaming and the waking worlds. (Irwin, 1994, p. 11)

Ultimately, dreaming provides a pathway of hope toward new decolonial futurities, because both emerge from the same sacred landscape—the landscape of the dreamer/visionary. They are deeply interrelated, with one blazing the path for the next. Dreaming has the capacity to initiate individual transformation spawning into collective transformation that will help bring about new decolonial futurities. Here I refer to the words of Anzaldúa in her revolutionary work "Now Let Us Shift," which can be found in *This Bridge We Call Home: Radical Visions for Transformation* (2002):

> At the lips of del mar you begin your ritual/prayer: with the heel of your left foot you draw a circle in the sand, then walk its circumference, stand at the center, and voice your intention: to increase awareness of Spirit, recognize our interrelatedness, and work for transformation. (p. 575)

Now is the time to once again value our dreams, to cultivate meaningful relationships with them so that they can chart our course to new decolonial futurities that heal the Cartesian split and ease the Baconian destructive need to control (Irwin, 1994; Shahjahan, 2005; Sheridan & Longboat, 2014; Tedlock, 1992), so that our dreams, through the Earth's love, can remind us of our origins and enable us to do the difficult work of summoning these decolonial futurities into existence through love, labor, and transformation. The next section will discuss the need for educational futurities to facilitate this journey of transformation that dreaming initiates.

Educational Futurities

Educational futurities provide a bridge between the individual transformation brought about by dreaming and the collective transformation that new decolonial futurities envision, and are achieved by promoting communal/classroom transformation. In some ways, educational futurities require a complete reimagining of our current educational system, one that does not participate or operate within the confines of the colonial matrix of power. This should help in fostering a spiritual transformation at the communal and classroom level. Educational futurities are systems of education that promote (a) cultivating a relationship with spiritual knowledges (i.e., dreaming, intuition, visioning, emotional and embodied knowledges); (b) integrating cyclical modes of time into the school-day learning; (c) a reconnecting with the Earth that takes place within school in some way in a tactile manner; and (d) achieving decolonial and spiritual transformation that benefits all students in the classroom. Educational futurities necessitate a shedding of the colonial skin and promote true diversity, thereby fostering a reverence and a true value for all of creation. The principle from which it originates is reconnection, because it is through reconnecting to ways of communing with the life force to overcome colonialism that the process of facilitating a decolonial resurgence blossoms. Educational futurities require connecting with the spiritual self, connecting with the Earth's modes of time, and connecting physically with the planet. In so doing a decolonial and spiritual transformation takes place. It should be noted that both decolonial transformation and spiritual transformation are not necessarily separate processes, but rather can coconstruct each other. Decolonial transformation involves the rupturing of previously held beliefs or worldviews, an unlearning and dismantling of colonial logics whereby the individual is now receptive to new possibilities. Thus, the process of seeking a sense of resonance and connection ensues, which can enable and facilitate a spiritual transformation, thus replacing old worldviews and giving rise to new worldviews that are inherently relational. Educational futurities envision providing students with a plethora of spiritual, emotional, and tactile tools as a means by which to tap into their spiritual selves and remind them of their belonging to the Earth and the responsibilities that come with that belonging. Therefore, what emerges and is proposed here in regard to decolonial and spiritual transformation could easily be introduced into the current education system provided, however, that there is a will and a desire to see such a transformation. In essence, what I outline here is a singular educational futurity, keeping in mind the previous definition as a framework. I also rely on the unpublished thesis of Marina Quattrocchi, which engages with dreamwork in a secondary school, and the work of Noelani Goodyear-Ka'ōpua, which centers Hawaiian Indigenous epistemology in the establishment of a Hawaiian charter school. First, however, two things need to be addressed, since they lay the groundwork for educational futurities to be successful—namely, the need for a study of ongoing colonialism and the absolute necessity for teachers to actively engage in dreamwork themselves.

The study of ongoing colonialism in school is an absolute necessity because students need to be exposed to colonial logics utilizing an anti-colonial framework, because it informs almost every component of their lives. As well, ongoing colonialism perpetuates violence, especially on Indigenous, colored, female, and LGBTQ bodies. Moreover, colonialism is taught as if it were a relic of the past, relegated to a particular era, that perpetuates ignorance—more specifically, settler ignorance. Glen Sean Coulthard, in his book *Red Skin, White Masks* (2014), discusses a poignant issue pertaining to the Truth and Reconciliation Commission and settler ignorance:

> In particular, the TRC temporally situates the harms of settler-colonialism in the past and focuses the bulk of its reconciliatory efforts on repairing the injurious legacy left in the wake of this history. Indigenous subjects are the primary object of repair, not the colonial relationship. (p. 217)

Understanding the colonial relationship by utilizing an anti-colonial approach is the first step in the process of decolonizing education and giving way to educational futurities. Ignorance will only further perpetuate the current system, and so unveiling the colonial logics should be the basis for an education system that helps to truly educate, emancipate, and awaken students to their potential.

Another important component for laying the groundwork for educational futurities is having teachers engage in dreamwork *prior* to their students. Since dreaming is a subjugated knowledge form and a knowledge that is rarely engaged in or utilized, it is important that teachers begin developing a relationship with dreaming to better understand its transformative nature. It needs to be experienced and cultivated by teachers so that they can understand the critical value that dreaming offers. This will provide teachers with an understanding of what the process entails, the challenges it presents, the benefits it can afford, and a basic understanding of their own dreamscape, which will help them to help their students become successful. It is therefore anticipated that with the particular experience of their own dreaming in hand, teachers will be able to create relevant and meaningful lessons that will help fully facilitate students' understanding of their own dreamscapes.

Developing a New Language

Cultivating a relationship with spiritual knowledges is an essential component of educational futurities, inasmuch as it develops and strengthens spiritual faculties, thereby facilitating further the process of decolonial transformation. Spiritual knowledges are guiding faculties that help in orienting, directing, and propelling progression in the same way that the five senses help to orient the individual in the world. By placing spiritual knowledges within the school system, students can be said to be unwaveringly empowered. Moreover, these spiritual knowledges will help to strengthen the community within the classroom by encouraging an openness to vulnerability, thereby fostering connections and friendship. Castellano (2010) refers to spiritual knowledges as revealed knowledges, and she defines them as follows: "*Revealed knowledge* is acquired through dreams, visions, and intuitions that are understood to be spiritual in origin" (p. 24). However, I would add to the list emotional and embodied ways of knowing, as they, too, can also be revelatory through a body, mind, and spirit connection. Any of these spiritual knowledges can be utilized in adhering to the educational futurities framework. In the following section, I will focus on the spiritual knowledge of dreaming and the significance of utilizing dreamwork in the classroom, using ideas based to a large extent on the unpublished thesis of Marina Quattrocchi entitled *Dreamwork in Secondary Schools: Its Educational Value and Personal Significance* (1995).

Utilizing dreaming in the classroom can be a powerful spiritual tool that works by acknowledging the entire being of the student, including engaging the emotional, ancestral, spiritual, mental, and physical awareness of the student. Dreaming is a spiritual praxis that is inherently decolonial and could provide significant assistance in subverting the eurocentric and colonial education system that has been born out of the four pillars of colonialism. In her thesis, Quattrocchi engaged in dreamwork with secondary school students by using a novel study that focused on dreaming as the curricular link (1995). Through her work, Quattrocchi found that there were many benefits to be obtained by integrating dreamwork within the classroom. These include strong class rapport, a better ability to problem-solve interpersonal problems, and a deepening spiritual connection (1995).

> Overall students considered their inner work with dreams a fascinating and valuable experience. Their initial scepticism dissipated when they were able to connect their first dream to their actual life experiences. The most prevalent outcomes reported by students were increased awareness and insights. This awareness led to an increased ability to problem solve, particularly in regards to relationships. They also felt dream discussion led to better class rapport. Many students experienced spiritual and prophetic dreams which helped them to make future psychological adjustments. The six students who did not present, overcompensated through the depth of their material. Their dream experiences were so personally meaningful that an overt presentation was not necessary. (p. 142)

Dreamwork in schools also provides a means of stepping away from and beyond the four pillars through which the colonial matrix has directly influenced schooling. The longer the dreamwork process is engaged in the school system, the more likely it is to bring about a decolonial transformation, as the dreams begin the process of stitching back together the division between matter and spirit and healing the Cartesian split. Tedlock, in the introduction to his *Dreaming: Anthropological and Psychological Interpretations* (1992), describes the Cartesian split as follows: "It must be remembered, however, that the Cartesian irreducible dualism of 'spirit' and 'matter,' which denies the common principle from which the terms of this duality proceeded by a process of polarization, was an historical development within Western philosophy" (p. 2). This separation of matter and spirit has been internalized and has degraded our understanding of what is sacred, and dreamwork can actually begin to heal this rift. Moreover, understanding a dream requires an understanding of the dreamer (Jung, 1974), and so this necessitates vulnerability, strong interpersonal skills, and the fostering of relationships built on trust. Therefore, integrating dreamwork throughout schools, from the elementary grades to middle school and eventually to high school, would be of immeasurable value for the students themselves and the collective decolonial and spiritual transformation that would ensue.

Furthermore, students should also learn the language of their dreams so that they may understand how to make sense of their dreams. This can be a valuable skill throughout their lives. Learning to understand the imagistic and symbolic content would require a strong sense of intuition, perception, and a vast of array of knowledge. In turn, this would require the study of psychology, mythologies, literature, history, world religions, and various other forms of texts that could easily be engaged with across the curriculum (Jung, 1974). In addition, technology could also easily be integrated into this learning process with a little creativity. Therefore, both dreamwork and the process of learning how to decode dreams could be systematically implemented into the public education systems and could be tailored to fit current curricular objectives.

Time

The introduction of a cyclical understanding of time into the school day might be regarded as helpful, inasmuch as it attunes students' minds, bodies, and hearts to cycles of creation. While there might be many ways in which to accomplish this heightened sense of awareness, many of the more meaningful methods involve physically reconnecting to celestial and terrestrial cycles. However, what I want to propose here is the introduction of "orality" in the classroom environment and the school community at large. Orality—that is, oral storytelling—is well recognized as one of the oldest forms of knowledge transmission, having the power to weave narratives of humanity, using anecdotes, family histories, and mythologies to disrupt western linear notions of time. As Paula Gunn Allen writes in *The Sacred Hoop: Recovering the Feminine in American Indian Traditions* (1992), "Traditional tribal narratives possess a circular structure incorporating event within event, piling meaning, until the accretion finally results in a story" (p. 79). The cyclical structure of orality helps attune students to nonlinear conceptions of time while imbuing love and wisdom through the unfolding of the storytelling process. In their essay "Speaking Truth to Power: Indigenous Storytelling as an Act of Living Resistance," Sium and Ritskes (2013) state the following about the power of orality:

> Whiteduck...speaks of how love motivates her grandfather's stories and, in Indigenous conceptions of love, connects all beings. These connections extend generationally—to the ancestors and to generations yet to come—as well as to the Earth and other beings. (p. 6)

Therefore, orality is based on relationality and is fostered through connection, attention, and deep whole-body listening. The knowledges and concomitant wisdom inherent in orality are powerful because it is a living knowledge.

Incorporating orality into the school day can be exceedingly valuable. I anticipate that relying exclusively on Indigenous elders would be quite taxing, as they have many responsibilities in their own communities. Thus, to reflect the student body, including the ancestries of the students and the oral traditions that reside within their own family units, bringing grandparents of the students themselves into the school would be greatly beneficial. I would propose this accommodation for all levels of schooling: elementary, middle school, and high school. There would have to be programs in place to facilitate this process of integrating grandparents into the school environment—for example, grandparents could have their own storytelling room and circulate throughout the school. In this way students would learn through the diversity that surrounds them, including knowledge about different parts of the world, about various religions, cultures, and communities, and about historical periods. Having grandparents present in the school system would be a method for students to learn in a relational way, one profoundly grounded in love, to hear stories of Land, struggles, resistance, history, proverbs, and mythology that fall outside the eurocentric curriculum (Sium & Riskes, 2013). Connecting students in the school system community to cyclical modes of time through presence, the circuitous way that stories unfold, and reciprocity that is given and received in the exchange, will help to further the decolonial transformational process. Since orality and Land are deeply interconnected, in the next section I propose to further explore reconnecting with the Earth as a necessary component of educational futurities.

Reconnection With the Earth

Reconnection with the Earth is another example of the way in which educational futurities can provide a bridge between individual and collective transformation. If schools begin to devote some of the school day to being outside and spending time in nature in productive and engaging ways, it would help to remind students of their origins. Nature is awe-inspiring, and extending the concept of the classroom by moving it outside takes down the walls of the classroom itself and, additionally, the epistemic walls of colonialism.

Reconnection with the Earth expands possibilities, connections, and a sense of belonging, because the Earth has always been the first teacher of humanity. In order to help illustrate the importance of reconnection with the Earth as far as schools are concerned, I point to Noelani Goodyear-Ka'ōpua's *The Seeds We Planted: Portraits of a Native Hawaiian Charter School* (2013). In this book she discusses the process, hurdles, and difficulties that went into setting up a Native Hawaiian charter school named Hālau Kū Māna (HKM) that utilized Hawaiian pedagogy, epistemologies, and values to teach students in holistic, embodied, and spiritual ways (Goodyear-Ka'ōpua, 2013). One of the most beautiful components of this book is the way in which communion with the Land and sea is emphasized as an essential part of the curriculum. Goodyear-Ka'ōpua expands on the notion of Land literacies to encapsulate this pedagogy:

> The recognition of what I am calling *land-centered literacies* extends upon the work to broaden older, outmoded understandings of literacy as simply about reading and writing printed text. Land-centered literacies include the ways Kanaka Oiwi developed practices of reading the stars and other celestial bodies and events; offering chants in our own human language and then observing and finding meaning in the responses of winds, rains, birds, waves, or stones; and writing ourselves into the landscape by drawing water through irrigation ditches to loi'kalo and then back to streams. Particularly in the era NCLB, in which only certain literacies are validated and assessed, it is important for Indigenous people to assert our own reading and expressive practices as equally valuable. (p. 34)

Land-centered literacies comprise a pedagogy that is actualized in the case of the Hawaiian charter school that Goodyear-Ka'ōpua discusses. Students engage in activities such as reconstructing irrigated agricultural terraces (known as *lo'i*) and taro cultivation (known as *kalo*), and are taught Hawaiian seafaring (known as *wa'a* pedagogy, a term that means "canoe") (Goodyear-Ka'ōpua, 2013). Incorporating Land-centered literacies that are grounded spiritually, pedagogically, and epistemologically in Hawaiian Indigenous knowledges required continual negotiation with the state; it was—and continues to be—a struggle (Goodyear-Ka'ōpua, 2013). However, Hālau Kū Māna is a testament to hope and demonstrates that a reconnection with the Earth can be fostered within the short time of a school day. More important, Hālau Kū Māna is a working example writ large of the process of communal decolonization on a school-wide scale.

What Are the Challenges of Pursuing This Educational Futurity?

It might be argued that the most formidable obstacle to be overcome in regard to any form of educational futurity, one that is inherently decolonial, is that most schooling is state controlled, particularly with regard to settler states—thus bringing us back to the fourth pillar of the colonial matrix of power, which is authority (Mignolo, 2011). The anti-colonial frameworks that teach students about ongoing colonial violence will inevitably invalidate the legitimacy of the nation-state in settler-state countries. Therefore, no state would condone—much less give their open-ended approval to—the introduction of such an educational futurity. Wrestling educational systems from the state's hands, or attempting to circumvent their power as much as possible, as Goodyear-Ka'ōpua (2013) and Quattrocchi (1995) have demonstrated through their tireless work, provides grounded and practical examples of hope. Moreover, it is easily anticipated that even the mention, much less the possibility, of integrating spirituality into school systems terrifies people. To be sure, there is a general lack of open-mindedness, fear, and skepticism surrounding spirituality and schooling. To many, dreaming is an invalid form of knowledge, and positioning it as a valuable knowledge is regarded as outright subversion. In today's world, however, people, communities, and nation-states are changing in response to the threat of change. Therefore, as long as people continue the decolonial work and stay grounded in new decolonial futurities, hope is on the horizon. Decolonizing people's minds is an imperative for all visions of educational futurities to flourish, and dreaming thus provides the pathway to hope, as the next section will demonstrate.

Dreaming Pathway of Hope

Dreaming is deeply interconnected with hope, because dreams reside on the pathway out of our colonial frameworks. Dreams are where hope is embodied, and they provide an entry point that is accessible to everyone. They chart the critical pathway for personal transformation, which is necessary if—communally and collectively—we are going to shed the colonial skin. Individually, however, we need to be open, receptive, and willing to reconnect, because for educational and new decolonial futurities to begin and continue requires a personal awakening. The imperative to decolonize resides with everyone, and dreams are a neglected resource and faculty that we need to begin accessing and cultivating as a decolonial tool. Dreaming also helps to bolster intuition, visions, and imagistic processes, because these faculties are all interconnected and help to speed up the decolonizing process through epistemic breaks in colonial worldviews. Thus, dreaming is our pathway to hope because it reawakens our ability to connect with all levels of creation. Through this process we can begin severing ourselves from the colonial matrix of power, thus ushering in new decolonial futurities with the help and support of educational futurities.

Conclusion

This chapter has sought to explain how the colonial matrix of power works on a global, modern scale. It has demonstrated the necessity for decolonial options and how spirituality is essential to decolonizing our way out of the colonial matrix of power. The chapter has invoked the envisioning of new decolonial futurities by Indigenous and decolonial scholars and further outlined how cultivating a relationship with dreaming can chart a pathway of hope to ushering in these decolonial worlds. Further, it has posited that educational futurities can help the catalyst that is dreaming by reinforcing the experiences that emerge in the dreamscape within the school day as a means of further propelling humanity to its destiny of decolonial transformation that gives rise to new decolonial futurities. In the words of Ama Mazama (2002), as she invokes African Indigenous knowledges:

> It is therefore fair to conclude from this that, in the African context, people do not conceive of themselves as separate from the cosmos but as being completely integrated into a universe that is much larger than any of them yet is centered around them. (p. 220)

In the spirit of Mazama's words, this chapter has sought to elevate the practice of valuing dreaming so that we can remember our origins and our interconnections and work toward a collective transformation that puts life at the heart of all that we value. Decolonial futurities illustrate our destinies, beckoning to us like a lighthouse amid a storm of colonial logics, while the act of cultivating a relationship with our dreams provides us the ship for which to chart our course and our educational futurities with our compass pointing us toward our home.

References

Allen, P.G. (1992). *The sacred hoop: Recovering the feminine in American Indian traditions*. Boston, MA: Beacon Press.

Anzaldúa, G. (1999). *Borderlands/La frontera: The new mestiza*. San Francisco, CA: Spinsters/Aunt Lute.

Anzaldúa, G. (2002). Now let us shift... the path of conocimiento... inner work, public acts. In G. Anzaldúa & Ana Louise Keating (Eds.), *This bridge we call home: Radical visions for transformation* (pp. 540–578). New York, NY: Routledge.

Battiste, M. (2013). *Decolonizing education: Nourishing the learning spirit*. Saskatoon, SK: Purich Publishing Ltd.

Berry, T. (1988). *The dream of the earth* (2nd ed.). San Francisco, CA: Sierra Club Books.

Castellano, M.B. (2000). Updating aboriginal traditions of knowledge. In G.J. Dei, B.L. Hall, & D.G. Rosenberg (Eds.), *Indigenous knowledges in global context: Multiple readings of our world*. Toronto, ON: University of Toronto Press.

Coulthard, G. (2014). *Red skin, white masks: Rejecting the colonial politics of recognition*. Minneapolis, MN: University of Minnesota Press.

Dei, G. (2003). Schooling and the dilemma of youth disengagement. *McGill Journal of Education, 38*(2), 241–256.

Dei, G.J.S. (2012). Suahunu: The trialectic space. *Journal of Black Studies, 43*(8), 823–846.

Goodyear-Ka'ōpua, N. (2013). *The seeds we planted: Portraits of a Native Hawaiian charter school.* Minneapolis, MN: University of Minnesota Press.
Hart, L. (2011). Nourishing the authentic self: Teaching with heart and soul. In N.N. Wane, E.L. Manyimo, & E.J. Ritskes (Eds.), *Spirituality, education & society: An integrated approach* (pp. 37–48). Rotterdam, Netherlands: Sense Publishers.
Irwin, L. (1994). *The dream seekers: Native American visionary traditions of the Great Plains.* Norman, OK: University of Oklahoma Press.
Jaenke, K. (2010). Earth dreaming. In C. Chalquist (Ed.), *Rebearths: Conversations with a world ensouled* (pp. 187–202). Walnut Creek, CA: World Soul Books.
Jung, C.G. (1974). *Dreams.* Princeton, NJ: Princeton University Press.
Keating, A. (2009). *The Gloria Anzaldúa reader.* Durham, NC: Duke University Press.
Lorde, A. (2007). *Sister outsider: Essays and speeches.* Berkeley, CA: Crossing Press.
Mazama, M.A. (2002). Afrocentricity and African spirituality. *Journal of Black Studies, 33*(2), 218–234.
Mignolo, W.D. (2011). *The darker side of western modernity: Global futures, decolonial options.* Durham, NC: Duke University Press.
Quattrocchi, M. (1995). *Dreamwork in secondary schools: Its educational value and personal significance.* Unpublished thesis, University of Toronto, Toronto, Ontario.
Shahjahan, R. (2005). Spirituality in the academy: Reclaiming from the margins and evoking a transformative way of knowing the world. *International Journal of Qualitative Studies in Education, 18*(6), 685–711.
Shahjahan, R.A. (2014). Being "lazy" and slowing down: Toward decolonizing time, our body, and pedagogy. *Educational Philosophy and Theory, 47*(5), 488–501. doi:10.1080/00131857.2014.880645
Sheridan, J., & Longboat, R. (2006, November). The Haudenosaunee imagination and the ecology of the sacred. *Space and Culture, 9*(4), 365–381. doi:10.1177/1206331206629250
Sheridan, J., & Longboat, R. (2014). Walking back into creation: Environmental apartheid and the eternal—Initiating an Indigenous mind claim. *Space and Culture, 17*(3), 308–324.
Simpson, L. (2011). *Dancing on our turtle's back.* Winnipeg, MN: Arbeiter Ring Publishing.
Sium, A., & Ritskes, E. (2013). Speaking truth to power: Indigenous storytelling as an act of living resistance. *Decolonization: Indigeneity, Education & Society, 2*(1), i–x.
Smith, A. (2013). Unsettling the privilege of self-reflexivity. In F.W. Twine & B. Gardener (Eds.), *Geographies of privilege.* New York, NY: Routledge.
Somé, M. (1994). *Of water and spirit: Ritual magic, and initiation in the life of an African Shaman.* New York, NY: G.P. Putnam's Sons.
Tedlock, B. (1992). *Dreaming: Anthropological and psychological interpretations.* Santa Fe, NM: School of American Research Press.
Thomas, M.K., Singh, P., & Klopfenstein, K. (2015). Arts education and the high school dropout problem. *Journal of Cultural Economics, 39*(4), 327–339. doi:10.1007/s10824-014-9238-x
Zine, J. (2007). Safe havens or religious "ghettos"? Narratives of Islamic schooling in Canada. *Race, Ethnicity and Education, 10*(1), 71–92.

Who Am I?

Phyllis McKenna

Who am I?
It took me 40 years to ask myself this.
Who am I?
We are greater than what we have been perceived to be.
History's deception of truth enabled me to fear what others thought of me.
Conditionings of shame, abuse, and trauma held me back from my greatness.
Looking back now, I see that this is how colonization wants me to feel. It was intended to set me up for failure.
The labels I hid behind so well were the pit of my downfall.
I wasn't good enough,
smart enough,
or worth the effort made me to fear life itself.
For many years I thought that life had somehow failed me, then it dawned on me....
This is not who I am!

Who am I?
I am an ogititaawe kwe (warrior woman).
My bloodline makes me a survivor not a victim. I am strong, noble, honest and fearless. I am a friend, mother, student and teacher.

The storms I have survived.
Have turned into the lessons that have brought me to a place of self-determination, resistance and resurgence.

"In essence, we need to not just figure out who we are; we need to re-establish the process by which we live who we are within the current context we find ourselves.... We need our Elders, our languages, and our lands, along with vision, intent, commitment, community and ultimately, action. We must move beyond resistance and survival, to flourish and mino bimaadiziwin (live the good life)."

—SIMPSON, 2011, P. 17

Reference

Simpson, L. (2011). *Dancing on our turtle's back: Stories of Nishnabeg re-creation, resurgence and a new emergence.* Winnipeg, MB: ARP Books.

Decolonization

Phyllis McKenna

Decolonizing education is more than just adding Indigeneity to the curriculum. There are deeply embedded systems of oppression in the classroom, from acceptable micro-racism to false knowledge of Indigenous peoples.

Learning about the Indian Act or residential schools does not enhance our existence; it hinders it. There is too much trauma taught in the curriculum in regard to Indigenous peoples. Going forward, we must look to the strength of our Nations—how it is that our people survived despite assimilation policies that nearly destroyed many Nations. This is worth learning.

Our resistance is that we still navigate these hallways, knowing that only 10% of my kind are successful in obtaining a postsecondary diploma at any level (King, 2017). We learn about eurocentric ideals, yet we know that what our Ancestors have taught us is more valuable and more truthful.

Our teachings of resistance, resurgence, strength, and kindness can only take us so far. We need our educators to understand that there is a whole other way of thinking, learning, and teaching.

Our Identity doesn't go away once we enter education; it becomes enhanced. It becomes more political. Now that we are considered to be in a place of privilege, we cannot just conform to settler ideals. We have the tools to think critically and challenge the status quo. The most important aspect of decolonizing education is to realize this, and allow me as a student to teach you about my resistance. Allow for others after me to do the same.

Our wisdom is not found behind our diplomas or degrees; it is found in what we do with this knowledge.

This is Decolonization.

Reference

King, T. (2017, September 7). Inclusiveness in Aboriginal hiring: Recognizing equivalencies. *Ryerson Works*. Retrieved from http://www.ryerson.ca/ryerson-works/articles/workplace-culture/2017/inclusiveness-aboriginal-hiring-recognizing-equivalencies/?utm_source=campaigner&utm_campaign=2017_sep_ryersonworks&utm_content=afcomms&cmp=1&utm_medium=e mail

Author Profiles

CRISTINA BIANCHI is a master of arts student in the Department of Applied Psychology and Human Development at the Ontario Institute for Studies in Education, University of Toronto (OISE/UT). Her professional experiences center on child development in the classroom. Her research interests lie in teacher influences on decolonization and anti-colonial education in the classroom, as well as overall student mental health and identity development.

JANELLE BRADY is a doctoral student in the Department of Social Justice Education at OISE/UT. Her research looks at Black mothering in education through an intersectional approach. Janelle draws on Black feminist thought and anti-racist/anti-colonial frameworks in addressing systemic injustices.

RACHEL BUCHANAN is currently completing her master's degree in curriculum studies and teacher development at OISE/UT. She has studied—and has been an educator—in settings in North America, India, Nepal, and Uganda, where she has come to recognize the colonizing effects of the western education model. Her research interests lie in the decolonization of curricula and in the development of anti-oppressive education systems.

GEORGE J. SEFA DEI is a professor in the Department of Social Justice Education and Director of the Centre for Integrative Anti-Racism Studies (CIARS) at the Ontario Institute for Studies in Education, University of Toronto (OISE/UT). He has published extensively on the subjects of decolonization, anti-colonialism, anti-racism, and Indigenous Knowledges. He is also a newly elected fellow of the Royal Society of Canada. In 2007, Professor Dei was installed as a traditional chief—specifically, as the Gyaasehene of the town of Asokore, Koforidua, in the New Juaben traditional area of Ghana. His stool name is Nana Adusei Sefa Tweneboah.

SHUKRI HILOWLE is a second-year PhD student in the social justice education program and also in the collaborative program Comparative, International and Development Education (CIDE) at OISE/UT. She currently works as an educator with the Toronto District School Board and the Peel District School Board. Her research interests include Islamophobia, anti-racism, gendered Islamophobia, nationalism, anti-immigrant injustice, and Islam in America.

CRISTINA SHERRY JAIMUNGAL is a PhD student in the Department of Social Justice Education at the Ontario Institute for Studies in Education, University of Toronto (OISE/UT). Anchored in anti-colonial research methods, anti-racism studies, and critical language theory, her research interests examine the racial politics embedded in the project of English-language education. Jaimungal holds a B.A. with honors in English and professional writing (York University) and an M.A. in curriculum, teaching, and learning, with a specialization in Comparative, International, and Development Education (OISE/UT).

MANDEEP JAJJ is a graduate student in the Department of Social Justice Education at OISE/UT. Her research interests lie in anti-colonialism, anti-racism, and decolonizing theories, along with development and modernization discourses. Mandeep's current research explores western "development" theories in relation to issues of economics and education. As a community educator, Mandeep places great importance on changing the frameworks and the languages we use to teach, so that we may subvert, resist, and overcome systems of marginality.

WAMBUI KARANJA is a PhD student in the Department of Social Justice Education at OISE/UT. She has a master's degree in law from the University of Toronto and has worked for over 25 years in community development in Canada, with a special interest in social justice, access, and equity issues. Her research interests lie in decolonizing theories on Indigeneity and Indigenous identity, Indigenous land rights, modernization, globalization, and research using decolonial, anti-racism, and critical race theoretical frameworks.

PHYLLIS MCKENNA is an Ojibwe/Odawa/Celtic woman who resides in Toronto, Ontario. Her roots are from M'Chigeeng First Nation Manitoulin Island, Ontario. She is the National Circle of First Nations Metis and Inuit Students chairperson for the Canadian Federation of Students, and vice president of equity at the Continuing Education Student Association of Ryerson. Phyllis is a student at Ryerson University, an award-winning writer, activist, and advocate. She's a public speaker and storyteller who inspires and shines. Phyllis has close ties to her Indigenous community and a strong desire to nurture and support the future generation of leaders who will follow her.

JESSICA PEDEN is an educator at the David Suzuki Secondary School in the Peel District School Board. She is an M.Ed. graduate of the Department of Social Justice Education at OISE/UT. Her research focuses on anti-colonial education, environmental social justice, and educational activism in the geography curriculum. Jessica supports student-led activist projects in her school community.

CAROLINA RIOS LEZAMA is an M.Ed. student in the Department of Social Justice Education at OISE/UT. She has worked in the Latin American community for several years on violence prevention and human rights projects. Her research interests include Latin American women's activism, Latinx feminist theory and praxis, decolonial spiritualities, and anti-racism.

HAGGER SAID is a recent graduate of the Master of Teaching Program at OISE/UT. She is a passionate advocate for diversity and inclusion in Ontario schools. Her research interests include decentralizing the English canon and diversifying literature at intermediate levels in Ontario. Her two-year thesis explored the effects of critical literacy and culturally relevant literature in English high school classrooms. As much as she loves teaching, she also loves conducting research, reading, and interacting with youth. Having completed her master's degree, she continues to pursue further research opportunities in the field of social justice and equity education, specifically within the English curriculum.

KIMBERLY L. TODD is a third-year PhD student in the Department of Social Justice Education at OISE/UT. She has a background in elementary education and has taught in South Korea, the United Arab Emirates, and on a First Nations reserve in Canada. Her research interests include dreaming, decolonization, spirituality, Indigenous epistemologies, and education. She has cocreated educational resources for organizations such as the David Suzuki Foundation and Amazon Watch.